OWEN DUDLEY EDWARDS, FRSE, FRHISTS, FSA (Scot.) was born in Dublin in 1938, studied at Belvedere College (for reference to which, see James Joyce's *A Portrait of the Artist as a Young Man*), and University College, Dublin, then at the John Hopkins University in Baltimore, Maryland, subsequently teaching in the University of Oregon. He then worked as a journalist for a year in Dublin. He taught in the University of Aberdeen for two years (1966–68), and since then at the University of Edinburgh whence he retired in 2005 but where he still gives occasional lectures. His subject is History but he frequently trespasses into Literature.

His wife Bonnie is American by birth and their three children are Scots. His most recent major work was *British Children's Fiction in the Second World War*. He was an SNP member in the 1970s but left when it expelled Alex Salmond, Stephen Maxwell, Kenny MacAskill and others. He rejoined later but in the interval supported his friend Nigel Griffiths MP (Labour) for Edinburgh South. He worked in the Yes campaign in 2014 and found it like the Civil Rights movements he knew in the USA and in Northern Ireland, the protest movements against the war in Vietnam in the USA, Ireland and Scotland, and the anti-Apartheid movement in Ireland. His next book is *Saint Johnny*, a fictional study of the friendship between St John the Evangelist and Jesus.

He has not met David Cameron, and probably never will.

By the same author:

Ireland (Deutsch, 1968)

The Sins of Our Fathers: Roots of Conflict in Northern Ireland
(Gill and Macmillan, 1970)

Burke and Hare (Polygon, 1984)

*Hare and Burke: As Performed around Greyfriars Churchyard and
Elsewhere: A Play* (Diehard, 1994)

British Children's Fiction in the Second World War
(Edinburgh University Press, 2007)

Dave Does the Right Thing (Luath Press, 2014)

HOW
DAVID CAMERON
SAVED
SCOTLAND,

AND MAY YET SAVE US ALL

OWEN DUDLEY EDWARDS

Luath Press Limited
EDINBURGH
www.luath.co.uk

First published 2015
Reprinted 2015

ISBN: 978-1-910021-69-9

The paper used in this book is recyclable. It is made from low
chlorine pulps produced in a low energy, low emission manner from
renewable forests.

Printed and bound by
Bell & Bain Ltd., Glasgow

Text background and parchment image
on the cover courtesy of Shutterstock.

Typeset in Mrs Eaves by
3btype.com

For Colin Affleck,
student, critic, friend

CONTENTS

CHAPTER ONE
Congratulations and Reflections 9

CHAPTER TWO
Who? What? A Definition of Prime Minister 19

CHAPTER THREE
The Etonian Education of a Prime Minister 64

CHAPTER FOUR
The Oxonian Education of a Prime Minister 91

CHAPTER FIVE
The Scottish Education of a Prime Minister............. 153

CHAPTER SIX
The National Education of a Prime Minister............ 191

CHAPTER SEVEN
The Dream That Will Never Die 248

Acknowledgements 277

'... Well, we won't go into the ethics of the thing. Eavesdropping, some people might call it, and I can imagine stern critics drawing in the breath to some extent. Considering it — I don't want to hurt your feelings, Tuppy — but considering it un-English. A bit un-English, Tuppy, old man, you must admit.'

'I'm Scotch.'

'Really?' I said. 'I never knew that before. Rummy how you don't suspect a man of being Scotch unless he's Mac-something and says "Och, aye" and things like that. I wonder', I went on, feeling that an academic discussion on some neutral topic might ease the tension, 'if you can tell me something that has puzzled me a good deal. What exactly is it that they put into haggis? I've often wondered about that.'

From the fact that his only response to the question was to leap over the bench and make a grab at me, I gathered his mind was not on haggis.

'However', I said, leaping over the bench in my turn, 'that is a side issue. ...'

P.G. WODEHOUSE, *Right Ho, Jeeves* (1934)

CHAPTER ONE

CONGRATULATIONS AND REFLECTIONS

MAJOR SWINDON [appalled]. Impossible!

GENERAL BURGOYNE [coldly]. I beg your pardon?

MAJOR SWINDON. I can't believe it! What will History say?

GENERAL BURGOYNE. History, sir, will tell lies, as usual.

GEORGE BERNARD SHAW, *The Devil's Disciple*, Act III

My dear Mr Cameron,

Congratulations! And quite genuine ones, with all the warmth to be expected in a message from enemy lines after an honourable defeat. You have won an impressive place in the line of Prime Ministers of the United Kingdom — the one existing since 1922 when most of Ireland left its predecessor, and that predecessor Union existing since 1801 when the Irish Parliament was melded into the British, and its predecessor, born in 1707, the one you were nominally trying to retain. Of course you never acknowledged that the Union of England (and Wales) and Scotland for which you claimed to fight had been abolished by its own act with effect from 1 January 1801. That would have admitted that the unmatchable trauma which you asserted would follow Scotland's departure from the UK had in fact been survived in 1922 when Ireland's presence in it had been reduced to one-sixth. A little learning is a dangerous thing, especially when there is a chance of the electorate learning it.

The congratulations are not as yet due (if ever) for the retention of Scotland's presence in the United Kingdom. You maintain humanity will benefit from it. I believe humanity will lose from it (notably since Scottish Independence would have meant the end of weapons of mass destruction on Scottish soil with others perhaps ultimately including the rest of the UK profiting by our example and relinquishing them in their turn). At the moment you declare that the surviving Union will be greatly reformed by you as a result of your present victory. The proof of that pudding (call it a haggis if you like) will be in the eating. Certainly you won on the plea that the future Union will radically differ from the one you started out to defend in 2011 when the Scots elected the Scottish National Party to majority government in the Scottish Parliament. We have yet to discover what you have saved, and for whom.

But whatever it proves to be, you may certainly be congratulated on the kind of victory that wins great applause in many history books. You had been faced by two opponents of considerably greater stature than yourself, Dr Gordon Brown and Mr Alex Salmond. You brilliantly ensured their fate would follow that of the detectives (in G.K. Chesterton's story 'The Sins of Prince Saradine' in his *The Innocence of Father Brown* (1911)) whom the criminal Flambeau ensured would one of them arrest the other. A folk-source for that may be the fairy-story of 'The Brave Little Taylor' who sits in a tree with two ferocious giants underneath whom he gets to attack one another by well-directed pebbles which each fancies the other has thrown on him. Wodehouse's 'The Ordeal of Osbert Mulliner' (*Mr Mulliner Speaking* (1929)) uses it when Osbert, a jade-collector, finds his apartment, his food, and (most importantly) his drinks annexed by two brutal burglars whose arguments over aristocratic social niceties end in mutual knockout after doing one another grievous bodily harm. You may have read it: Wodehouse is enjoyed by intelligent Etonians. The police assume Osbert (actually hidden during the conflict) was responsible for the mayhem and smilingly reprove him, and a muscle-preening, Africa-exploring rival in love hitherto threatening Osbert's life now vanishes in horror-stricken response.

It's worth taking a close look at Chesterton's 'The Sins of Prince Saradine'. It's a fantastic tale in its way, even for him, but turns on a threatened prince adapting Flambeau's trick. Prince Paul Saradine having murdered a Sicilian and abducted his wife is in danger of vendetta from his victims' son, while his own brother Stephen (holding proof of the murder lacked by the son) blackmails him. Father Brown continues:

> Instead of resisting his two antagonists, he surrendered suddenly to both of them. He gave way, like a Japanese wrestler, and his foes fell prostrate before him. He gave up the race round the world, and he gave up his address to young Antonelli; then he gave up everything to his brother. He sent Stephen money enough for smart clothes and easy travel, with a letter saying roughly: "This is all I have left. You have cleaned me out. I still have a little house in Norfolk, with servants and a cellar, and if you want more from me you must take that. Come and take possession if you like, and I will live there quietly as your friend or agent or anything." He knew that the Sicilian had never seen the Saradine brothers save, perhaps, in pictures; he knew they were somewhat alike, both having grey, pointed beards. Then he shaved his own face and waited. The trap worked. The unhappy captain, in his new clothes, entered the house in triumph as a prince, and walked upon the Sicilian's sword. ...

Now, any parallel here has nothing to do with the private lives of any of you three: in fact whatever criticisms of your public lives may be just, your private lives seem to be examples to the rest of us. And the actors in the story do not always prefigure any specific one of you the whole time. Dr Brown is not a blackmailer and did not take your place, you rather took his. If anything he could be taken for the vendettisto Antonelli rather than for the blackmailer Stephen: he has been accused of vindictiveness, but I suspect he has been vindictive purely on the instructions of prime ministerial cosmeticians whose bad advice he follows with the credulity of a respectful patient in inadequate medical hands. I know him to have a generous heart. Yet you of all people know him to have cause for a vendetta. During his premiership you assailed him day after day in that filthy orgy of mutual vituperation 'Prime Minister's Questions' which has done so much to bring the House of Commons into universal contempt.

And you dishonoured your old school by the viciousness of your incessant cascade: until your performances we believed that, whatever its other inadequacies, Eton bred gentlemen. In your own premiership, you scarcely permitted a day to elapse without implication your predecessor had caused a world depression, an absurd canard which invited derision for its user. You certainly ensured that if ever a statesman had cause for revenge, it was Dr Gordon Brown against yourself.

But as soon as the political lines for battle on Scottish Independence were drawn, you took yourself out of the line of fire and besought the Scots to follow the judgment of Dr Brown, and his former follower and more recent critic Mr Alistair Darling. It was doubly clever. You had directed enough barbs at Mr Darling as Dr Brown's accomplice for him to posture as Dr Brown's successor in form if never in

meaning, and to guarantee his acceptance of the apparently
rejected Brown role in your casting. The psychology was
excellent. Dr Brown had too much pride and too much
dignity to scamper into position at your behest or at Mr
Darling's, but would never resist the call to take up the cause
of Scotland in the Union in which you made only guest
appearances and Mr Darling bored humanity into either
indifference or anger. You knew that Mr Salmond's gallantry
would take on any opponent. You are fond of citing English
historical examples, all the more if they are irrelevant to
Scottish history. (We will come back to that later.) Chesterton (a great Englishman all the more for being something of
a Scottish nationalist) remarked in his *Short History of England*
(1917) that at Bosworth in 1485 Richard III called again and
again for his opponent Henry Tudor to do battle with him
but the future Henry VII was far too shrewd a modernist to
do anything of the kind. And again and again Alex Salmond
called on you to meet him in debate, but you were your own
Tudor, and you left Mr Darling, Mr Jim Murphy, Mr
Douglas Alexander, Mr George Galloway, and many another
empty suit of armour to rouse Dr Brown to heroic combat
by their inadequacy as matadors. You may not be the greatest
British statesman of our times, but you may well be the
shrewdest.

Your own guest appearances were masterpieces of chore-
ography. Whatever may be said in criticism of your tears they
certainly were no idle ones. 'Thou tellest my flittings; put
my tears into thy bottle; are not these things noted in thy
book?' demands the *English Prayer Book* of 1662 (56:8). The
tears naturally proved symptoms of heartbreak, whose
condition you certainly did not stint. And it improved upon
your earlier diagnoses. In the twilight of the Brown administration, you made much of Britain being broken, with a

querulous note almost recalling the Nanny Thatcher sworn
to discipline those children who broke it. Since quite a
number of Britons were broke themselves in 2010 it had its
apposition, although few of your friends seem noticeably
broke. But however slow your awareness of the Scottish
relevance of your reflections it must have struck you that a
broken Britain might well leave Scotland on the other side
of the break. So Britain's breakage was sidelined in favour of
reports on your own cardiac brittleness. It was mildly
ludicrous, yet rebuking mockery; it was masculine if morbid.
Thus silenced, you mutely and tearfully signalled Operation
Heartbreak, reaching above sordid politics to Housman's
aristocratic poem 'The Stars Have Not Dealt Me':

> Oh, grant me the ease that is granted so free,
> The birthright of multitudes, give it to me,
> That relish their victuals and rest on their bed,
> With flint in the bosom and guts in the head.

So you suffered in supposed silence, while your minions
mouthed menaces at the rebellious Scots.

As minions go, we might cavil at your Tory lieutenants.
Had it not been for Dr Gordon Brown, the sneers of Mr
George Osborne might well have struck fire into undecided
voters among whom he had sought to strike fear. Yet your
strategy was so sure of the ultimate certainty of St Gordon
discombobulating the Scottish dragon that you could hope
Mr Osborne's fiscal threats would offset their propaganda
dangers; Mr Osborne might be dismissed by insufficiently
respectful plebs but his message was ammunition when
reworked in the relentlessly Scottish accent of Dr Brown, in
contrast to the Scottish intonation of your coalesced hench-
man Mr Danny Alexander giving way to Thames Valley
Anglicisation, much as Mr Tony Blair, Sir Menzies Campbell

and other chameleons now pass for white. And Mr Ed Balls, frisking, barking, and tail-wagging his devotion to the Osborne doctrine of currency refusal to an independent Scotland, eloquently drove home the lesson that whatever your weaknesses as master of the Tory party, your mastery of the Labour party is so complete as to require a dog-licence.

The Liberal Democrats are even better Tory house-trained, in particular for the conviction that cul-de-sacs are race-courses. And for the grand farewell, you wept among the Scottish Widows as worthily as Nixon after his Checkers speech and Reagan at his first Inaugural, while Mr Ed Milib-and found Scottish shoppers rough and rude in contrast to the respectful English to whom he is accustomed, and Mr Nick Clegg fled from the very newsmen in Selkirk. You, the top-level pre-Referendum invaders are all, of course, far above us, but you at least let your tears fall on us where Messrs Miliband, Clegg, Farage &c left us only their whines.

On your first acquaintance with him Mr Alex Salmond must have seemed alarmingly over-educated, all the more deplorable for his being a graduate of St Andrews University, best known on your horizon as an outpost of fashionable England ultimately sanctified as a marriage-market for the Royal Family. And Dr Gordon Brown was clearly too big-brained for you to tackle seriously, whence your understudy of another David against him, when you stood well protected by the famous despatch-box and slung stones. When it came to Mr Salmond, Mr Patrick Harvie and the YES forces, Dr Brown himself was the biggest of the stones you slung while standing in what seemed Scottish safety, insured by Scottish Widows. Did you select your emporia by some ironic little self-mockery of your own, or merely by idea-association with tears? Or was your manipulation of your rival for

Scotland's affections into the front line of battle also reminiscent of the earlier King David? It was easy to calculate that Mr Darling would prove too limited to play Captain Hook, and run out of steam while confusing it with his own emissions of gas. And by coupling their names as the persons on whom the defence of the Union must rest — Beh-eh-eh-ter Togeh-eh-eh-ther, so to speak — you could ensure that they would never advance in time or tandem, but at the dwindle of the Darling dance the Brunonian Can-Can would polk its ponderous Plutonium. I suspect Dr Brown surprised even you, for all of his professional embodiment of your diagnosed necessities. And you would certainly have been gratified by the scattering of his Lilliputian Labour colleagues under his seven-league boots.

It certainly must be comforting to look on the period from your kissing Her Majesty's hands to denote acceptance of office, until Scotland voted NO, as a coherent whole, reflecting a total victorious strategy rather than an overall margin of tactical wins. You certainly did not expect, and can hardly have desired, a total Scottish Referendum vote of 84.6 per cent of Scotland's population. Yet if you had an overall strategy, and perhaps you did, its execution must have begun with your first privatisation in office, selling off Scotland to the Liberal Democrats when carving the job-cake in 2010. It was judicious: Scottish jobs for LibDems meant so much more English loot for your own party to enjoy. It was offset by at least one major job for a ScotLibDem, Mr Danny Alexander, admittedly as a reslice when an initial English LibDem nominee for Treasury sidekick proved unfit for purpose. But what it meant was that Scotland's future could be evaded by you until the last minute, for the most part. You amused yourself by allowing the LibDems to change warhorses in midstream in October 2013, Mr Michael

Moore SNP for Berwickshire, Roxburgh, and Selkirk, being arbitrarily dumped from the Secretariate of State for Scotland in favour of Mr Alistair Carmichael MP for Orkney and Shetland. The supposed reason was that Mr Moore was too much of a gentleman (without being an Etonian) for the work of keeping his fellow-countrymen in line, whereas Mr Carmichael is impaired by no such delicacies.

Do party Whips and constituency association chairpersons and local ward mechanics bend the aristocratic ears of a coalesced cabinet? At some point, my dear Mr Cameron, you must have concluded that the LibDems would suffer much more potential electoral punishment for having signed up to the coalition than your own hardened Tory veterans. I suspect you drew that conclusion earlier than did Mr Nicholas Clegg. This meant that vulnerable seats in a LibDem holocaust in Election 2015 would need careful previous calculation. Mr Michael Moore sits for a seat in the Scottish Borders, part of it previously held by one of the few surviving LibDem grandees, Sir David (in Scotland) Lord (in Westminster) Steel. Sir David's career as first Presiding Officer of the restored Scottish Parliament enhanced the lustre of his name, and his goodwill might cling to Mr Moore. Yet (whether David, Sir David, or my Lord) Steel was a name linked to achievement, accomplishment, or at the very least, attempt, whereas when ditched by the Deputy Prime Minister (a proceeding allegedly unimpaired by influence from the Prime Minister) Mr Moore would have failure written large over his career. At Election 2015 his seat will have superficial hopes of LibDem retention, given its 5,000-odd majority, but that may disappear in a massacre of the junior partner in Government, and a possible killer is the senior partner in Government. Mr Carmichael on the other hand is the most likely LibDem to retain a Scottish seat in Westminster, heading Election 2010's result by a yawning majority (and, for him, it is the right adjective) with the Tories buried somewhere around fourth or fifth. I suspect that any hint you dropped in the ear of Mr Clegg ripened with no appreciable retention of its origin by your innocent partner.

In any case, Mr Moore seems on his way to his political grave, while Selkirk duly gave a hard Border welcome to Mr Clegg himself on Referendum eve, Wednesday 17 September 2014. He was duly accompanied by Mr Moore, but the latter's humiliation was symbolically reaffirmed by his conscription alongside the much less graceful contours of Mr Carmichael. The LibDems (as you most certainly do not need to be told) exude unpleasant memories among the Scots of their previous butchery of Scottish statesmen, notably the rapid ouster of Mr Charles Kennedy and Sir Menzies Campbell from the party leadership to make room (as it proved) for Mr Clegg. Mr Clegg may have imagined that Selkirk must be true LibDem territory what with Steel domestic proximity. Alas, Sir David (or Lord) Steel was nowhere in sight to reprimand the more boisterous local yokels, and Lady Steel was reported to intend voting YES. And you, my dear Mr Cameron, sat remote from the burial of Mr Clegg's Selkirk hopes as you graced the Scottish Widows with handshakes as clean as might be expected of Pontius Pilate.

You would seem to have added a new meaning to the office of Prime Minister.

CHAPTER TWO

WHO? WHAT? A DEFINITION OF PRIME MINISTER

'... there's a sort of man under him [the King] called the Prime Min'ster that sort of helps him govern an' he's chosen out of a general election.'

'Like the man they have in It'ly called the duck', said Douglas, anxious to air his knowledge.

'You're thinking of the dog', said Ginger scornfully, 'the man we had in history what ruled a place called Venice an' was called a dog.'

'I'd have called myself somethin' better than a dog or a duck if I was goin' to be a ruler', said William. 'I'd be called a lion or an eagle or somethin' like that.'

RICHMAL CROMPTON, 'William, Prime Min'ster' in *William the Bad* (1930)

Who, at the time of reading, is the Prime Minister? It is a question one might ask if one had a black-out and were then examined in hospital. It is taken as a yardstick on one's mental balance. To know who is the Prime Minister means that one is probably sane rather than insane. As we are now in 2014 and have witnessed two changes of Prime Minister in the last ten years, another in the previous ten, another in the ten before that, it seems a good test, not too easy, not too hard. There may be a risk in it, if the thought of who is a specific Prime Minister could be mentally distressing: to utter Tony Blair's name might prompt anger, especially after his taking us into war in Iraq on false premises, to utter Margaret Thatcher's might also, especially because of her tone which many found patronising, but that doesn't seem to have deterred doctors or nurses from using the test. So the Prime Minister's identity is medically reckoned an acceptable scientific method of measuring our command of our own identities.

This is not to say that the Prime Minister means more to people than, say, the Queen, but she would clearly be a more ominous test, being far better known than a Prime Minister since she has been Queen for all lives under 60. If one doesn't know who is the monarch of the UK, one's mental condition is much more serious than if one can't tell Cameron from Brown, or from Blair, or from Thatcher. That it might seem a much bigger sign of insanity to confuse Cameron with Thatcher than with any of the males who succeeded her breaks down because of Thatcher's forceful personality: any sane person might reasonably think of her as male chauvinist.

Similar tests in the USA would face different pitfalls. Since President Barack Obama has a visible physical contrast from previous Presidents by his skin-colour, a patient's awareness of his Presidency might seem too simple a test for reliability. As against that, the longer he stays in power the less (it might be felt) his policies seem to differ from those of his predecessors. Sometimes Prime Ministers don't seem too ready to distinguish President Obama from President Bush, President Bush from President Clinton. If President Obama is succeeded by Hillary Clinton, everyone should be able to distinguish them from one another, but a patient in 2001–2009 might have faced too hard a test not to confuse one President Bush with another, and should Governor Jeb Bush be elected in 2016, the test might be less satisfactory still. On the other hand, voice must play a large part in such assessments. What a President or Prime Minister sounds like must be important in identification. Let us suppose (only suppose, my dear Prime Minister) that you are succeeded by Ms Theresa May, and both female Prime Ministerial voices might be thought similar as bossy and posh, but Thatcher was chiefly zealous to impress, Ms May to inform, or, to rephrase it, Thatcher sounded authoritarian, Ms May sounds authoritative. It is thus that Thatcher was resented where Ms May might not be. The Bush Presidents also differed here: the first President Bush sounded like an incompetent sales-man trying to make himself understood in a kindergarten, the second like a moronic Texas millionaire. As to a third, I trust we will not have to wait and see.

A head of government will be the more readily identifia-ble if there is some phrase or turn of speech which she/he favours. It may not be memorable in itself but the context may give it a chance of immortality. Tony Blair popularised the words 'moving on' when more and more people wanted him to move off. Some which were signature-tunes in the speaker's lifetime can vanish and be replaced by others less well known at the time. President Kennedy in office was somewhat affectionately taken to make much use of 'with vigor' (pronounced 'vigah'); after his traumatic death people identified him more with key phrases from his Inaugural. Speech-writers artificialise this sort of utterance, and it becomes interesting to determine whether a phrase identified with a world leader is really natural to them. In your case, your notorious fondness for the words 'doing the right thing' or speaking of this or that as 'the right thing' has become so famous that Luath Press, publishers of this book are also issuing an anthology of your fondness for it. You know far better than I whether for you it is a mantra, a refuge, a mnemonic or a boy-scout rule. You may remember having adopted it, or whether imperceptibly it grew on you. Or you may one day have noticed your use of it, or had it pointed out to you. And how often are such habits irritating to others? Does your right thing set teeth on edge? Does your wife find it idyllic or soporific? Did your speechwriters invent it or did they have to learn it? Was it the result of your having studied the works of Peter Drucker when nominally or otherwise you embarked on a business career (and you might have gone to many worse authors)?

To be less personal about it, Harold Wilson, for instance, may very well have received phrase-graft before he started repeating that 'a week is a long time in politics' but probably 'I'm going to be very frank and open and honest about this' was his own home-made article. That kind of signature-tune, original or artificial, often uses citation of some household name as mantra or (it would be hoped) crowd-pleaser. Wilson, the more his preferences became Right-wing, cited the late Aneurin Bevan as 'Nye' to proclaim his devotion to Left-wing Labour traditions. Paul Foot's *The Politics of Harold Wilson*, one of the best critical studies of a modern politician, had a fairly savage demonstration of this in a chapter entitled 'The Mantle of Nye'. Thatcher, similarly, would make familiar allusions to 'Winston' as though claiming a personal intimacy of a kind Winston Churchill would never have tolerated from her. It is of course two-edged. I dare say you are by now sufficiently aware that while a few delicate allusions to Thatcher when campaigning in Essex may make whatever medicine you are administering go down (or would you risk having U-PUKE claim to be more Thatcherite than thou?), any cuddly allusions to the Iron Lady when you are north of Hadrian's Wall are best avoided (and perhaps no very welcome prescription north of Grantham). Even quoting Robert Burns is dangerous for an English Tory in Scotland, after Thatcher's quease-making efforts at it. A genuine Burns enthusiast from anywhere on earth is another matter. As a matter of fact an apprenticeship in Burns studies would probably do you and your policies a lot of good.

You could seek to become known as an event in yourself although it could become dangerously akin to adoption of the part of Buttons in a pantomime with Thatcher as the ghost of the wicked stepmother and a Scottish Cinderella or Snow White. A genuine phrase-maker heading a government is unlikely to repeat his personal products. Churchill's most memorable lines were articulated in response to some political, military, or diplomatic event, their value retained in part by not wearing out their welcome. Churchill being half-American knew more naturally how to sell himself, and knew that to appear somewhat ridiculous though very good-humoured may be a first-class means of winning: he learned it above all from studying President Theodore Roosevelt in office 1901–1909. Your erstwhile fellow-Bullingdonian London Mayor Boris Johnson today plays the same tactic, although his Churchillian or Rooseveltian stature remains open to doubt. Arguably a US President starts with the advantage of an Inaugural which can flash a shop-window of gems, although Theodore Roosevelt, the prize self-publicist of all time, entered the office by succeeding on McKinley's assassination, and thus served almost a full term before delivering an Inaugural (on his re-election). Usually it is a lesser statesman (or politician) who becomes identified with a single turn of phrase, such as Prime Minister H. H. Asquith in 1910 'We had better wait and see'. It may be immortalised when subsequent events turn its recollection into bitter recrimination as with Lloyd George's 'make Britain a fit country for heroes to live in' when answered by the mass unemployment of World War I survivors.

But the converse can hold good. Some words, phrases or sentences from a national leader may make limited impact on first use, and then for various reasons be recalled, respoken, reprinted and win immortality because of their vital renewal of national morale. This was more likely before radio, the classic instance being what may very well be the greatest speech ever delivered, and also one of the shortest — Lincoln's address on 19 November 1863 when opening the National Cemetery at Gettysburg where the USA had won its crucial victory over its rebel opponents the Confederate States of America on the preceding 4 July. Lincoln as President was only required to say a few words, and his words were indeed few. The event of the afternoon was the standard Great Speech in which American public figures had sought immortality during the preceding half-century and Edward Everett of Massachusetts gave it to general satisfaction orating for an hour or two. He was not there purely for art's sake or because he had been President of Harvard. He had been Vice-Presidential candidate in the 1860 election when Lincoln was chosen, and he had been on another ticket whose front-runner, John Bell of Tennessee, had then sided with his seceded home state, so Everett was needed to symbolise support for Lincoln among his political rivals for national office. It took a couple of days for the country to realise that in addition to making one of his very few public utterances during the war away from Washington DC, itself under frequent rebel fire, Lincoln had given the country a masterstroke in arousing morale and justifying the fratricidal defence of the Union. And now who remembers Everett's speech? Not you, I suspect, my dear Mr Cameron, although as we will see I know you to be exceptionally well educated in the history of government. (We will not see any discussion of Simon Cameron, the most corrupt member of Lincoln's cabinet, interested though we have to be in your namesakes.)

The role of head of government in rousing national morale was never more urgent than when Franklin Delano Roosevelt delivered his first Inaugural, on 4 March 1932 with the USA famed across the earth as the supposed Eldorado where the streets were paved with gold had crashed into what seemed universal poverty. It had survived at least four major depressions previously but this seemingly stretched out into a hopeless future. Roosevelt faced it above all in the words:

> Let me assert my firm belief that the only thing we have to fear is fear itself — nameless, unreasoning, unjustified terror, which paralyzes needed efforts to convert retreat into advance.

Professor H. W. Brands of Texas in his useful and attractive biography of FDR, *Traitor to his Class* (2008) notes this as to be hailed before long 'as a landmark of presidential rhetoric. At the time it didn't seem so, not least since it was patently false. Americans had plenty to fear, starting with massive unemployment, widespread hunger, and a collapsing financial system' (p. 283). But it was not false. Roosevelt was a diagnostician superior to his biographer, no doubt partly because in his 12-year battle with polio he had learned much in trying conquer or at least offset the incurable. And the manner of delivery threw strength, which no longer sustained his legs, into an almost physical conflict as he spoke. His cadences made the word fear almost take hideous form before his listeners' eyes, then be smashed down and down and down in the violence with which his oratorical style assailed it. Absence of TV meant that his hearers and even witnesses hardly realised how crippled he was, but the word 'paralyzes' asserted the country's enemy to be his own. And his prescription was absolutely right. Capitalism depends on confidence, much of it frequently misplaced. That immortal Inaugural was literally a confidence trick, not to perpetrate a swindle but to win the first victory where it had to be won – in the human mind of an entire people. H. L. Mencken mockingly spoke of Roosevelt's 'Christian Science smile' but that too was good diagnosis. Christian Science at its wisest recognises the need to begin by fighting illness with the mind as the battlefield. Roosevelt was not a Christian scientist but he had an American's instinctive reaction to treat the world as an adventure where the first combat had to be with oneself.

We are speaking of a head of government who was also a head of state, and the US Presidency has been built from its own inaugurator, Washington, to be hero-priest-king as required. The United Kingdom having retained a separate head of state will find it less easy to recognise the sublime in the Prime Minister. To the present writer the present queen's greatest achievement in words were those she spoke in a language alien to her in Dublin during her first state visit. It was simply the correct formal greeting – O President and friends – but the trouble she had obviously taken to develop the beautiful intonation she correctly gave it, and for all of her regal solemnity the implicit laughter at the surprise she knew she would give her Irish audience, meant that never had so few words won so much peace and love and eradication of hatred and bitterness. In a very different way the courage of her father George VI in rallying the nation in wartime wireless Christmas messages despite his speech impediment gave fresh confidence to his hearers. We don't have much comment on it since comment on the King was more or less outlawed, but if we listeners who were not his subjects were inspired by his gallantry it is surely correct to think of unspoken reactions 'if 'e can keep going so can we'. They wouldn't have known that he practiced revolver-shooting in his garden fully intending to be killed if his people were successfully invaded. But of course Winston Churchill used his headship of government to shore up morale despite the fortunes of war. Probably no Prime Minister has ever used radio more effectively in national crisis. But if the wartime allies Roosevelt and Churchill were the sublime in national leadership by radio — the nadir being Hitler, Goebbels, and in the USA Father Coughlin — the post-war omnipresence of TV displaced it for a much more uncertain medium. Imagine Roosevelt's fireside chats or Churchill's war broadcasts by soundbite!

And that in its turn makes historical comparisons less easy as we seek Prime Ministerial quality. You, David Cameron, whether personally good, bad, or indifferent, are to a large extent the creation of cosmeticians. You have been taught what to sound like, what to look like, what to dress like, what to think like, what to say like. What these 'like' yardsticks really are can be deduced but seldom firmly defined. At its most basic a head of government may have a disability it is necessary to minimise, such as Franklin Roosevelt's paralysed legs or Eamon de Valera's virtual blindness. Neither would seem likely to have survived TV scrutiny as demanded today. But apart from these grand deceptions, FDR and 'Dev' were their own creations, while demanding essential aid from wives, children, and friends (real friends, not simply professional followers). Truman was his own very real self, Eisenhower was partly recreated although the best reworking seems to have been his own, Kennedy was cosmetised but strictly under family recipes especially from his Napoleonic mother, Johnson was working his way back to his left-wing youth offset by his utter dependence on others for foreign affairs (including Vietnam) in which he had no deep interest. Richard Nixon may have been a seismic shift: he really was remade between 1962 and 1968, although his inner core of identity was in fact far more consistent than even his enemies realised. The British succession of Prime Ministers were less obvious artificial products.

For one thing they were installed under Class and Authority. A US President has visibly started among the people. There was certainly some hokum about it. The early Presidents were chosen much less democratically and from prominent pre-revolutionary families, but the fourth and fifth, James Madison and James Monroe, died poor, while the first President from poverty-stricken roots, Andrew Jackson, concealed his status as frontier plutocrat and oligarch in Tennessee. If more recently an aspirant for the Presidency has some well-heeled dynasty or aristocratic-sounding surname it could well be to her/his disadvantage. New York Governor Nelson Rockefeller, perhaps personally an even more attractive candidate than the incumbent President Kennedy, was weakened in his major run in 1961–64 by his famous and wealthy name, and before his election Kennedy himself — however aided by his father's wealth — was probably disadvantaged by his reputation. (Harry Truman put it characteristically: 'his biggest trouble isn't the Pope, it's Pop'.) Hillary Clinton might never have started as a Presidential candidate had it not been for her husband, but her quest for the Presidency in 2008 was more impaired than advanced by being always thought of as ex-President Clinton's wife. He was popular, but the public did not want to give him a third term by the back door; and if she would have been set on being her own President nobody was sure he would take the same view. It may be different if she tries for 2016, certainly.

Premierships involve succession when one's party is in power. Curiously for all we are told about the Americanisation of British politics, Presidential dynasties have been much more visible in recent years while Prime Ministerial families are now much less so, save for publicity purposes. Arthur James Balfour as nephew of Robert Cecil third Marquis of Salisbury (and partly brought up by him) inherited the premiership in 1902, but then was ousted in what eventuated as the Liberal landslide of 1906. Neville Chamberlain owed much to his father Joe, and was displaced in 1940 by another son of a political grandee, Winston Churchill. Such genealogy was reinforced by the sense of their belonging to a political class, respected as Authority. Northern Ireland was governed by the Ulster Unionists in alliance with the Westminster Tories for 50 years and ready to supply it with a majority when needed, and presumably one-party states are even more family-ruled than most. Dame Dehra Parker, Minister for Agriculture, kept the seat warm for her son, and then after he was killed in World War II, for her grandson Major James Chichester-Clarke who would ultimately succeed his cousin Captain Terence O'Neill as Prime Minister of Northern Ireland. Dame Dehra was the first woman in any cabinet in these islands (unless one counts the illegal cabinet set up by Dáil Eireann which included Constance, Countess Markiewicz, also the first woman elected to the House of Commons but consonant with Sinn Féin policy never taking her seat).

The actual roots of a premier's natural and personal authority would vary, sometimes drastically: the actual two obvious embodiments of such authority in their identities as premier were Sir Alec Douglas-Home (from his ancient earldom) and Harold Wilson (from his academic excellence). After that new images of Authority were needed. Aristocracy was by no means as dead as it looked (Douglas-Home's Scotland had voted for the Tories under Sir Anthony Eden in 1955 in their last majority there). Meritocracy never displaced it (Wilson's exceptional intellect was widely denounced as being 'too clever by half' meaning literally that anything too obviously eclipsing mediocrity was deplorable; Michael Foot as candidate for the premiership in the 1983 General Election was jeered at for being one of the greatest bookmen of his time; Gordon Brown's intellect was likewise held against him, all the more because his degrees were from Edinburgh instead of the usual Oxbridge forcing-house). But meritocracy was not visibly undervalued in Scotland or in Wales, a consideration in claims for devolution and beyond.

The new remaking of the political leader was first brought to a truly fine art in Margaret Thatcher's case, and after some initial temporising it was frankly admitted that she owed much to public relations people in open profession (e.g. Saatchi and Saatchi) or to civil service conjuring (Bernard Ingham). But neither deserved their reputation, their best achievements being to have their lack of scruple confused with actual success. The real genius in selling Margaret Thatcher was Denis Thatcher, who must have been amused by Saatchi's and Ingham's usurpation of laurels actually his but never claimed by him. To plant a wildly successful supposed satire on oneself and one's Prime Ministerial spouse in the most notorious lampoon paper of the day (with subsequent West End show spinoff) thus trivialising ostensible hostility into a comic soap opera was a process of unequalled mastery. It recalls Disraeli and Charles

11 in its creative objectivity and genuine self-mockery. A true artist, Denis doesn't seem to have interfered with actual cosmetics: his wife deferred to appropriate elocutionists, hair-colourists, &c, as required. Instructively, it was Margaret Thatcher's voice and manner that alienated Scots spectrum-wide from High Tories to born-again Trotskyites, and they were acquired at considerable financial cost, which Denis would not have grudged. Voice and manner did their best work for her in the Home Counties where chiefly required and if their effect was reversed north of The Wash it could at least dress for class war against the miners: in Margaret Thatcher's fairy-book (supposing such a thing possible) Snow White would have prioritised breaking the Seven Dwarfs' trade union. Denis's area of expertise was limited, and South African investments under Apartheid meant far more to him than Scottish squirearchy, but he did train her to make jokes about his consumption of malt whisky (as publicised in *Private Eye*) rather than have her punctuate her recitals with jokes about mean Scots recalled from Donald McGill postcards on sale in inter-war Grantham. Her idea of European diplomatic finesse was to tell European diplomats stereotype English witticisms at their countries' expense. But their susceptibilities presumably meant as little to Denis as did Scottish theology. He was content to perfect his Pygmalion-ship in home territory. However diligently he sculpted, the clay whence came the results was unsuited to travel across the Channel – or the Tweed. Margaret Thatcher was too coarse a creature for tragedy, but there is a touch of pathos in her delusion after Denis's death, that he was still alive, a little like Trilby still in thrall to her dead Svengali.

Despite brave, if banal, attempts to classify you as Margaret Thatcher's offspring, you (my dear Mr Cameron) are much closer to what she vainly tried to appear. For you are

of the manor born, you are begat by Feilden Earls of
Denbigh one of whom fell fighting for Charles I (you are
only collaterally descended from his son who fought against
Charles), you are begat also by the Talbot lords of Shrews-
bury one (John) killed trying to reconquer France in 1453
while another (Charles) proved the decisive courtier to ensure
that in 1714 the dying Queen Anne would be succeeded by
her distant but Protestant cousin George of Hanover rather
than her Roman Catholic half-brother James, you are begat
once more by the Earls of Errol whose most famous laird
fought for Bonnie Prince Charlie, and you are begat yet
again by William IV (or William III of Scotland), illegitimately, and thus are descended from George III who vainly
sought to hold on to his American colonies, and from
George II who valued Hanover above these islands, and from
George I and the wife whom he imprisoned for life and thus
never saw these islands to whose Queenship she was entitled,
and therefore you descend from James I and VI whose
homosexuality did not prevent his siring the entire line of
British monarchs ever since, and from all his predecessor
Scottish monarchs back to Robert Bruce, and in England
from Henry VII, Edward IV, Edward III, Edward II, Edward I,
Henry III, John, Henry II, Henry I, and William the
Conqueror. No Prime Minister has ever sported blood as
blue in such profusion, though the Duke of Grafton (1768–
70) may run you close, being illegitimately descended from
Charles II and so from Charles I and thence from James VI
and I and so back to your lot. He isn't much to live up to,
though no doubt not as wretched as he appears in the lacer-
ating letters of Junius. As for the Cecils ennobled as Salis-
burys who closed the reigns of Elizabeth I and Victoria, or
the Churchills who ensured the triumph of invasion from
Europe in 1688 and prevented invasion from Europe in

1940, they are but yesterday in comparison. Your ancestral line from King William to King William outshines all your predecessors however disreputable the individual ancestral rulers, although as we will see later your claim on heroic ancestry is even more illustrious than your claim on royalty (Robert Bruce triumphs under both categories, but the heroic is the more important since he would not have lasted as king without it).

The Scots assert the principle of equality with the aphorism that 'we are all Jock Tamson's bairns', Jock Tamson being the progenitive principle with whose variant you may be familiar from *Lady Chatterley's Lover*. The English counterpart is from the medieval priest of the Peasants' Revolt, John Ball:

When Adam delved, and Eve span,
Who was then the gentleman?

Those derived from two different countries, but they are the last word on genealogy wherever we are from.

Your ancestry throws light on an otherwise neglected feature of your politics – their possessiveness. Capitalists in characteristic self-portraits diligently fulfilling what Marxists expect of them no doubt articulate the romance of acquisition, the bloodier the better, and you radiate enough of such ambience to validate your credentials with your party's owners. We would not wish to discredit you by minimising your greed. But your eye seems to sparkle with less glee at mere grab than, say, your friend and colleague George (originally Gideon) Osborne, whose Irish landlord ancestors came from a class of limited paternalism: at least one Osborne was saluted by the authoritative Arthur Young as the best landlord he encountered in late 18th-century

Ireland, but Gideon and/or George too obviously melts his habitual sneer when his hosts are moneyed. Irish tenantry saw their hopes dashed when acquisitive heirs followed benevolent patriarchy. He may have managed to secrete sanguinary drops of blue via the occasional ancestress who (in P. G. Wodehouse's classification) didn't know how to say 'No' to Charles II, but you could swim in yours. This may help explain the tone of your few public interventions (as opposed to the many supposedly secret) in the Great Scotland Referendum debate. You really sounded personal about it. You made much of your patriotism which, as you phrased it, entitled you to demand the retention of Scotland, as though it were part of a regal equipage of which you were the leading practical custodian. We might not have realised your ancestral animation, but the tone had a genuine regal demand where your allies/rivals/sidekicks merely radiated their indigestion at this threat to their jobs and salaries. I except Gordon Brown, but I suspect that though he would never admit it, his descent from Church of Scotland clergy plays a crucial part, and his heroic turnpike road in the cause of NO he took with the vehemence of John Knox at his bravest, and some of his impatience with accuracy. And the term 'resurrection' applied to his entry into the Referendum fray was quite exceptionally apposite.

Your own capacity for quiet command, when you were sufficiently self-controlled, was effective by scenting itself with the spirit of vanished kingship. You occasionally put a foot wrong by the ministerial yen to claim intimacy with your distant cousin in Windsor and Balmoral. Your post-Referendum claim of oracular clues to the Queen's mind was a toe-stub in a generation gap: the English establishment in the late 1960s made a purring sound to acknowledge receipt of an oral communication when expressions of approval or

disapproval were undesirable. In today's usage ît is compre-
hended by the phrase 'I hear you'. Her Majesty certainly
used ît in Edinburgh in the 1970s as Dr Gordon Brown
could have told you. But be ît said on your behalf that you
generally seem to have avoided the proprietorial where the
Queen was concerned, unlike Thatcher's grab for royal
status in her ridiculous 'We are a grandmother', or Tony
Blair as busybody necessîtating four-lettered dismissal from
the Duke of Edinburgh. Your invisible but not wholly
inaudible royalty had a realîty lacking in the Thatcher-Blair
posturings. It was not what the job specifications of Premiership required, but ît enhanced your otherwise slightly ragged
electoral credentials. You had — have — a certain something:
perhaps what François Sagan might have called Un Certain
Sourire. We may discover a reason for ît later.

This partly contextualises your interesting if unexpected
hymn of praise for H. E. Marshall's *Our Island Story* (1905), a
Scottish publication of female Canadian authorship. Like
you, I enjoyed ît in early youth (the 1940s in my case, the
1970s in yours). Did you have the same shock of recognîtion
that I did when finding, very early on, her remark that all the
four countries in our island story were unîted, England,
Ireland, Scotland, and Wales, and of these the first to be
unîted were England and Ireland? I read this as a lîttle boy
in Dublin, very surprised that this book which had such
interesting things in ît had something as wrong as that. Irish
Catholics in the 1940s believed that Ireland and England
were never unîted, except that sometimes, indeed often, the
English tried to force us into things we did not want, like
Protestantism, but Catholic Ireland won in the end, and
here we were, outside the Second World War which most of
us hoped the English, or British, would win. By the time I
was reading, H. E. Marshall's confident assurance was as

alien to British Tories as ît was to the Irish Catholics, and îts comfortable Edwardian imperialism was replaced by unspoken agreement between the ruling class in Britain and that in Catholic Ireland that Ireland (26-county Ireland) and Britain never could be unîted, so that England had not failed in Ireland, ît simply had faced an impossible task. Was that the way the new sîtuation was explained to you in the 1970s? I take ît you were given Marshall at your prep school, Heatherdown (îtself still very old-fashioned and not deŝtined to survive your pupillage by many years). In any case you would have got quîte a lot of hiŝtory of the four countries from Marshall, including a thrilling poŝt-Macaulay account of 'the ŝtory of brave Londonderry', which worried me somewhat as being a true ŝtory of heroes but heroes on what for me was the wrong side. For you, of course, ît was the right side, but in the 1970s Brîtish Tories were not as certain of the virtue of Northern Ireland as they had been. If you or your prep school noticed, I doubt if either cared. Your acceptance of Marshall did not require you to be purely Whig or Hanoverian. She put you firmly on the Whig side in Ireland, but in Scotland she became increasingly Jacobite. If she was old-fashioned, she was also a premature poŝt-Moderniŝt. Did you have any clue to the value of her inconsiŝtency from what your name might have told you?

It helps us to determine the origin of your royally proclaimed love for the Unîted Kingdom, as yet without worry about which Unîted Kingdom you meant. Your (if not my) sense of royal anceŝtry could flourish in the Marshall prose, moŝt events seen through the prism of successive kingships, since 'brave Londonderry' was happily contextualised in the advent firŝt to England and then to Ireland, of what Marshall called 'William the Deliverer' (to whom, do you remember, she gave this tîtle in sharp, deliberate contrast to your unpleasant ancestor William the Conqueror whose oppression of the brave English she scorned — a very interesting distinction from where I was reading). Alas, you weren't descended from William the Deliverer, his homosexuality not being sidelined for procreation, unlike those of his great-grandfather James I and VI, or his cousin and successor Anne. But Marshall taught us one thing without saying it. The real definition of a king is heroic (all the Greek heroes in the Iliad seem to be Kings of some place or other). William III of England and Ireland, II of Scotland, was the last hero-king, damn nearly getting himself killed in the traditional manner as extolled by G.K. Chesterton for Richard III (and not for William III). Since power had subsequently passed to the Prime Minister, could there be a hero Prime Minister, all the more so today when many of us can still remember the one unquestionable case of it — Winston Churchill. I remember liking his voice because of a kind of growly fun in it, rather like an uncle who would be good at playing bears. Marshall didn't sell me on the Whig/Protestant side of William in Ireland, and she called Derry by the wrong name. But she censured William for Glencoe, and was all for Bonnie Prince Charlie as against the Redcoats and the Butcher Cumberland. Some of this was further inflamed by the 20th-century Tory and 18th-century Jacobite D.C. Thomson of Dundee whose *Adventure* comics carried enormous stories with fascinating detail about Scotland, a place I had never seen. To assure you of the complexity of my own inheritance, the worst villains in *Adventure* were the Hanoverian Campbells, and my godfather whom I loved very much was a Campbell. I also loved Stevenson who began *Kidnapped* with a kindly Campbell but had them very much on the wrong side by the end of the story.

You wouldn't have known *Adventure*, and in any case by your time comics had lost their fascinating acres of print and gone wholly tabloid. But I think I can point to the locus classicus in *Our Island Story* in the matter of your professed love of the UK. She didn't much care for Anne (neither does Macaulay) but she tried to give every monarch good or bad a chapter-theme and Anne's was 'How the Union Jack was Made'. She had a fine illustration showing St George's Cross, and St Andrew's Cross, and a flag of 1707 showing the Union of England and Scotland and she then explained that not until 1801 did they get it right when Ireland (although united for centuries with England) had her Parliament included in the British Parliament and so the Union Jack could now be made properly with St Patrick's Cross for Ireland being added. I felt suitably contemptuous of the flag before it got its Irish contribution. Of course we were glad to be outside the United Kingdom but it seemed good that we had helped to make the Union Jack.

And that should bring it home to you what happens when a country leaves the UK. It goes. And it doesn't. And thanks to Scottish nationalism Scotland's hope for Independence has nothing of the violence which made it so tragic in Ireland and had rubbed off from the Great War.

You yourself are very much aware of your family link with Churchill's heroic wartime premiership, to wit his Minister for Information, Duff Cooper, himself a hero by resignation from Neville Chamberlain's cabinet over the Munich agreement with Hitler – Eden and he were Churchill's only allies among the leading Tories in the run-up to the Second World War. William IV's great-granddaughter Lady Agnes Duff was Duff Cooper's mother, her other daughters included your great-grandmother. Another daughter, Sybil

Hart-Davis, was the mother of my first mentor in literary research, and leading benefactor of my career, Sir Rupert Hart-Davis, incomparable editor and publisher. Cooper wrote several remarkable books, some published by his nephew, among them *Operation Heartbreak*, a lyric war tragedy, whose name may well have supplied a motif for your pleas against Scottish Independence.

It is a thesis of this present treatise, my dear Mr Cameron, that you are much more intelligent than you deem it safe to reveal, and thus we have to take your mental measurements with allowances for deeper wisdom below the surface. You give a better performance of Bertie Wooster than Hugh Laurie, though if Osborne played Jeeves a wise employer would keep the silver spoons well counted every night. And the Wooster identity is well affirmed by your aura of what Bertie himself calls 'the young Master', in happy ignorance of the intricacies woven by his employees. You triumph in the art of alibi. Bertie's need in moments of crisis with Jeeves to remember that his ancestors did dashed well at Crecy is matched by your own silent invocations of their conquest at Hastings (silent lest your treacherous Europhobes associate Hastings with acute Europhilia). But we have to allow for your Woosterisms being not merely prattle or patter, especially when you sink Wooster benevolence in the nauseating priggishness of Bertie's cousin Edwin the Boy Scout justifying one of his devastating acts of kindness. Your allusions to Thatcher carefully understudy Aunt Agatha's son young Thos. when in love with Greta Garbo. If we are to perturb your prose in the interest of a deeper resonance, an obvious point of departure lies in your comments on former Prime Ministers.

Crude parallels afflict us nowadays in which Prime Ministers are confusingly likened to Presidents. Now, for all of your charming Woosterisms, we know you to have received a training in constitutionalism second to none (of which again more later). You clearly feel it necessary that your own party do not unmask you as a swot (like Gordon Brown). You may even have horrid memories of real-life events where the Bullingdon wreaked its oafish vengeance on wretches who had come to Oxford to study, and more directly you are likely to know the fate of the hero of Evelyn Waugh's *Decline and Fall* at the hands of the Buller an aeon before your time.

Waugh had even immortalised your collateral ancestor Duff Cooper's wife Lady Diana as Mrs Stitch in *Scoop* and their correspondence when published won justifiable celebrity (*Mr Wu and Mrs Stitch*). I dislike alluding to the Bullingdon and we will find good reasons to find much better subjects to absorb us in your Oxford career, but its graduates include your somewhat sinister money-man, and your aspirant rival still in his Mayoralty. So even on questions as relevant to your statesmanship as reflections on the historical realities of being Prime Minister you nowadays insist on writing and speaking well below your intellect. You need to vindicate the role of Prime Minister as thaumaturge in its own right, but you must not strain Tory minds.

Hence your conversation in May 2008 with Dylan Jones (*Cameron on Cameron* (2010), p. 312): 'Change in a political party is constant, and a party that stops changing and stops understanding the society it's trying to represent would be finished.' This at least fulfils the demand of the prophet Habbakuk (IX.2): 'Write the vision and make it plain upon tables, that he may run that readeth it'. It is a clear repudiation of Thatcher's absurd denial of the existence of Society (God knows what primeval Grantham superstition first

articulated that gibberish). We'll look at its Scottish implications later.

'The Conservative Party's brilliance over centuries has
been to change to reflect society.' Translated, this means that
since Thatcher said Society didn't exist, the Thatcher years
showed no reflection at all, the party stuck in immobile
swamp, the mirror unable even to grant its current owner
Snow White Stepmother status. But remove your disguise,
and no touch of the poisoned apple prevents your witness,
although you have to disguise yourself by remaining
surrounded by (disunionised) dwarfs:

> Disraeli understood the conservatism of the suburbs, Peel
> understood that there was a growing urban population and we
> had to repeal the corn laws, Salisbury understood the impor-
> tance of patriotism, Churchill understood the importance of
> home ownership, Mrs Thatcher understood the importance
> of giving trade unions back to their members.

The last is the master-touch, telegraphing its origin as 'Mrs
Thatcher understood the importance of dismembering
trade unions' to those capable of decoding it, but otherwise
assuring us that Mr Cameron understands the importance
of being earnest.

The other four theses appear simplistic enough to absolve
the proponent from the charge of intelligence, but in fact
contain much cunning and some wisdom. And here let us
benchmark for future discussion the undoubted fact that
you received as intelligent and informed a training in the
history of modern British politics as anyone could have. As
to the verdicts on your more reputable predecessors, you
phrased yourself with the air of a jay in eagle's feathers,
almost inviting demolition, but in fact your intent was to
conceal rather than reveal your glory.

This view of Sir Robert Peel, for instance, was a very perceptive awareness of his confrontation by the deluge of Irish migrants. They were migrants, not immigrants, Ireland now being part of your beloved UK by Union as well as by conquest, but as Paul Foot pointed out in his pioneer Penguin Special *Immigration and Race in British Politics* (1965) the sudden rise in Irish intake for the larger island won the nativist hostility which would rebubble its nausea 120 years later against incomers from the British Empire or Commonwealth. Although from within the same country, the Irish in mid-19th-century Britain were shunned, despised and underemployed because of what was declared to be their alien religion, their alien language, and their not so alien diseases. Peel – a hero putting humanity above party – reached beyond his time in fighting the Great Famine by relief food, by public works to provide employment, and by repealing the Corn Laws. I know that you know all that already, but you weren't going to produce a historical reference implying undue compassion on your part for what might be thought immigrants, were you? Yet this touches on one of the main phenomena recording Scotland's growing distance from England: we in Scotland need immigrants and want to welcome them, you surrender to odious xenophobia. Yet Peel faced a far greater challenge from incomers than today's UK, and he sacrificed his career to meet it, being ejected from the premiership by the knife-manship in his Conservative party at that point declining to 'change to reflect society' – for you to cite Peel as exemplary of the progress of the party which destroyed him indicates that among your other qualifications for premiership is a neck of sounding brass.

Bad as these tricks with history appear, they are less nauseating than Blair's repulsive apology for the Great

Famine. Unless he was admitting his descent from the parasite bringing the potato blight, his action was a repulsive egregious stage-grab ingratiating himself with presumably vote-bearing descendants of Famine migrants. By contrast your apology for Bloody Sunday in (London)Derry was appropriate, as you had inherited the responsibility for events (just) within your time, carried out under the regime of one of your predecessors in ruling party and country, and a response when the facts became finally and unarguably clear was essential. Everyone in the archipelago might well be proud of your dignity and honesty. You acted as the Prime Minister of the UK should act.

Your book with Dylan Jones is copyright you both, and hence however close to your original conversations must also be accepted as a written text, which you have revised and passed for publication so I'm not confronting you with your judgments made on the spot and never cleared (or cleansed) by you. You are far too intelligent not to have done this, and are in any case used to making your reported words spoken in the House of Commons what you want yourself to have said rather than what you actually said: and so do all MPs (and MSPs, I wouldn't dream of implying perpetual political innocence for the Scots). Forgive my road diversion here, but it's as well for people to be reminded of that, isn't it?

Isn't it?

I'm very glad you mentioned Peel, because he was a truly great man, extraordinarily hardworking, responsive to the written reports or letters he saw, ready to alter his judgments on mature consideration, judicious in assessment in a conservative way (if you like) but determined on reform where it was really needed. And by 'reform' he meant what it said, eradicating abuses, not simply finding some public possession in good running order and then selling it perhaps to the advantage of useful friends. Since he was a strong Protestant who stood out against Catholic Emancipation until Daniel O'Connell confronted him with a Catholic election in Clare in 1828–29, let's admit that when he thought or talked of reform the word recalled Martin Luther's courageous insistence that Catholicism must be swept away and an uncorrupt church put in its place. (Did I tell you that I am an active Roman Catholic?) He might not have wanted to think Catholic Emancipation a reform, and he would have been grimly aware of what Martin Luther would have called it, and in language Peel himself was too polite to use.

Peel is certainly a model for you in your protestations of love for the United Kingdom, because UK Prime Ministers have seldom tried to think of a home front beyond England, but he did. Scotland was sewn up under the Lord Advocate appointed by the Prime Minister but having been Chief Secretary for Ireland 1812–18 Peel really thought across ancient frontier lines and older seas. For the 32 remaining years of his life after his Irish stint, he built up one of the best private libraries of books from and about Ireland (how is your Scottish library, Prime Minister?). It wasn't usual. Ireland has been commonly if unwisely declared the grave-yard of aspiring political careers (and yet look at the Prime Ministers previously serving in Irish office – Wellington, Melbourne, Peel, Derby, Balfour, Campbell-Bannerman; the same superstition clung to the Welsh Office in recent years, but your distinguished colleagues William Hague and John Redwood owed their political prominence to it). Melbourne for one showed little sign of further interest in Ireland after his time there (beyond the unwelcome Parliamentary necessity of allying with Daniel O'Connell), and, as Prime Ministers go, he was exceptionally literate. In the case of your tribute to Peel's urban awareness (not a Tory characteristic before him, I agree), I think you may have simplified which in your case too often becomes oversimplification, something people prefer less than you have imagined. You would have been thinking of the Tamworth Manifesto of 1834, when Peel committed the Conservative party to acceptance of the Reform Act of 1832 and at least some of the implications of the industrial revolution (of which his father had formed a significant part, if not as great a part as its workers).

The iconoclastic historian George Dangerfield (famous for *The Strange Death of Liberal England* with its account of the Tory rebellion against constitutionalism in 1912–14) reflected in his *Victoria's Heir* that when Peel died, poor men wept in the streets of London. Some of their successors may have done so for Churchill, or Attlee. Could any Prime Minister ask for greater honour?

Historians admire Peel (other things being equal) once they get into his papers, so impressively archived in the British Library. It is good to feel the tug of a real mind pulling from the past in answer to your own, and doing what it could to see you get a good hold, for he played a great part in building up historical archives of the state. His old Parliamentary opponent and Whig historian Thomas Babington Macaulay, found himself in unexpected admiration for the Tory former Prime Minister when they met in a small group to professionalise archival maintenance and administration. All of us should feel small as we confront the past: it is good to know that when Peel did so, the leading British historian thought him at his greatest.

D. H. Lawrence wrote of Herman Melville (in his explosive *Studies in Classic American Literature*): 'Melville knew'.

Similarly I would say, Peel knew, if we are thinking about ruling the United Kingdom. How many others did, including yourself for all your professed love of it? As too many people could tell us, to love is not always to know.

Apart from his unquestionable value as a Cabinet Minister (who from then till now could match his intelligent industry?), Peel's visible awareness of the United Kingdom was to do with Ireland, which he studied: most UK politicians know a little England, at best. But Peel's occasional collisions with Scotland open up another aspect. I encountered him when in 1829 he was made aware of the Burke and Hare murders, and the overwhelming sense I got from the surviving correspondence between himself as Home Secretary and the Lord Advocate Sir William Rae was of men supposedly united under Prime Minister the Duke of Wellington, but actually separated not only by space but by time. Rae was still in a very long 18th century ready to assume that arrangements between gentlemen (not to be called corruption) were a fact of life: Peel was well and truly 19th century believing that if the law was being defied, denied, or circumnavigated, it must be reformed. (It makes one understand why the UK — but mostly England — should have given birth to H. G. Wells's *The Time Machine*, and to the BBC's *Dr Who*.) In a way the point was made by the smart-ass joke sidestepping metropolitan responsibility for one of the casualties of the UK, the failure to prevent apartheid in Northern Ireland before 1969: 'you are approaching Northern Ireland, set your watches back 300 years'. G. S. R. Kitson-Clark in his *Peel and the Conservative Party* (1929) was an ambitious, sophisticated, documents-driven historian but when the young writer looking back a century earlier followed the young Peel of 1812 to his first major post, Chief Secretary for Ireland (where Peel lived while in office, in contrast to salaried holders of that office in most of the 18th century), he concluded that 'When Peel turned his attention to Irish administration, it was rather like the severe cold all-intrusive light of morning breaking in on the weird shadows of a haunted wood' (p. 10). In part, Kitson-Clark for all his new professionalism was not immune to the spirit of his own time, the post-war 1920s whose urban English iconoclasm still shivered to the music of Yeats. And Scotland? Peel could claim a far stronger hold on the United Kingdom's ideological convictions than most of his fellow-English politicians when we remember that in the 1820s the time-lord Walter Scott acknowledged him to be his political Master first in opposition to Catholic Emancipation and then in its enactment. Yet Scott's whole array of 20-odd masterpiece novels, which inaugurated social history and historical fiction, brought into play an intoxication with the past as alien from Peel's England as Ireland's haunted wood. The three lands were now united in the same kingdom, and as formerly the same kingship, but not in the same country. And however great the challenges time-differentiation between the lands gave Peel, he faced them bravely, learning to change his mind, reorder his troops, and be damned as a time-server for his trouble.

Few of Peel's fellow-premiers would even try to imitate him in this regard, unless they came from beyond English time themselves, like Wellington from Ireland, Lloyd George from Wales, or Gladstone by bi-parental origin from Scotland. Peel's greatest critic, whose name you even placed ahead of him as a maker of the Conservative Party, the young Benjamin Disraeli, was ready to play Time-Lord in his own way, although seldom crossing any of the three peripheral frontiers to Wales, Scotland or Ireland, but even his admirers (and he had many, far more than merely

Tories) would refer to him as 'alien'. He was a Christianised Jew whose great novels deliberately identified himself with a bewildering orientalism. In fact his career makes for further time-alienation from England, so that, correctly interpreted, his self-distancing from England bears ominous comparability to that of Scott, Lloyd George, and his own bitter adversary Daniel O'Connell. That the native Irish O'Connell and the half-Scots Macaulay went on directly from their successful championship of Catholic Emancipation to a vehement if (for some decades) unsuccessful fight to abolish the exclusion of unChristianised Jews from Parliament, in part reflected their instinctive recognition of their own common qualities, for all that both of them occasionally fell into London habits of casually derisive references to the people for whose rights they had actually worked so hard. It did not stop them hating Disraeli, or deploring his meteor-like rise, although neither would live to see him ensconced in your present residence, my dear Mr Cameron. And neither can have hated him as thoroughly as he was hated in his own party, above all by his successor as its leader, Robert Cecil third Marquis of Salisbury. In fact Salisbury's private allusions to Disraeli make your antagonists Blair and Brown seem positively chummy.

What you meant by 'Disraeli understood the conservation of the suburbs... Salisbury understood the importance of patriotism' is fairly moot. If anything Disraeli was the master-manipulator of patriotism in party service and, however reluctantly, Salisbury's contribution in that regard was learned from him. Disraeli knew how to entertain them in or out of suburbs and enchant them with his patriotism (but did he carry Scotland, Ireland, and Wales with the England he pied-piped in his exotic wake?). He certainly charmed Queen Victoria whose romantic Scottish obsession increased her dependence on her servant (and possible morganatic husband) John Brown. Disraeli would speak of the two Johns he must always enlist in his plans, John Bull and John Brown. Salisbury despised them both, and quite possibly despised Victoria too. Cecils were Tudor Reformation new rich, and highly conscious of what their ancestor and founder of their great fortune Lord Burghley had told Queen Elizabeth on anything and everything. They certainly felt that put them above mere electors of Hanover imported to England in 1714 purely for their Protestantism (about which the Cecils in general seem more devout than the early Georges). Your citation of Salisbury, while somewhat haphazard, presumably arose from a historiographical cult bursting out under three different authorships in time for the millennium, and for the centenary of Salisbury's retirement from his third premiership in 1902 (albeit all his governments were either minority or coalition, whose appropriateness for yourself had not dawned when you were talking to Dylan Jones). At least one Salisbury bibliography made its author Andrew Roberts a Tory house historian, and keepers of the Thatcher flame could rejoice in Salisbury's having been quite as rude as Thatcher in public utterances with the slight distinction that he always meant his insults and hers may sometimes have originated in mere incompetence. He was not quite an icon fit for Tory democracy (in fact he destroyed the career of Lord Randolph Churchill, its leading exponent in his time, after Disraeli himself). There is a faint charm that he, the first Prime Minister of the 20th century, had opposed the great extensions of the franchise in the Reform Bills of 1867 and 1884. But surely it should eliminate him from a respectable UK Prime Minister's search in our day for appropriate exemplars!

You cannot declare your love of a democratic country entrusting (or at least partly entrusting) you with its rule while you publicly and privately invoke the shade of a predecessor who opposed democratisation at its two major constitutional advances, and heartily despised it. You might secretly seek to emulate his characteristically Cecilian subtlety in political intrigue and destruction of opponents in his own or anyone else's party, or his readiness to use and anonymously write for newspapers and magazines for that end. In fairness to Salisbury (not that he would give a damn whether I was fair to him or not), he did his own writing, and you are intelligent enough if not always wise enough to do yours. But Salisbury rejoiced in so rich a cynicism that the super-patriotic *Daily Mail* only meant to him something 'by office-boys for office-boys', as opposed to the press for which he wrote himself. He may have been a master-diplomat, but he sneered his way to the ends of the earth. He may invite more respect than we ought accord to modern Downing Street adventurers, informing the House of Lords on 30 January 1900 in the high tide of the Boer War 'I do not believe in the perfection of the British Constitution as an instrument of war'; imagine Blair admitting that, or imagine its equivalent from his American employer George W. Bush ('Yo Blair!'), although it sums up their public ethics exactly.

How would you like to meet him? I doubt if you would. His mocking lips would curl that massive beard in your diminution, with little concern as to your royal ancestors having shed their blue blood for England and Scotland (and Normandy) centuries before his first visible progenitors were telling others to shed theirs. The earliest known Cecils were Welsh marauders on the most successful of all their raids on England, under the command of the future Henry VII. Salisbury's most diplomatic son, Lord Robert Cecil, noted at the Paris Peace Conference in 1919 that his leader of the UK delegation Prime Minister David Lloyd George 'assured me that I was a Welshman and that the original name of my family was Seissyllt, which he wrote down on a bit of the menu'. Cecil had just resigned from Lloyd George's govern-ment on its (unduly deferred) Disestablishment of the (Episcopalian) Church of Wales and any attempt at patching up a Celtic peace between the little Welsh solicitor and the multi-centuried house of Salisbury was doomed. Disestab-lishing the Welsh Church reflected majority Welsh popular sentiment while the Cecils would always have known what was better for the Welsh than the Welsh could possibly know themselves. Lord Robert had come of age in the year his father began his first year in 10 Downing Street where he ruled for most of the next 20 years retiring from a govern-ment casually known as the Hotel Cecil (as in aristocratic 17th-century Paris NOT as in the UK world of commerce).

But how would you like to meet Disraeli? Can you think of any Prime Minister in whose personal company you would rather be? He would have extolled the romance of your Jewish ancestors, by way of a start, and made the most of any romance in your more numerous gentile ones. He would have a very refreshing honesty, more medical than cynical, as in his speech of 17 March 1845 'A Conservative Government is an organised hypocrisy'. You can hardly tell us how much you agree with that, though your Opposition thirst here as elsewhere to rival the Tories. You had excellent reasons for mentioning Disraeli first in your list of Conserv-ative premiers. Your Oxford tutor Vernon Bogdanor was fond of many quotations from Disraeli (chiefly from his most political novel *Coningsby*) for their sheer value in teach-ing, and himself introduced an edition of Disraeli's 1870 novel *Lothair* (Oxford English Novels (1975)) for which he most appropriately quoted the great if ferociously authoritarian F. R. Leavis on Disraeli's possessing 'the interests of a supremely intelligent politician who has a sociologist's understanding of civilisation and its movement in his time', interests Leavis found 'so mature'. Michael Foot on the eve of himself becoming Leader of the Opposition in 1980 also quoted *Coningsby* in his essay 'The Good Tory' (*Debts of Honour* (1980)), p. 45): 'A great man is one who affects the mind of his generation... Great minds must trust to great truths and great talents for their rise, and nothing else.' But while charmingly enthusiastic about their divide in party and period, Michael Foot smiled that 'Disraeli was never foolhardy enough to rely on his noble prescription'. You are no fictionist (except perhaps when under pressure from the necessity for economy with the truth), and so far you seem even less ready than Disraeli to rely on that 'noble prescription'. But Foot's insight, applied to you, suggests you may possess a touch of Disraelian independence, to which so far you have rarely allowed the breathing-space he gave his own variety. If nothing else you have momentarily seen the Disraelian vision of statesmanship, and here seems more productive research-ground than in Peel's dedication to work or in Salisbury's complacent contempt. And to be Disraeli you must have humour, not just smartness. You have to know how best to weather ridicule.

In one way you won't be Disraeli, and probably in the future Parliaments of your time nobody will. There was one Disraeli figure in your Referendum story, Alex Salmond, and as we look at him we may glimpse how far Disraeli is above the rest of us. That instant wit, that skill in political anatomisation, that delight in absurdity, that deployment of his own enemies and critics, that occasional towering rage at real evil, that elegance in riposte compelling the admiration of its victims, that quite unsparing invisible self-analysis, that very firm unyielding privacy, that eternal youth at any age — those things they shared, and it is heavy work for others to make mileage in them. Disraeli's was probably the most profound mind among your choice of Tory Prime Ministers, searing its way through the socio-political genealogical layers of his world and beyond them to what his world thought it knew and had scarcely discovered. *Sybil* told the polite world from what human degradation and exploitation its pleasure and leisure were possible; *Coningsby* mingled exact science and comic mastery in showing the microbes who rule our political world. Michael Foot speaks of Disraeli's understanding of Ireland in his Commons speech of February 1845 on the very eve of the Great Famine as 'a speech which seems to have compressed into it something of the whole ensuing century of Irish history, a foretaste of the famine, the Fenians, 1916, the founding of the Republic and more modern events still'; that extraordinary compression here and elsewhere resembles a mining process of unimaginable speed drawing ream upon ream into his reach and diagnoses, and Foot's 'a foretaste of the famine' perfectly glosses the horror Disraeli beheld ahead of Ireland.

The speech itself is vital to your own problem of loving the United Kingdom, and since you speak of its 300-year history the place of Ireland among those kingdoms however United must instruct us on the place of Scotland whether or not bereft of Ireland, or of a portion thereof. Disraeli showed unanswerably how metropolitan voices groped for understanding of the periphery, and his genius as a prophet can be felt in our recent debate on Scottish Independence, however different the visible features and questionable the mercenaries:

I want to see a public man come forward and say what the Irish question is. One says that it is a physical question: another a spiritual. Now it is the absence of the aristocracy; now the absence of railways. It is the Pope one day and potatoes the next... A starving population, an alien Church, and in addition the weakest executive in the world. Well, what then would gentlemen say if they were reading of a country in that position. They would say at once, 'The remedy is revolution'. But the Irish could not have a revolution and why? Because Ireland is connected with another and a more powerful country. Then what is the consequence? The connection with England became the cause of the present state of Ireland. If the connection with England prevented a revolution and a revolution was the only remedy, England logically is in the odious position of being the cause of all the misery of Ireland. What then is the duty of an English Minister? To effect by his policy all those changes which a revolution would affect by force. That is the Irish question in its integrity.

It is merely wasteful to dismiss this as something in another time and another place — as who should say, that was in another country, and besides, a million and a half are dead. It is your beloved Union of which Disraeli spoke, and asked the serious question whether the connection created the misery, or, as we might modernise it, induced the alienation. Disraeli did not speak of the Act of Union itself, using instead the word 'connection' which Theobald Wolfe Tone used in his Francophile revolutionary years before the Irish Act of Union which he would not live to see. And it would be equally wasteful to reproach Disraeli with having done little to answer the Irish question, since his obvious answer was that he could rule the Tory party from what he rightly called the greasy pole, but he could not direct the eyes of his reluctant followers as far or deep as understanding and revolutionising the periphery required. Your image of the

Conservative Party exhibiting its multi-century brilliance in changing to reflect society is slightly warped by its perpetual yearning to change back, and all too frequently its main response to Disraeli's leadership was to try to get rid of it. It is in reality no surprise to you to think of a Tory tradition of hopes of anticipated palace coups and stabs behind the arras.

But you yourself do share with Disraeli the benefits of this isolation on top of the greasy pole. He had very few friends in politics (Michael Foot points out that one was the anti-war Radical John Bright, a link whose charm contrasts with the dearth of Dizzy's Tory friendships. Like you, he knew how to manipulate his enemies. But like you (to quote Michael Foot once more) 'His victories were always tactical, not strategical; he did not lead, he followed'. (Isn't it pleasant to read an author who understood the difference between tactics and strategy, when every oaf today talks about strategy while usually meaning tactics?)

How isolated is that top-of-the-pole isolation? Do you reign or rule? Do you preside like some modern constitutional monarch, or remain the dominant figure in the discussions among your Cabinet whether you are there or not? It isn't always clear which you are, and since the US President has to be both King and Prime Minister it may be useful to return to the alternatives there. Franklin D. Roosevelt was a ruling President, not merely reigning: being wheelchair-bound he needed to show everyone including himself that he was perpetually activist, continually synthesising opposing opinions among his cabinet members and White House administrators, making Presidential intervention part of his essential therapy. It also meant that regardless of how crippled they thought he was, the public automatically thought of him as an activist, not as a patient. The other extreme was Dwight Eisenhower, letting his subordinates get on with it. Naturally, both symbols are misleading: the interventionist if he has any sense will ration his interventions, the serene potentate will know when to use his power, not merely to flourish it. The situation was clarified, indeed defined, when Peel's immediate predecessor Melbourne determined what has been the rule since, the collective responsibility of the Cabinet (or, as *1066 And All That* put it unkindly, that it did not matter what the Cabinet said so long as they all spoke at once). Melbourne in the 1820s had served in governments whose members were at loggerheads with one another over Catholic Emancipation, and when under Wellington and Peel the pro-Emancipationists were left outside, it was the anti-Emancipationist administration which found it had to grant it.

There may still be points of clear ideological or administrative difference among government members, but seldom on crisis issues. It meant that when Peel was Prime Minister in the 1840s, his devoted supporter Wellington complained that Peel was in a damned fright about those rotten potatoes, but that meant that Wellington and all the Cabinet must support the measures to fight Irish famine which Peel took, however revolutionary such government activism on an economic question might be. In general the periphery would be least likely to have its relevant minister continually subject to invigilations by the Great Man, but Burke and Hare seem to have taught Peel that Scotland could no longer be left so confidently to its Lord Advocate. Yet that situation could carry its own deceptions. Under the younger Pitt, the Scottish Lord Advocate, Henry Dundas, was the most powerful man in the government next to the Prime Minister. But that arose from the friendship — indeed partnership — of the two men in question. The next time the periphery was closely linked to the Prime Minister was when Salisbury gave his nephew and ultimate successor Arthur James Balfour his first job, in 1886, and since it was well known the premier was Balfour's Uncle Robert (so addressed in their official correspondence) the Music Halls invented the classic explanation for jobbery 'Bob's your Uncle!' which then survived across the English-speaking world after Uncle Robert and Nephew Arthur had vanished from public memory. The job was that of the recently-invented Scottish Secretary, whose necessity was disputed by non-Scots (it was first filled by the Tories in 1885 but created in response to pressure on Gladstone from the political boss of his Midlothian constituency, Archibald fifth Earl of Rosebery who would become Gladstone's successor in 1894). The Scottish post was a test flight — its interest for Salisbury would be to see how well young Arthur sustained trial gallops. Since his sister had married a wealthy Scot in Balfour's father, who died early having installed her in the great house Whittinghame conveniently near Edinburgh, it was useful as a political centre whence Scottish Toryism could be built up, and to that extent Scotland became less peripheral though more for personal than political reasons. Balfour and Rosebery eyed one another with unfailing courtesy from their great houses and while both of their premierships were failures they brought public interest back to aspiring Scottish politicians. It was relevant to Scottish foci that the next Liberal and the next Tory premiers were also Scots, Sir Henry Campbell-Bannerman and Andrew Bonar Law, though neither were welcomed by their Scottish predecessors: the first Labour Prime Minister was also a Scot, James Ramsay MacDonald. Stanley Baldwin raised the Scottish Secretariate to Cabinet level in 1926, a compliment to his rival MacDonald's origin perhaps but also symbolising Scottish status reverting to shadow in place of substance.

In any case all of them won their rewarding notoriety for their work outside of Scotland, Rosebery in the London County Council and as Foreign Secretary, MacDonald as an intellectual London journalist, Balfour on transfer to the Irish Chief Secretariate in 1887 which proved a real testing-ground in which the seemingly lackadaisical nephew won the title 'Bloody Balfour'. It did not mean implacable hatred. Edward Carson (whose career Balfour ignited by making him Crown prosecutor against land agitators and Home Rule politicians) told Balfour's niece and biographer Blanche Dugdale:

> Look at the fund he raised, and the arrangements he made, when the potato crop failed. That was what made them call it 'Balfour's famine'. – Thanks be to Mary and all the saints, and to Bloody Balfour, ould Ireland will be saved yet! – as an old woman said at the time – and she was right.

Carson wasn't being funny, although enjoying the humour of the thing. He was Protestant Ulster's great leader in the fight against Home Rule in 1910–14, but his own Christianity was agnostically non-sectarian, and he seems to have loved the beauty of Roman Catholic rural devotion. Scotland watched Irish politics, its crofters' revolts inspired by the Irish land leagues in the 1880s, its Toryism tinged by the discovery that the indolent Balfour was proving a local hero. He was chosen for the Chancellorship of the University of Edinburgh in a gesture of Unionist solidarity in 1891. As the Orange societies swelled into defiance against imminent Home Rule before World War I, Scotland produced echoes although seldom much more. The Independence Referendum a century later was all the more revolutionary because ît was îts own thing, not a shadow or a clone. You may not think ît the Right Thing but as the ſtruggle maximised, ît became more and more aware of îts indigenous integrîty.

'I made Carson in a way' Balfour told his niece (Dugdale, *Arthur James Balfour* (1936), I. p. 147). 'I made Carson and Carson made me.' In fact this was coalîtion polîtics, all under Salisbury's watchful eye. Carson began as a Liberal Unioniſt who revered Joe Chamberlain, leader of the Radical defection from the Liberals during the parliamentary ſtruggle for the firſt Irish Home Rule Bill in early 1886. Balfour's reliance on Carson as fearless law enforcement officer was an intereſting anticipation of your use of the Liberal Democrats in the battle for Scotland – Danny Alexander, Secretary of State for Scotland, then on his promotion Michael Moore, then when you decided (surely you and not the amiable Clegg) that the fight was going to get dirty – out goes the gentleman Moore and in comes Aliſtair Carmichael, serenaded by the press as the available tough. It was the same principle: let the junior partners do the dirty work, although the flabby Carmichael seemed lîttle more than animated blubber by comparison wîth the heroic and skeletal Carson. (How Carson would have despised a House of Commons pretending conflict for the purpose of lodging sycophantic queſtions to get unctuous answers!) Balfour's previous tenancy of Scotland's infant secretariate was not necessarily a certain troublefree billet – the embattled crofters were learning from the Irish land war and their men in the Commons (such as Dr Charles Cameron) were among the moſt dependable Liberal allies for the Irish Home party.

Balfour's insouciance and affection for his brother's slightly alarmed children at Whîttinghame might seem to dismiss one possible incursion of Irish affairs into Scotland, in the shape of assassination of the Irish Chief Secretary. Five years before, Chief Secretary Lord Frederick Cavendish had been stabbed to death in Phoenix Park on 6 May 1882. Scotland was of significance not because of its Secretariate for all of Rosebery's hopes for its strengthening national sentiment, but because of the potential fate of the former incumbent. Originally Salisbury seemed to have personalised Scotland as a somewhat prickly aristocratic hermit, and his first choice to inaugurate the new post of Scottish Secretary in 1885 was the Duke of Richmond and Gordon (whose first Dukedom indeed derived from his ancestress's refusal to say NO to Charles II and who thought the post offered to him was unnecessary). Salisbury, oblivious for the moment of his own nephew, told the Duke he was the only possible choice since otherwise:

> the Scotch people would declare that we were despising Scotland & treating her as if she were a West Indian colony. It really is a matter where the effulgence of two Dukedoms and the best salmon river in Scotland will go a long way.

One could hardly ask for a clearer vision of what the Tories saw in the Scottish part of the United Kingdom. It remained the Unionist ideal Scotland until the Second World War, as even would-be native makers of a more Scottish Tory Scotland such as John Buchan seemed to sanctify the salmon river as its heart (though his finest epiphany *John Macnab* (1923) requires an infant tinker poacher to complete the work). George Orwell's posthumous 'Such, Such Were the Joys' (1952) remembered Scotland as an English pleasure-ground, claims to whose ownership marked the means for prep-school children of plutocrats to despise their inferiors:

> The school was pervaded by a curious cult of Scotland, which brought out the fundamental contradiction in our standard

of values. ... Ostensibly we were supposed to admire the Scots because they were 'grim' and 'dour' ('stern' was perhaps the key word), and irresistible on the field of battle. In the big school-room there was a steel engraving of the charge of the Scots Greys at Waterloo, all looking as though they enjoyed every moment of it. Our picture of Scotland was made up of burns, braes, kilts, sporrans, claymores, bagpipes and the like, all somehow mixed up with the invigorating effects of porridge, Protestantism and a cold climate. But underlying this was something quite different. The real reason for the cult of Scotland was that only very rich people could spend their summers there. And the pretended belief in Scottish superiority was a cover for the bad conscience of the occupying English, who had pushed the Highland peasantry off their farms to make way for the deer forests, and then compensated them by turning them into servants... Scotland was a private paradise which a few initiates could talk about and make outsiders feel small.

'You going to Scotland this hols?'

'Rather! We go every year.'

'My pater's got three miles of river.'

'My pater's giving me a new gun for the twelfth. There's jolly good black game where we go. Get out, Smith! What are you listening for? You've never been to Scotland. I bet you don't know what a black-cock looks like.'

The 'twelfth', of course, was the twelfth of August, when grouse-shooting began. In Protestant Ulster, the twelfth was of July. When Orwell was at pre-school leading Tories would have needed to celebrate both since in 1912–14 the great guns of the party collectively committed treason, declaring intent of resisting a Home Rule Act by force if necessary. A suitable link drawing the peripheral countries together was formidably present in the Tory leader, Andrew Bonar Law, Scots but implacable in readiness to lead his party against government and law. His father had been a Presbyterian minister for a time serving in Belfast to which young Law learning the trade of an iron merchant in Glasgow would travel for weekends attending his father's sermons. Their theological effect appears to have been minimal or negative as he remained an atheist or agnostic for life. But their political effect and that of the congregation on him made the defence of Protestant Ulster the great cause of his life.

There was one version of your beloved UK, my dear Mr Cameron, while the Orwell reduction of Scotland to a plutocratic hunting-ground gives you another facet. Orwell's memory seems representative of his times, save that it was not (for the most part) the English who had evicted the Highlanders but their own Anglified chieftains, as bitterly recorded in Walter Scott's preface to his *A Legend of Montrose* and in the anonymous 'Canadian Boat Song' (probably his work also). Modern Scottish nationalism educated itself in the 1970s by the evangelistic touring show *The Cheviot, the Stag and the Black, Black Oil* by John McGrath and the 7:84 company. The image of the Scots as Sunday-schooled cannon-fodder survived in Orwell's 1984 where Winston Smith (bearing the outcast proto-Orwell's surname from 'Such, Such Were the Joys,' is shown when still at liberty and as part of his work inventing a Scots-named icon for Ingsoc youth, Ogilvy. As a pre-school boy Orwell read the *Magnet*, the boys' weekly bringing to its devoted readers the doings of Billy Bunter, Harry Wharton, and their schoolmates at Greyfriars, where the Scots boy, Donald Ogilvy, has six brothers in the UK forces in World War I (e.g. *Magnet*, 4 May 1918). *Nineteen Eighty-Four* here as elsewhere is simultaneously satire against Left and Right:

At the age of three Comrade Ogilvy had refused all toys except a drum, a sub-machine gun and a model helicopter. At six — a year early, by a special relaxation of the rules — he had joined the Spies; at nine he had been a troop leader.

Here Orwell was mocking Baden-Powell's Boy Scouts, launched in his prep-school years, and the mockery suggested their work shaded naturally into informing (not to be thought of as sneaking).

At eleven he had denounced his uncle to the Thought Police after overhearing a conversation which appeared to him to have criminal tendencies.

At seventeen he had been a district organiser of the Junior Anti-Sex League.

At nineteen he had designed a hand grenade which had been adopted by the Ministry of Peace and which, at its first trial, had killed thirty-one Eurasian prisoners at one burst. At twenty-three he had perished in action.

Thus Scotland, depopulated for aristocratic and pseudo-aristocratic blood-sports, gave up its evicted refugees for international slaughter. It gives it a sure place in the history and literature of the UK. That, my dear Mr Cameron, was what you were crying about.

CHAPTER THREE

THE ETONIAN EDUCATION OF A PRIME MINISTER

Alas! regardless of their doom
The little victims play!
No sense have they of ills to come
Nor care beyond to-day:
Yet see how all around them wait
The Ministers of human fate
And black Misfortune's baleful train!
Ah show them where in ambush stand
To seize their prey, the murderous band!
Ah, tell them they are men!

— THOMAS GRAY, 'Ode on a Distant Prospect
of Eton College'

You have been cultivating the image of a cosseted mediocrity, my dear Prime Minister, partly with a view to luring your enemies to their destruction. I am obliged to divest you of your Hallowe'en mask. Conceal it as you may, confuse your enemies and still more your rivals as you pretend, huddle away from any similarity to the intellectualism of Harold Wilson, Harold Macmillan, Winston Churchill or Michael Foot — but you are probably their mental equal save that they did not clutter their intelligence by persistence in its concealment.

Your adventures in that concealment as you stride throughout Europe and the world are not our primary concern, although we have to notice them in appreciating how you saved Scotland. Moliére would have done much with them, seeing his concern with characters trying to prove what they aren't. The great Scottish comic actor Rikki Fulton would go into long broodings to determine what stage business, movements, gestures &c Molière himself would have given to the part: this was for triumphant productions of Molière in Scots – did your love for the.UK lead you to come up here to see such things? How much delight do you take in our archipelago's linguistic diversity? Your training and intellect may not have prompted that logical step.

You certainly showed your shrewd use of your education in that list of Prime Ministers from which you have been learning. Its prime quality lay in the names you carefully left out. It might seem that the Conservative Party (be its merits what they may) can hardly be proved in direct descent from early 18th-century ancestors. But the Conservative Party (Scotland) thinks it can in its Commission on the Future of Scotland, Chair Lord Strathclyde (2014), which brightly begins:

> The Conservative Party is and always has been the party of the Union... 'The Union is a Tory accomplishment – first under Queen Anne in 1707, then under Pitt the Younger (with Ireland) in 1801... The Conservative Party is and always has been flexible about how the Union should be encouraged to evolve.

It seems unfair to quibble with artistry like this. Yes, there were Tories involved in making the Union like Robert Harley the Northern Secretary of State, Tories who would later be Jacobites like Henry St John the Secretary at War, Tories like the Treasurer Lord Godolphin and the Commander-in-Chief the Duke of Marlborough both of whom were rapidly becoming Whigs. Never mind the Union, the Tory party itself had no union from George I's arrival, many Tories would have preferred a return of the exiled Stuarts, and few were enthusiastic about the Union of Parliaments. The Tories at the time of the Union of 1707 were prepared to contemplate a Catholic on the throne and Godolphin and Marlborough had intrigued with the Catholic Stuart claimants. Pitt sought to pass the Union with Ireland conditionally on Catholic Emancipation but had to resign when it was blocked by George III, and the Tories were then the party against Emancipation. The Union with Ireland never really worked until O'Connell was elected to Parliament, where he proved its greatest orator and kept a government in office for the later 1830s at which point the entire archipelago was evidently represented and therefore the Union's leading enemy was making it work for the first time. This attempt to declare the Tory party the party of Union on the basis of one or two facts wildly out of context and isolated from the natural progress of history simply tells us that if present-day attitudes of the Tories to the Union are based on this in-and-out vision of history, we can have no confidence whatsoever in their Unionism. In other words, my dear Mr Cameron, what is unalterable Unionism with you today may be Unionism in fragments the day after tomorrow. And any healthy state may prefer to avoid your Unionism when it involves stirring the army to mutiny and arming a sectarian civilian populace all against a constitutional act of Parliament. An appeal to history from you is much more dangerous because you are not the average ignoramus heading a Tory government, such as Heath or Home or Sir John Major. (When John Major became Prime Minister the relevant Irish diplomat reported as follows: 'The good news is that he says we shouldn't be bound by history. The bad news is that he

doesn't know any history.') You are light-years beyond
Thatcher, the worst student imaginable since she fancied she
knew any thing of importance anyway. You may be as well
informed as Macmillan, who read many of the books he
published, and certainly better than Eden. You can't
compete with Churchill or Gordon Brown, good historians
when their biases were not imprisoning them. But as we will
see you are one of the best students of history to have ruled
in 10 Downing Street.

You have not been a much more reliable commentator
on history than Lord Strathclyde, but this looks like high
Machiavellian deception in you whereas he and his committee
are clearly three-card-trick pseudo-historians. Without
making an ass of yourself playing Whigs and Tories under
Queen Anne, you have consistently spoken as though the
United Kingdom had been formed in 1707 and prospered
to the satisfaction of all — at least of all within it — until the
second decade of the 21st century. Age cannot wither your
UK nor custom stale its infinite virginity. Your whole strategy
necessitated avoidance of all mention of Ireland and its
increase of Union and then part decrease: indeed you all too
often avoided mentioning Northern Ireland when it was
honest, courteous and politic to include it. This was not
only relative to the debate on Scottish Independence: your
idolisation of the Olympic 'Team GB' revealed your premature limitation of UK frontiers, since it excluded Northern
Ireland. It was particularly short-sighted and ungracious in
its treatment of Northern Ireland Catholics who were beginning to think of themselves as UK citizens rather than
hopeless Irish anti-partitionists. After your predecessors
have spent incalculable blood and treasure trying to hold
Northern Ireland in the Union as wished by the majority of
its inhabitants, you exclude it from the supreme sport

celebration. Do you look on Northern Ireland as a possible discard, and that the predatory shark-teeth of Mr Gerry Adams will be ultimately invited to devour the victims for whom he has panted so long? You use the word 'Britain' far too often when you should say 'UK'. Yet what of the actual creation of the United Kingdom of Great Britain in 1707 (which lasted until 1 January 1801 when 'Great Britain' ceased to have a constitutional existence being superseded by the United Kingdom of Great Britain and Ireland)? Yet despite the recent historiographical attempts to suggest that Scots in the Scottish Parliament of 1707 may often have believed in the value of Union with England while also being happy to take any money England spent in persuading them, you seldom invoke founding fathers on either side of the Border, not even Marlborough, the first great Churchill, that self-enriching warlord whose armies may have silently proved the most alarming of all pressures on the Scots. Lord Strathclyde and friends have inexpertly shown that the devil is in the detail, but you seem to leave the Union at best unprofaned by the hands of its votaries.

Naturally historians have advanced and occasionally enriched themselves by finding birth-dates for the Tory party, but little or no agreement seems to exist for any date before the last premier of the 18th century, William Pitt the younger. Lord Strathclyde and his friends lay down the law about 1707 with a brazen confidence which hardly augurs well for any other alleged facts emanating from the Scottish Tory party, and indeed you showed us your own view of them in telling us to follow the judgment of Gordon Brown and Alistair Darling on Scotland while withdrawing none of your perennial implications that they caused a world depression. Your predecessor as party leader and subsequently your subordinate as Foreign Secretary William Hague has suitably revered the younger Pitt. But in your list of great Tory premiers you passed Pitt by, for all of the glory of his 17-year innings overshadowing poor Thatcher (1979–1990) and the longlasting Lord Liverpool (1812–27) alike, not to speak of Pitt's second and final two-year term. He is your exemplar in isolation, granting his companionship with Henry Dundas some likeness to George Osborne yet in both cases retaining the strength of solitude. He had some of your master-skill in manoeuvring amongst your enemies and knowledge of when to seek and discard alliances and underlings with varying temperatures according to your needs. But of course Pitt was unmentionable since he was the architect of the unmentionable Union (or mentionable only by Lord Strathclyde and his pals), the one with Ireland which sullied the purity of the one with Scotland. Moreover, Pitt resigned office in 1801 when he was prevented by George III from delivering Catholic Emancipation as promised by him when getting the Union through the Irish Parliament and persuading the prominent Catholics spiritual and temporal to support it. He seems to have regarded himself as bound by a Vow. It was safer to leave that scrupulousness in 1801. You hardly desire such a precedent round your neck, even before you became associated with Vows for the support of Unions.

Similarly you omitted Balfour and Bonar Law, although theirs were rich precedents as Prime Ministers famous for defence of the Union. And you know a great deal about them. Commentators and political opponents alike make much of your being an Etonian, but they seldom ask what you studied there, or how much, or with whom. The snobs want to luxuriate in the thought of Eton, the pseudo-egalitarians want to deny its democracy. As it happened, you were taught there by one of the leading Irish historians of our time, and graduated from Eton with a mastery of the Union with Ireland which you would later so carefully conceal. There was no coincidence about it: Eton has produced the best Irish history-teaching of any English school in the last half-century. As a teacher of Irish history in Scotland I found the quality of English public school products no more predictable than those of any Scottish comprehensives, save that they were sometimes too quick to exhibit a high opinion of themselves. But any student from Eton came to a university's Irish history courses with excellent groundwork. As a freelance Edinburgh Festival Fringe theatre critic I also noted that Eton schoolboys in most years gave the best schoolchild performances, but alone among secondary schools they seldom mentioned their school in their publicity – they called themselves 'Double Edge'. They realised the likelihood of the name of Eton putting Scottish audiences and critics off. Like you – and like Alex Salmond – they knew how to manage their enemies.

Your exceptionally useful biography, *Cameron: Practically a Conservative* by Francis Elliott and James Hanning (2007, 2012) has obtained reminiscences of you from one of your Eton teachers, Dr Andrew Gailey, whose subject 'Northern Ireland: a Study in Conflict' you took, later getting him as tutor for more advanced work. I doubt if anyone could have easily found a better teacher. He is thorough, austere, kindly, stimulating, conscientious, diplomatic, and quick to see how errors and omissions can best be averted. To any Irish historian he is invaluable for 20th-century history. He resembles his fellow-Irishman Professor R. F. Foster of Oxford in making the most of relevant creative literature, his publication topics extending from the Irish novelist (and Church of Ireland canon) who wrote novels as George Birmingham to Jack Sayers, the great editor of the best mid-20th-century Northern Ireland newspaper . He taught you History of Art amongst much else, and in fact ensured that whatever you learned about Ireland you assimilated in multi-cultural terms. When you studied with him your diligence and his dedication must have ensured that your subsequent supposed erroneousness in leaving Northern Ireland out of your panegyrics for the UK was entirely deliberate. You know what you are doing far better than your critics understand why you are doing it.

In your time at Eton Dr Gailey was working on his major book *Ireland and the Death of Kindness: The Experience of Constructive Unionism 1890–1905* (1987). The book is a historian's delight as its author brings its various characters to life in deeply informative portraits and fascinating commentary on their doings. We can never recover the past, but the book at times makes the reader think himself/herself there with illumination from a generous but unsentimental guide. It may be doubted if any other book outshines its understanding of A. J. Balfour, for instance. No doubt you stay in touch with Dr Gailey, now Vice-Provost of Eton, whose Provost is a Crown appointment and thus presumably under your jurisdiction. So if you didn't read *Ireland and the Death of Kindness* published when you were an Oxford undergraduate, you will surely have seen it since. In any case, its first page of text carries three epigraphs each of which could stand as theses for your Prime Ministerial relationships with Scotland. The first quotation was from Prime Minister Salisbury to outgoing Chief Secretary for Ireland Sir Michael Hicks Beach on 28 February 1887:

> I agree with [General Sir Redvers] Buller that you cannot govern the Irish or anybody else by severity alone; but I think he's fundamentally wrong in believing that conciliation and severity must go together. The severity must come first. They must 'take a licking' before conciliation will do them any good.

With this in mind he transferred Balfour to the office Hicks Beach was resigning for reasons of health (and possibly safety). The language reminds us how close to his schooldays Salisbury remained — like Hicks Beach and Balfour he was an Etonian but left it after five years because of bullying, but like many victims of bullying he seems to have made it more of a virtue in retrospect.

Dr Gailey's third epigraph was from nephew Arthur in the same year, assurance he had learned the lesson his uncle was teaching:

> I shall be as relentless as Cromwell in enforcing obedience to the law, but, at the same time, I shall be as radical as any reformer in redressing grievances ... It is on the two-fold aspect of my policy that I rely for success. Hitherto English governments ... have been all for repression or all for reform. I am for both: repression as stern as Cromwell; reform as thorough as Mr Parnell or anyone else can desire.

It showed some independence of the surrogate parent Uncle Robert (always so addressed by Balfour: the Cecils did not care to be rejuvenated by Music Halls). Balfour was at least prepared to contemplate Buller's tandem procedures rather than Salisbury's sequential timing. Balfour's next 15 years were to require his slow takeover of Salisbury's domestic policy-making to the point of ultimate near-ventriloquism. But initially he had to cater to Salisbury's hopelessly crude paternalism for the periphery. Salisbury's present-day biographical apologist the Tory historian Andrew Roberts quoted him in the *Quarterly Review* in 1872:

> Is it not just conceivable that there is no remedy that we can apply for the Irish hatred of ourselves? ... May it not, on the contrary, be our incessant doctoring and meddling, awakening the passions now of this party, now of that, raising at every

ſtage a fresh crop of resentments by the side of the old growth, that puts off the day when these feelings will decay quietly away and be forgotten?

Whatever else this might have asserted, ît was not the United Kingdom. 'We' was England, though when nephew Arthur had come of age ît might be permîtted to include Scotland (limîted to the Scottish great houses). Its idea of Ireland recalls US Republican party members in Senator Joe McCarthy's time, insiſting the opposed party had 'loſt China', that these subordinate and subhuman peoples could never assert their dreams of independence wîthout the metropolîtan polîticians (in London or in Washington DC) prompting them to do so. Ten years later, in 1883, Salisbury told the *Quarterly*'s readers in his essay 'Disintegration':

> Possession of Ireland is our peculiar punishment, our unique affliction, among the family of nations. What crime have we committed, wîth what particular vice is our national character chargeable, that this chaſtisement should have befallen us?
>
> Andrew Roberts, *Salisbury*, 442–43

Dr Roberts dignifies this by terming Salisbury 'Ever the fataliſt'. It may simply have been an intellectually lazy man's self-exculpation from dealing wîth public queſtions which his opponents at leaſt tried to face. It would be a Tory response to Ireland all too frequently, sometimes wîth force as the idler's resort, sometimes wîth sheer inanîtion. The young Balfour was credîted wîth physical laziness, hence to prove himself to his uncle and the world he could not afford to languish in his uncle's formula. To assume he had Cromwell as an appropriate model was certainly idiotic, since however bloody-minded Balfour might be he could hardly start butchering the inhabîtants of disrespectful towns. But Balfour had matured on Macaulay whose rhetoric argued that Cromwell's methods were superior to the petty persecutions of penal days, and on Carlyle, who saw them as superior to any possible alternatives. Theodore Roosevelt, nurtured on the same exhilarating breast-feeding, argued in private correspondence for the same choice, Cromwell or Parnell, though not their combination. It was an intellectualised version of carrot and stick, and as such a tempting but foolish policy for future Unionist leaders whether facing Ireland or Scotland. Irrespective of whether Ireland be in the Union or not, the viewing mechanism from London can remain ominously familiar.

Dr Gailey's second epigraph was again from A. J. Balfour, in a letter to Colonel Milward in 1892 five months after leaving office as Chief Secretary. It reads as though it might have inspired you, my dear Mr Cameron, on taking office as Prime Minister:

> [The government party] is not a conservative party but a unionist party – a unionist party in which no doubt that conservative element greatly predominates, but one nevertheless of which the liberal element forms an essential and more important part. Now such a party can act heartily together only if by the exercise of a certain amount of mutual forbearance.

I think neither Balfour nor you made the mistake of equating the 'liberal element' with Liberal party members alone. But to what did Irish Liberal Unionism in 1892 amount? And what was Liberal Democracy in Scotland after it had seen its UK chieftains, Charles Kennedy and Menzies Campbell, successively decapitated? I suspect that you saw the weaknesses of your partners on the Scottish front which you so shrewdly entrusted to them, while Mr Clegg – the ultimate beneficiary of the Scottish decapitations – retained rose-garden coloured spectacles. Balfour was right: so long as Liberal Democrats would stay liberal, they could preserve an identity for their outlying followers. He would be even more right when his doctrine be applied to the settlement of 2010 and its sequels. In both cases, the sweets of office were too powerful for the memory of former principles. You were clever enough – and courteous enough – to sound like the most liberal Unionist of the entire Scottish drama. Your lieutenants then easily induced the Liberal Democrats to sound as Conservative as possible to justify their places in the sun and the tacit assumption that big boys must show themselves big bullies. The public, if it wanted big bullies, knew the party which had specialised in their production and hence was unlikely to prefer the new variety, but the realities were obvious enough. We may not all have been to Eton but most of us have been to school.

Dr Gailey's *Ireland and the Death of Kindness* opened up the idea of constructive unionism in theory and practice, and you can gain much profit in re-reading it and considering what it tells you with an eye to constructive Unionism in Scotland. And I mean you. Do not insult the intelligence of the Scots by pretending that constructive Unionism in Scotland is left entirely to the Scottish Tory party and what it can amalgamate from Scottish Labour and Scottish LibDems. We all know that nothing can come from Scottish Unionism against the will of their London lords (or, if you think we should go native, lairds). This is not to dismiss the Holyrood Unionists. Willie Rennie may sound like the barman in the Last Chance Saloon fearing the liquor is about to run out, but he would probably make a better fist of Scottish business at Westminster than the insults to the Scottish people who now hold the lucrative posts. Ruth Davidson, Colonel in the Territorials, may never quite win the universal respect in which her predecessor as Holyrood

Tory leader Annabel Goldie is held, but she has had her moments: her speech on same-sex marriage was probably the best in that debate, and one of the best I have heard. Her genius in dignified gratitude to her own family for giving her so happy a childhood and showing her own yearning to have a comparably happy family herself struck to the heart of the dishonest argument clothing a bigoted opposition to lesbian and gay marriage with the pretence of protecting the family. To offer a precedent dearer to me than to you, she played the role of Marx unmasking Hegel and standing him on his head. As she made clear, we were all in this together, Unionists and Nationalists (or, as we say nowadays, NO and YES): and in your own Parliament you showed leadership and courage on same-sex marriage comparable to that of Alex Salmond and the great majority of the Scottish Parliament. The air is more honest with those measures on the statute books. But while I have little doubt that while the Colonel would have led as many of her forces as she could in supporting her just cause even if you had not shown that courage at Westminster, her leadership in general exists by your command, as those of the other Unionist parties for their Westminster masters. After the Referendum poor Johann Lamont became our star witness as to the Labour party's form of London rule. Everyone knows now that the Unionist parties at Holyrood are merely London fiefs and this alone was a sufficient reason for many voters to vote for the SNP who, whatever their drawbacks, are not likely to be ruled from London.

You are personally credited here with the ouster of Annabel Goldie from the Holyrood Tory leadership, although she was the woman who proved that Scotland could love a woman Tory leader – so much for the thesis that Scottish anti-Thatcherism was male chauvinism. You are also credited with stopping Murdo Fraser's bid for the Scottish

Tory leadership when he called for a born-again party with names such as Conservative or Tory blotted out. Whatever your other merits, you live in a world of admanship and brandnames, and your cosmeticians in London will have told you the brand must stay, rechristening in Scotland would be bad for the image in England. I have no regrets, not being a Tory and never intending to vote for one, and the Colonel has a much better sense of humour than the martyred Fraser (if not quite equal to Annabel Goldie's which has played a fine part in ennobling the spirit of Holyrood). But it will convince nobody for you to echo the words of the hero of a non-Scottish play 'Thou canst not say I did it, never shake thy gory locks at me'.

Dr Andrew Gailey showed himself a historian wisely warning against excessive political party self-congratulation, but that lesson is no harm to your party or mine. He showed how Tory governments responded impressively and from time to time imaginatively, with recognition of individual agrarian reform movements, notably those giving the Irish agricultural labourer his first sense of assurance. And it was a time when important understandings developed between people of very different political, religious, economic and social backgrounds. You may have been very clever in your insistence that the Scots did not like you and hence others would have to preach the Unionist crusade, and for all of our rude remarks about your being a new edition of Blair who was a new edition of Thatcher, you had the wit to know what they did not, that a Unionist London politician openly giving orders to the Scots sends voters in shoals to other camps. In Thatcher's later years the wretched Scottish Tories were virtually on their knees either to God or her (and they scarcely could distinguish between them) that she stay south of the border, but back she would come, patronising smile and roguish finger at the ready as she closed in on Scots who thereafter would never vote Tory again. Blair would do the same thing thus causing Alex Salmond to offer him a second-class railway ticket to Scotland any time he would like, with a Scottish Nationalist harvest to follow. So you were wiser in your generation, and other crusaders in other parties were left carrying the Unionist can. But the LibDem, Labour and Tory hearts you united up to and into the pre-Referendum Vow are now sundered far apart, and you may even have to dictate future Scottish policy in the open!

Even the Tories could not sustain Salisbury's sneer, half-rising to a whine, about the Irish hating the English, or him personally (he easily equated them), and his nephews the Balfour brothers at least found it wise to perpetrate the doctrine of killing Home Rule by kindness however haphazard its actual realisation. It would not need you to invoke the spirit of Oliver Cromwell for all that he was the first creator of the United Kingdom by his summons to all three kingdoms to send their representatives to his Parliament. But it would need you to pursue the principle of creative Unionism, instead of avoiding, sidelining or offloading Scotland. It worked for a time, but if you are serious about your love for the UK you should now be capable of more than singing its praises to the Scottish Widows. And the starting place is that very example of the Balfours in at least recognising the existence of gross social injustice in the condition of the agricultural labourers. The equivalent is now at hand. Instead of running from the field where you declare you were hated, turn now to the nadir of your popularity. You won the Referendum, but you lost in four key areas, Glasgow, North Lanark, West Dumbarton and Dundee. These are also places with some of the worst poverty in the UK. Their YES votes were a rejection of the Union and all it stood for, all along the line, and in countless cases the cause of that rejection was hatred of a society dooming them into hopelessness. You can begin by thinking what you and the Colonel and the First Minister can do to end that shame, those livid weals on the face of your beloved Union.

Dr Andrew Gailey's Special Subject in which you studied 'Northern Ireland: a Study in Conflict' must have its long shadows when your aim to win the General Election of 2010 turned on an unsuccessful attempt to reap victory from incorporation with the Ulster Unionists, the supposedly moderate Protestant party in danger of being outflanked by the more extreme Democratic Unionists under the late Revd Dr Ian Richard Kyle Paisley. When you were studying Northern Ireland at Eton, your teacher could not have been bettered, but the time in which you were studying was misleading, being about 1983. Thatcher was entrenched in one of her most perverse and silly performances, dragging the problem down to lower depths yet, in the worst traditions of a schoolyard brawl. Garret Fitzgerald, Irish Taoiseach from 1982, was probably the finest intellect among heads of government in his time, and certainly the finest Ireland has ever sustained north or south of the border. He was also an utterly honest, charmingly innocent person. As journalist and academician in economics he educated his countrymen into belief in and use of the European Union which he probably understood better than anyone else. In 1984 Thatcher made some ignorant remark about economics in his presence and with his almost religious anxiety to teach truth and dispel error at all times, he painstakingly corrected her. Surrounded as she was by a court whose denizens knew never to contradict or correct her, and to preserve their patience through her incessant monologues, she was thunderstruck and (when she had recovered) livid.

She used an early opportunity at a press conference on talks she had had with him on Northern Ireland to assert that three proposals had been made by Fitzgerald (they had not) and after enunciating each one as contemptuously as possible, bawled 'OUT!' Presumably she had got the idea from youthful critics of her government who used to shout 'Maggie! Maggie! Maggie! OUT!, OUT!, OUT!' This was an utter humiliation of Fitzgerald. It might be compared to the accuracy of Goebbels when inducing a rant from Hitler. It certainly solidified her status with her Tory Right and (for the very last time) the Ulster Unionists. It gave enormous moral support to the utterly unscrupulous leader of the Irish parliamentary Opposition Charles J. Haughey, who would certainly capitalise on it to his chauvinist best regardless of its benefit to the murderous IRA, whooping up fires of Anglophobia over all the island of Ireland. Fitzgerald was derided as the butt of Thatcher's performance, the Republic of Ireland swinging round to the view that nobody but a crook like Haughey could deal with Thatcher. The IRA were thus reassured of an increase in their credibility and acceptability amongst Irish Catholics on either side of the border who were not themselves violent but who would now be more easily persuadable to be what Mao called water in which the fish (i.e. the guerrilla fighters) could swim. This would have been the archipelago's background to Northern Ireland when you were studying at Eton, where I take it neither Dr Gailey nor yourself realised how fraudulent the Thatcher 'OUT! … OUT! … OUT!' actually was. And whatever Dr Gailey's views on Margaret Thatcher, you would not have questioned her perspicacity or integrity, however ungentlemanly she might sound.

Her stance was electorally quite foolish, UK-wise, apart from its toxic effects on Ireland. Irish-born or Irish-descended Catholics voting in Britain had usually voted Labour since the 1920s, but a more affluent generation, more seriously concerned with the decline in public morals (especially sexual morals) was drifting towards the Tories. Few of them had any affection for the IRA and might well have plenty of criticisms of the Republic, but humiliation of the land of their fathers in the gracious intellectual and obviously good-natured person of Garret Fitzgerald would distance them from Thatcher. Tory nuts-and-bolts men (and what Disraeli would call the Tadpoles and Tapers) could not afford to chuckle too heartily in private over Thatcher's freak-out, however much they might publicly admire it when so required. The same Rightward drift among Irish-descended Catholics was taking place in the USA where the Republicans under the Irish-descended Ronald Reagan (elected President in 1980) were making gains they wished to consolidate and enlarge. They were decidedly open to assist a process of ameliorating relations between the UK and Ireland with a view to pacification in Northern Ireland, the whole to be clearly if vaguely attributable to President Reagan. Fortunately for them, self-ingratiation with Reagan was one of Thatcher's delights — she had grown up in the generation of Hollywood-stardust collectors — although Fitzgerald retained his place in Thatcher's personal Inferno, probably even more than Haughey (the rough trade attracts Tory chemistry), despite which the Anglo-Irish Agreement of 1985 was born, and the Ulster Unionists were convinced that London had betrayed them having been ignored in its creation. Thatcher in fact cared nothing for them, her mental UK being actually coterminous with England, and seldom north of Grantham. But her language adopted for purposes of pomp and circumstance was somewhat Edwardian when on patriotic occasions, and the Unionist non-Paisleyîte elîte when on parade liked to keep îts official language Edwardian as in the days of Sir Edward Carson and Sir James Craig. So the Ulster Unionists remained bîtter and outcast while the Revd Dr Paisley continued to declare London a Sodom. But this would have been a lîttle remote from you when the Anglo-Irish Agreement happened and the Unionist alienation hardened: your view when you were studying at Oxford would have been informed, but you would have lacked the intensîty of personal research wîth a view to authorship, as you had at Eton thanks to Andrew Gailey.

This wholly exceptional training was an excellent preparation for Prime Ministerial office in general, insofar as you, unlike Thatcher, think of yourself primarily as Prime Minister of the Unîted Kingdom, and if you don't do as much as (from your point of view) you should, you certainly have tried to study ît better than she. You certainly were better prepared on Northern Ireland before taking office than any Prime Minister other than Winston Churchill (whose life was threatened by Unionists when he visited ît as a Home Rule minister in the Liberal Cabinet in 1912) and James Callaghan (who took a tour of duty in 1969 and wrote a book about ît). Harold Macmillan was an enthusiastic publisher of great Irish lîterature but wîth lîttle reference to modern Ulster. A Scottish list would be larger as regards actual visîtors to Downing Street residence, but many would simply have qualified somewhat closer to the Orwell definîtion. (Not that Northern Ireland under the Unionists did not seek to rival the Scottish sporting trade: one tourist authorîty slogan, dropped in the 1970s, read 'Come to Northern Ireland for the Shooting!')

It's important in mapping your UK patriotism to see how far your education may have directly affected your sentiments and perspectives on the peripheral countries of our archipelago, and here your relationship to Northern Ireland is instructive. One slightly odd blip on the radar is given by Francis Elliott and James Hanning, having reached your time at Oxford in their *Cameron* (pp. 69–70):

> In March 1987 he [you] caused some unhappiness among those who felt he was not pulling his weight ideologically when, during one of his generally passive encounters with the [Oxford student debating] Union, he supported the decision to allow Sinn Fein leader Gerry Adams to speak there. Cameron's view was that he should be allowed to have his say and that his audience should be able to make an informed judgment, in favour or against. He tried this line on his tutor Vernon Bogdanor, who disagreed, saying that Sinn Fein's relationship with the IRA was unhealthily close and that the normal democratic rules should not apply. Having heard Adams speak, Cameron told a friend that he felt 'grubby' about listening to the Northern Irishman, and that Bogdanor had been right.

I would not willingly bite the hand that has fed me, and Messrs Elliott and Hanning have in my view given a superior biographical performance on a Prime Minister's early life, far superior to such works on the early life of Gordon Brown, for instance. But our text here, with the best auctorial will in the world, may be misleading. Put like this, it sounds like a wealthy Oxford pup rearing back from the spectacle of the Union's hospitality to a person from the bottom drawer best left below the salt. As Mr Gerry Adams would know all too well how to milk left-wing sympathies, the implication of your disdain for his poverty-stricken roots in industrial grime and sectarian discrimination seems that it was grounded in snobbery rather than (as it was) humanity. Worse, the passage also implies that Mr Adams was just another nationalist, merely a little unthinking in his liberalism towards persons of violence. It could easily lead to lifelong assumptions that all nationalists are the same kind of nationalist, not bombers and gunmen themselves, but sadly wanting in responsible self-distance from gunmen, shadows of gunmen, you might say, if you had heard of Sean O'Casey and hadn't studied his plays.

During the Referendum fight, the Ulster Unionist leader David Trimble, who had now settled into the House of Lords and the Tory party, declared that 'we' had beaten the nationalists in Northern Ireland and 'we' would beat them in Scotland. He may very well have been conscripted by you as one of your heterogeneous rag-tag-and-bobtail aka 'Better Together'. To an observer such as myself, who admired Trimble's courage and enjoyed his wintry humour, this was tragic. My Lord Trimble surely knows that the Scottish National Party throughout its history has been utterly hostile to violence and eradicated any suspicion of it from the party's ranks. The relationship of Sinn Féin in general and Mr Adams in particular to the IRA was well summed up by one of the PhDs in history whom I had the privilege of supervising, Dr Christopher McGimpsey, a prominent member of Trimble's Ulster Unionist party, who was asked to address a Fringe meeting on Northern Ireland at a Labour party conference, with Mr Gerry Adams as the other speaker. Dr McGimpsey warmed up the crowd by asking what was the difference between the IRA and the Spice Girls. His answer was that Geri had definitely left the Spice Girls. Professor Bogdanor's euphemism 'unhealthily close' was all too apt: many people are believed to have lost their lives from the unhealthiness of that closeness.

There had been non-violent protesters in Northern Ireland against its apartheid state before the IRA brought its angels of death over Ulster. Some left; some retired; some joined the IRA. No such traffic between non-violent and violent nationalists would be permissible in Scottish Nationalism. The difficulty about Tory perceptions of violent nationalism is that ideologically the Tories are rather enthusiastic about the martial virtues, which boiled over into the threat of violent rebellion in Ulster before world war broke out in 1914. The Tories come to Scotland for the shooting of the brute creation, and the resultant activity may make them sound as though their classification of brutes might include the human variety. Their heroes in popular literature became particularly heroic in taking the law into their own hands, from Bulldog Drummond to James Bond. To claim that James Bond is legalised by his licence to kill might inspire Mr Gerry Adams (were he ever to be honest) with the thought that it depends on whose is the licensing power. And you may remember, my dear Mr Cameron (unless you have never read an Ian Fleming treatise or seen a Bond movie), Bond sometimes outruns his license (as for instance in *For Your Eyes Only* title-story). Moreover neither the ethics nor the vocabulary of this form of discipleship can be confined to gentlemen. Even the Revd Dr Paisley's choice of epithets could run beyond Biblical limits: he denounced the Tory Secretary for Northern Ireland Tom King as a 'lily-livered cur', a rubric frequently employed by Uncle Bulldog himself. (But we cannot think the lecherous Bond would have passed muster with him.)

The problem about you British, Irish, and even Scottish Tories facing an unarmed nationalism is that your own nationalism is iconographically armed, pictures of violent patriotism such as Scots Greys charging at Waterloo as recalled by Orwell. You have never found it easy to face non-violent hostility whether from Daniel O'Connell or

Mahatma Gandhi, and you frequently convinced yourselves that it must be a cover for secret violence. Salisbury became fixated on Parnell's being a secret assassin-creator, and was brazenly indifferent when the evidence on which he, his followers and allies, and the obedient *Times* relied, were proved forgeries. In the 20th century it certainly became true that violent Irish nationalists stole weapons of non-violence such as the hunger strike — the IRA martyrs in Northern Ireland were certainly not non-combatants, but sought and found the sympathy once accorded to pacifists only. Non-violent civil rights agitators of 1969 sometimes abandoned that principle in later years, and took to IRA violence including supporters of all the slaughterhouse policies that entailed. But it found no place in Scottish Nationalism. The SNP held consistently to its philosophy of non-violence, nor could all your tears wash out a word of it. It expresses itself most obviously in the failure of Unionism to acknowledge that whatever its hatreds of the SNP, the party has saved Scotland from drinking at the Irish poisoned chalice. But as Bernard Shaw begins the Preface to his *Androcles and the Lion*, Barabbas has consistently stolen the identity of Jesus. Conversely, followers of Barabbas who claim discipleship to Jesus will always assume real followers of Jesus actually worship Barabbas. And I fear that you, my dear Mr Cameron, are a follower of Barabbas. Your Christianity when mentioned appears a matter of courtesy to some ancient custom of less importance than the monarchy, and nowhere requiring the ravening delight with which you congratulate the UK on the size of its 'defence' establishment, weapons of mass destruction and all. You are a Barabbite, however gentlemanly.

Your being a gentleman limited you in Northern Ireland. The Ulster Unionist party you had studied in Eton under

Andrew Gailey was led by gentlemen, some of them having cultivated English accents (especially if, like Robin Chichester-Clark MP, they were chiefly based in London), some not (especially if, like his brother Major James Chichester-Clark, they were chiefly in Northern Ireland). They were no longer too obviously anti-Catholic (and many, such as Chris McGimpsey, were not anti-Catholic at all). In 2010 you built an alliance with Ulster Unionist party then under Sir Reg Empey. Twenty-five years ago Empey and I had a very agreeable meeting in part of which we talked of one of my daughters being at that point a nun. I could not have asked for a more courteous and sympathetic listener. He was not just not anti-Catholic, he readily recognised Catholics as his fellow-Christians, provided they weren't homicidal or covering up for homicides. But by the time you were seeking allies in Northern Ireland, the common gentility had become as obsolete as the common Christianity. Ian Paisley's unquestionable liking and friendship for Martin McGuinness, once they had begun to work in Government together, presumably operated on the presumption that since all Catholics were damned one lot could hardly be more damned than another. Martin McGuinness shows every sign of a reciprocal theology. And when the most visible effect of your linkage with the Ulster Unionist party was that its sole MP defected in protest against her party's engagement with you, I think you showed what Dr Gailey described to Elliott and Hanning: 'There is a mindset which is crucial in all winners which is the ability to think of what is to come, not what has just passed, to be able to move on' (p. 488). You had not thrown Northern Ireland aside as being too much trouble to understand, after the manner of Reginald Maudling's exit line from a tour of duty there 'What a bloody awful country! Get me a double gin, somebody.' You had

studied it, won the applause of an exceptionally well-
informed specialist on it, and now in 2010 you saw no
further future in it. The UK shrank to GB, and you deluged
the epoch of the London Olympics in canonisation of Team
GB when to consolidate the pacification of Northern Ireland
what was needed was Team UK. Instead, you appointed Owen
Patterson to the Northern Ireland office, as negative a gesture
as could be imagined. Whether or not you are a one-nation
Tory, you have certainly proclaimed yourself a one-island
Tory. Will you similarly turn your back on Scotland?

In case you want to tell us Team GB was its own creator
(something into which you would not dream of intruding),
alas your credibility as a non-interventionist vanished
during the Referendum as prominent person after prominent person from Spain to Saturn came popping out with
their doubts about the fate of Scotland in the event of
Independence. We recognised that for all of your nurseling
status on Thatcher's snatched milk, you are unrivalled as an
international manipulator, even if your initial efforts to
mobilise great names to pronounce on Scotland's danger
had to begin in some cases with explaining that Scotland
existed, and where. Admittedly your conscripts invited to
step up to the plate (more likely to the glass) and explain that
Scotland would not retain status within the European Union
if Independent then turned rather savagely on you in some
instances, and having been taught to threaten Scotland,
warmed to their work and threatened England as well. You
had in fact shown yourself a good tactician, diplomatically,
but a bad strategist. And your underlings in the European
Parliament were now allying themselves with Rightists who
in their less malevolent moments may have been genial, but
seldom gentlemen, whereas its gentlemen preferred moder-
ation, centrism, calm. You lost some good diplomats by

parting company with previous Tory MEPs. I suppose you lacked the experience of Northern Ireland in the European Union to realise that persons who could be quite ungentlemanly and ferociously Protestant, and apparently Europhobic, notably the Revd Dr Paisley, worked very effectively with ostensible enemies such as John Hume to further European investment in Northern Ireland. (The Reverend Doctor's ostensible reasons for hostility to the EU was the foundation of the EEC in terms of the 1957 Treaty of Rome, rousing his expectant congregations and mobs by proclaiming it a treaty *with* Rome, including the Vatican which however nonsensical was more rational than most Tory and U-PUKE forms of Europhobia.) And your gentility would have been less alive than Paisley, Hume and Winifred Ewing to the effectiveness of poverty as a diplomatic weapon, which at that stage had fewer users than the European community subsequently acquired. Winifred Ewing elected MEP in 1979 turned the SNP from Europhobe to Europhile by her own instincts and energy, and automatically recognised that Irish geniality (whether Paisleyite or Papist) made inroads closed to UK pride and Thatcherite parochialism. Irish diplomatic genius could not foresee or forestall the squandering of the fruits of its European victories by its domestic rulers, replicating a thousand-fold the UK idolatry to banks. You could call it a peculiarly painful example of neo-colonialism, by which having noisily shaken off the rule of the official oppressor, all of the oppressors' economic follies are then slavishly copied and endlessly replicated by the liberated province. An Independent Scotland must be very careful to immunise itself from that disease, while retaining what wisdom is on offer from England. It will be easier since a Scottish break from England cannot be the result of violence with its corresponding boomerang effect. But neo-colonialism is a much more real danger for Independent Scotland than the magic monsters dreamed up by think-tanks narrating nursery nightmares.

And before we leave Eton, perhaps we might hope that you would remember the poor boys for whose education it was founded, and whom the poet Gray commemorates at the beginning of his Ode, the nearest post-Norman England came to a saint King, and surely the most sympathetic English king drawn by Shakespeare with his sorrow for the sufferings of his fellow English.

CHAPTER FOUR

THE OXONIAN EDUCATION OF A PRIME MINISTER

LADY BRACKNELL: Untruthful? My nephew Algernon? Impossible! He is an Oxonian.

— OSCAR WILDE, *The Importance of Being Earnest*, Act III

I t is a sad reflection on the maturation process in human beings that an appropriate symbol of Eton should be its beautiful chapel whose visitors may mingle devotion to God and Henry VI in solitude and in community, while that of Oxford in your time seems omnipresently a brawling club of destructive drunks. It has been served up for the contempt of posterity in Evelyn Waugh's *Decline and Fall*, bearing its specific extra damnation that the University discriminates in the aristocratic alcoholics' favour at the expense of serious, impecunious, scholarly students. You were fool enough to join the Bullingdon Club. I have been as stupid in my time, if less expensively so.

Contrary to so much that has been written about you, Oxford gave you real scholarship in which to wallow, as you did. It concerns us because, as at Eton, you found an absolutely outstanding mind whence to be trained, Professor Vernon Bogdanor, and your mentor trained you for mastery of the possible uses of Devolution and Referendum in these islands of which he was becoming the leading scholar. Dr Matt Qvortrup edited *The British Constitution — Continuity and Change* (2013) a Festschrift in his honour, opening with an epigraph from yourself without date, and hence possibly written by you for the occasion: 'Vernon Bogdanor understands like few others the connection between history, politics and institutions – and that is what makes him such an authority on the British system of Government'. It would probably have been more accurate to say 'systems' – the singular number suggests a single intelligent design which Bogdanor would emphatically deny – but otherwise I don't think it could be put better. Bogdanor also has the distinction that in lectures and writings he has a beautiful and instructive clarity.

Vernon Bogdanor must have been a delight to work with. He avoids social science jargon and contextualises political science in the most appropriate and most interesting history. His wisdom in fact taught you a vast amount of relevance to your post-graduation career. He followed your formation of government in 2010 with his *The Coalition and the Constitution* (2011) which makes no visible capital from his tutorship of yourself 25 years earlier. It provides an invaluable historical and constitutional framework on a subject on which the British media were (even for them) quite extraordinarily ignorant, your post-election coalition being frequently treated as unspeakable, unknown, and unEnglish. It was easier for me having first encountered the phenomenon in 1948 Dublin at the age of ten. But Bogdanor is in fact exceptional in his mastery of both Irelands and their polities and politics, useful as they are in building up practical examples of Devolution, Referendum and Coalition for students and teachers alike.

While biographers of politicians are to be deplored in ignoring their possible mentors and instead pursuing preferably disreputable anecdotes of their school and student lives (Messrs Elliott and Hanning are admirable exceptions to this), we may make too much of the importance of mentors. My grandfather had a modern version of Jesus's parable of the Pharisee and the publican in which the Pharisee walks triumphantly up the church and informs God who successful he has been and how much money he has made and what major political achievements he has ensured and what magnificent acts of philanthropy he has set on foot, while at the back of the church a wretched, threadbare, insignificant little man beats his breast and says 'Forgive me, God. I taught him'. And it is much easier to begin assessment of the influence of Vernon Bogdanor's mentor, Professor Geoffrey Marshall of Oxford, on Bogdanor than Bogdanor's on you. And teaching is far less valuable if it simply makes for unquestioning regurgitation. Professor Bogdanor doesn't need to complain much about that, where you are concerned. Since the Referendum he has condemned as constitutionally unsound your notion of restricting Commons business of exclusively English content (where that can be determined) to English MPs. The SNP MPs try to keep out of English business anyway, but a courtesy is a long way from a regulation. For all of his punctilious depersonalisation of your possible differences it is hard not to hear an echo of the Irish Lord Chief Baron Palles sitting on an appeal alongside his former pupil, now Irish Lord Chief Justice O'Brien of Kilfenora whose judgment Palles followed with the commencement 'Oh Peter, Peter, you never learned that law from me!'

Bogdanor's *The Coalition and the Constitution* is essentially an overture to the Cameron government whose music included warning notes:

The Conservative/Liberal Democrat coalition could threaten the unity of the United Kingdom... The coalition is very far from enjoying a majority in either Scotland or Wales. So, although it may appear to enjoy a clear mandate in England, critics in Scotland and Wales will argue that it has no mandate to govern the non-English parts of the United Kingdom... This could give rise to serious problems, especially when cuts in public expenditure come to be implemented. For these cuts are likely to be felt with particular severity in Scotland and Wales, which are more dependent upon public sector jobs than the south of England. Labour might dispute the mandate of the coalition in Scotland and Wales, but the nationalists will claim that these territories could avoid the cuts altogether by becoming independent. (P. 41.)

And he went on to point to Thatcher's introduction of the poll-tax to Scotland when representing only a Scottish minority (actually one-seventh when being implemented), strengthening both Labour and the SNP 'and to fuel the argument for devolution', reflecting that cuts 'will similarly strengthen both the radical devolutionists and the nationalists'. This was an excellent refresher course for you, but obviously Bogdanor in 2011 spoke to the world as well as to you. You had been trained by him, but others would find his prose an easy taskmaster. His greatest importance for you and your potential opponents was to show the importance of thinking constitutionally which meant clear instead of fuzzy lines of thought provided Bogdanor was doing the thinking. Looking back on what he wrote we may see the casualty in the 'radical devolutionists' among whom were the probable plurality in favour of the compromise between Independence and status quo, a vast increase in powers of the devolved Scottish Parliament, to be known as 'Devo-Max'. Your elimination of Devo-Max from the Referendum ballot paper and the restriction of the alternatives to the extreme two you may (or may not) have assumed would finalise the debate with those against Independence however devolutionary they might think themselves opting for NO and the YES voters being a minority of one-quarter or one-third to judge by polls at the time you concluded your 2012 Edinburgh Agreement and therefore radical devolutionists and nationalists being separately silenced. But Bogdanor was writing between the 2010 Commons election when Scotland held every seat for Labour of those won the previous time, and the 2011 Holyrood election when the minority SNP government swept in to a majority. And various other developments brought Devo-Max, the radical devolutionists, into the YES camp in large numbers, with a probably large group vacillating, ultimately voting NO, and probably regretting it. Whether your decisions followed a reading or misreading of Bogdanor we don't know, but whatever individual errors there might have been, he ensured you would function on a higher level on constitutional matters than the lumpen-Westminster.

When you became his pupil, Bogdanor had already edited *Coalition Governments in Western Europe* (1983). Oracular but lucid, contemporary but historical he is probably England's best scholar of the constitution since Walter Bagehot (1826–77), infinitely superior to the ferociously partisan Unionist grand-pamphleteer Albert Venn Dicey (1835–1922) whose pioneer status in Oxford constitutional thought seems to attract somewhat excessive piety. Dicey fostered identification of English nationalism and parliamentary sovereignty in the prevailing undemocratic first-past-the-post form. Bogdanor preaches proportional representation as well as the use of the referendum: his piety to Dicey clothes the richness of his alternative constitutionalism. Like all of us, he can make mistakes. *The Coalition and the Constitution* (p. 61) tells us that 'Gladstone's government of 1886 was followed [having been defeated on Irish Home Rule in the Commons and then in General Election], until 1892, by a purely

Conservative administration, the Liberal Unionists prefer-
ring to offer support from outside the Government'. But
when in a bid for power Lord Randolph Churchill, Tory
Chancellor of the Exchequer, resigned from Salisbury's
Government at the end of 1886, the Liberal Unionist
George Joachim Goschen accepted the post at the beginning
of 1887 though he had fought two by-elections to occupy it
having been defeated in Edinburgh East in the 1886 General
Election that had brought Salisbury to power, and failing to
win in another constituency on his first attempt in 1887
after the appointment. He was the only non-Tory in the
Cabinet, but that post was Exchequer and his acceptance
saved the Prime Minister from loss of power in name or in
fact, and that made a coalition. Goschen did join the Tories
in 1893, but only after the end of that Salisbury Government
in 1892. As Randolph Churchill said of himself, Bogdanor
'forgot Goschen'. This display of pedantry on my part
merely serves to show how deeply and subtly he transmits the
entertainment as well as the scholarship of constitutionalism
and its history. There is a faintly amusing touch about the
personnel of 1886–7. The leader of the Liberal Unionist
secession from Gladstone over Irish Home Rule was the
Marquess of Hartington and future Duke of Devonshire, an
exotic name and the inheritor of two centuries of Whig
oligarchy, in that sense exotic but not very bright. Perhaps
his most endearing observation is 'I dreamed I was addressing the House of Lords. I awoke and found that I was'. Up to
the schism he hardly cared for the Radical Unionist secession leader Joe Chamberlain, of Chamberlain & Nettlefold,
screw-manufacturers, of Birmingham. Goschen had come
to prominence through his father's success in banking. In
Hartington there might have been a Clegg essential to enable
a Tory government to form but not joining it. In Chamber-

lain there might have been a potential Charles Kennedy if only possessed of ruthlessness. Goschen's expertise might prefigure Vince Cable, in both cases a recruit to the Tory Cabinet really valuable for his own expertise, as opposed to a personal popularity or a driving force. Did Bogdanor's training in general lead your thoughts to such models in Cabinet-forming? Where you would prove superior to Salisbury was in recruiting your Parliamentary Opposition to your Unionist crusade. Your removal of Devo-Max left them little alternative, and the one Labour leader who could have made something of that, Gordon Brown, Scottish devolutionist leader for almost 40 years, was necessarily only available for grand guest appearances since his retirement to the back benches – he could have played Devo-Max, and in fact, he played it though chiefly when it had been excluded from the ballot paper. Yet that also you may have foreseen. You had after all been begging his leadership and abusing his economics for your entire premiership. At all events Bogdanor had ensured if you would be the first Prime Minister to face a serious threat of Scottish Independence, you had been better trained than any of your predecessors in the scholarly apparatus necessary to come to terms with it, however much you have tried to disguise the fact.

Bogdanor not only shows himself at home in history, but easily summons literature to his aid. This again made valuable training available to you. In earlier days only one Prime Minister seems to have become a great novelist but about a dozen were either figures of literary consequence or else enthusiastic readers. Your immediate predecessor Gordon Brown may well have been the leading student publisher of his time, playing a vital part in the Anglicisation of Gramsci as well as producing the great blueprint or *Red Paper on Scotland*. Macmillan was a great publisher of poetry, prose and plays.

Churchill's speeches are great literature. Baldwin made use of his first cousin Rudyard Kipling. Balfour published philosophy. Gladstone was a literary critic and theological essayist. Canning was a masterly polemicist. There have been more bogus reputations, and you may well prefer to enjoy reading in private rather than trumpet it in public. But Bogdanor had certainly shown you how to read literature about politics and society. *The Coalition and the Constitution* opens on an epigraph from Disraeli's *Coningsby*:

> 'Society in this country is perplexed, almost paralysed; in time it will move, and it will devise. How are the elements of the nation to be again blended together? In what spirit is that reorganisation to take place?'

> 'To know that', replied Coningsby, 'would be to know everything.'

The first lesson to draw from that is that you, very fortunately for yourself, had fallen into the hands of a tutor with a fine sense of humour, and where you were going, you badly needed it. Also, like Nicholas in Christopher Fry's *The Lady's Not for Burning*, once you know his qualities Bogdanor 'can drop back into a quite brilliant humility'. Coediting *The Law, Politics and the Constitution* (1999), a Festschrift in honour of his Oxford Mentor Professor Geoffrey Marshall, Bogdanor's essay 'Devolution and the British Constitution' began appropriately if formidably:

> Many years ago, Geoffrey Marshall was my tutor in politics. For my first essay, instead of the standard fare on the power of the Prime Minister or the role of Congress, Geoffrey asked me to write on Dicey's constitutional principles. This was a complex exercise for a beginner, but I wrote what I thought to be a decent summary of Dicey's views. Geoffrey, in the gentlest possible way, showed me that Dicey was a more subtle thinker

than was commonly imagined, but also that his principles were in many respects inadequate as an explanation of the British constitution. I retired, shamefaced.

Dicey was a querulous Unionist, somewhat of an invalid, and capable of marshalling extensive scholarship in support of his view on the anti-devolutionary essence of the British Constitution on which many Unionists were very anxious to give him veneration and publicity. Did he teach? His Chair was at All Souls College which suggests not. That would tell us a lot. Bogdanor's — and Geoffrey Marshall's — work was greatly strengthened by their being teachers. To put forward your ideas before the sceptical eye of a student is a great test. That Dicey held his own for most of the 20th century as the leading academic authority on the Constitution says less for his successors than for him. Bogdanor by the present date towers over him. Bogdanor, no more than Gailey, was a natural Tory. Both were admirers of political dissidents (Gailey of the liberal Unionist Jack Sayers, mid-century editor of the *Belfast Telegraph*, Bogdanor of the former Labour Foreign Secretary and Social Democrat leader David Owen). Bogdanor shared with Gailey a great sense of humanity in history; his establishment of political realities evolved from the past gave his readers a real sense of the characters he quoted. One could see the social being behind the minds. And he probably could see those behind the minds he was helping to shape. He probably shares some common ground with you on non-European foreign relations, enjoying as he does status in the Henry M. Jackson society whose icon was a Cold War Senator known because of his advocacy of big weapons as 'The Senator from Boeing' whose lethal products he championed throughout his 30-year service in the US Senate (1953–83). Had Professor Bogdanor been prominent in the 1950s and 1960s one might have expected him to bob up in *Encounter*. These neo-Jacksonians seem a bright bunch in their way. They include Michael Gove and David Willetts, the most conspicuous intellectuals in your Government if not so happy in practice.

Bogdanor has been quoted as declaring you the best student he ever taught. If he really had said that, his view would be worthless. No tutor teaching for 40-odd years could possibly declare a single pupil the superior of all others. But of course Bogdanor did not say that, having been victimised as usual by the slovenliness and superlatives of the modern media. Elliott and Hanning have him putting you among the 'brightest 5 per cent he has ever taught', and that is a computation to which most British university tutors of today are accustomed. He looked back from 2007, saying of you (p. 56):

> He was liked by his tutors since he was both courteous and stimulating to teach. He enjoyed an argument. It was clear from the moment he arrived that he was likely to secure a very good degree. I would have been surprised if he had not achieved a First... He is one of the ablest and nicest students whom I had taught.

This is positive enough to be inescapable. Bogdanor's own judgments of historical evidence, whether completely accurate or not, are so sound in their bases that we must assume the same mastery in his assessment of his best pupils. (Academics are much less reliable in judgments on colleagues.) You are intelligent, my dear Mr Cameron, and there is no point in further attempts at concealment.

And you are exceptionally able.
And you are exceptionally nice.

Let us take the last point first. It isn't particularly obvious in TV lights, and still less in what the media make of you. But it has an eerie ring of my own judgment on an Edinburgh History student who got a First, and with whom I worked, although I was never his tutor. He was 'one of the ablest and nicest students' under my assessment. His name was Gordon Brown.

The common factor here is that in both cases you and Dr Brown are under close media scrutiny, and the constant diminution of the intellects and niceness of you both is evidently a tool of the TV interviewer's trade. It may not be habitual practice for all their victims, but something about the two of you evidently brings out the worst in them, that niceness makes them ugly, partly because they take Thersites or some other scurrilous cynic for the ideal of true objective judgment. Their work may most frequently be seen while TV sets in pubs drown conversation and so you are assailed by your TV interviewers with all the dignity and judgment of a pub bore for ever spouting his profundities, all the more embittered because of the absence of immediate potations. But you become entrapped by their conventions and take them for democracy, and bait and blast one another according to the specifications you believe your tormenters require of you. And so you and Dr Gordon Brown lose the nobility which once was yours.

Professor Bogdanor's magnificent wisdom and literary productivity carry some innocence with them. This must always be true of the theorist, although it is invaluable for the theorist to be also a teacher: it has been true from Socrates down that the greater the scepticism of the students, the stronger the theory from the teacher. But when the theory is enclosed in a book, and the student has reached the political heights, the invaluable links may rust and risk breaking. Bogdanor is surely the supreme authority on monarchy in relation to the Constitution. (We are speaking here of relatively abstract theorising, in which the academic or private scholar seeks first of all to let the evidence speak for itself as best it can, avoiding the premature formulation of a thesis where possible: a scholar with a political agenda such as Dicey is another matter since evidence is then likely to be hammered into wherever will benefit the Dicey prejudices.) Bogdanor wrote in his Introduction to *The British Constitution in the Twentieth Century* (2003) which he edited (p.6):

> By the end of the nineteenth century … it had been widely accepted, both by politicians and constitutional theorists, if not by the sovereign herself, that she should not intervene in party politics.

He had rightly pointed out that Victoria in 1894 chose Rosebery as Prime Minister when Gladstone finally retired, ignoring the convention of asking advice from appropriate quarters of which the most appropriate at this point was Gladstone himself. But the last Prime Minister who openly sought royal intervention in his favour had been Disraeli, even to such Napoleonic detail as pushing his chair slightly closer to the Queen's at the end of an audience so that their intimacy would seem greater in the eyes of her servants (whose political importance he would not underestimate). And yet you, my dear Mr Cameron, returned to the Disraelian hints of greater agreement between Queen and Prime Minister, and (almost certainly inaccurately) implied in chatting to the former Mayor of New York that the Queen agreed with bias on your part against the Referendum choosing Independence (while retaining the Queen whose place as Queen of Scots is senior to her other titles and in a choice might be presumed to outlive them — had you thought of that?). When your folly had been brought home to you, you might juſtly have mourned that you had not re-read your old tutor and followed what was done by Gladſtone (out of respect), by Salisbury (out of contempt), and by Rosebery (out of insecurîty) that monarchs do not intervene in party polîtics and the Disraelian musical chairs were obsolete. Admittedly the present Queen had juſt improved relations between Ireland and the UK far more dramatically and effec- tively than her miniſters could hope to do but Royal diplo- macy is highly conſtîtutional when public — for one thing, she speaks more beautiful Irish than you are likely to do unless you have been brushing up your anceſtral Gaelic.

But the point is that whether or not you disregarded your Maſter's voice, he had grounded you in conſtîtutional tradi- tions, conventions and possibilîties, and he was the leading scholar on Devolution and on Referendum, and thus you were armed and warned when as Prime Miniſter you confronted both. As a ſtudent encouraged by Bogdanor to think out personal fulfilment of the several roles throughout hiſtory it would be natural to day-dream 'If I were Prime Miniſter what would I do in a Devolution/Referendum crisis?' The average young Tory wîth mildly careeriſt ambîtions might have wrîtten off devolution after 1979 and the clear signal that Thatcher would dîtch Douglas-Home's promise of a better Scottish Parliament, but Bogdanor ensured you would not be the average young Tory. Similarly after his back-breaking, sight-endangering hard work fight- ing for devolution Gordon Brown fought off pressures to drop ît and ſtayed alongside John Smîth's resolution to return to ît. That zeal on his part would bring him back from the polîtical graveyard in 2014. Others including the brilliant debater Robin Cook played an out-in-out game wîth devolution, and many of the Labour old guard (we might call them Bourbons) made devolution and îts advocates (particularly Dr Brown) objects of venomous continued attack, and in the 1990s Blair kicked it into the long grass (otherwise George Robertson) but Brown – and Donald Dewar – held true. In fact he took great diplomatic trouble to ensure Dewar would be the man to bring it back.

But to return to yourself at Oxford, whatever might be said about devolution, the 1979 contradictions would surely have offered the basis of an interesting essay, including (since it was Politics or Government, not History) an exploration of whether a fresh instalment of devolution was possible, likely, or inevitable. You would have been in Tory employment at Smith Square by 1989 when Michael Forsyth, Margaret Thatcher and kindred spirits had dinners in Edinburgh and London to celebrate ten years of having denied the Scots what they had voted for. You should have known about them, if not actually present, whether as guest or gofer. Were you sent as a runner-boy to bring final orders from the London celebration to its cheap edition, and, if so, was that your first visit? Did the 1989 dinners revise what you had learned at the feet of Bogdanor, or did your Oxford wisdom and Thatcher's shrinking Scottish support convince you that Scottish Tory doomsday was on its way? You had shrewd business in your blood – did it cross your mind to cut Scottish Tory losses? After all, you were exceptionally intelligent, probably far more than the usual apprentice Tory careerists, all greed and no gumption. You evidently kept a very straight face while intoning devotions to Thatcher when in Oxford and London. It was the intellectual equivalent of cheering the new clothes of the empress as she smirked her way stark naked. One thing is certain. Your brains must have found transfer from Bogdanor to Thatcher a departure from the sublime to the ridiculous. It suggests anthropological parallels to the medieval ceremony of devotions paid to the King of Fools, or the sailing ship *rîtes de passage* crossing the equator when neophytes were formally washed on the inſtructions of a patently bogus King Neptune accompanied by a repulsive mock consort in drag. At leaſt ît trained you for performance at her funeral.

And I mean that. To have given her a ſtate funeral was an insult to Winſton Churchill, the heroic laſt recipient. Some things in her funeral, regardless of îts subject, were moving: Thatcher's granddaughter proved a beautiful reader of Sacred Scripture. The same could not be said of you, when you declaimed from the pulpît 'Let not your heart be troubled: ye believe in God, believe also in me' (John xiv.1.). Whether the congregation and the TV audience were to underſtand from this that you thought you were Jesus Chriſt, or that you thought Thatcher was, or that you invîted is to make our faith in God receive a corollary of belief in you or Thatcher or both, ît is not easy to say, but to a worshipper of Jesus that use of Scripture was ſtraight blasphemy. That she had devised such a use for the holy Gospel was not particularly surprising: the sermoniser before the General Assembly of the Church of Scotland was ſtupid enough to entîtle herself to any such comparisons. The moſt offensively anti-Chriſtian seculariſt could not have devised anything more potentially hurtful to believing Chriſtians. For you to perform in this manner tells us much of the ethics of your disguises. It is at all events consiſtent wîth your pretence of ſtupidîty to win the anti-intellectual vote. Your Thatcherite followers should have forgiven you any of the sins they had tabulated againſt you. It ſtinks worse than Southey's 'A Vision of Judgment' recording Heaven's gratîtude to George III for condescending to go there, for which Byron so juſtly mocked that Poet Laureate in his great poem of the same tîtle. He too had George admîtted to

Heaven, but quietly. Anyhow, God forgive her, and you —
and all of us, every one.

To move from the theological back to the political, what
were your full motives in accordance with your professed
love for the UK to decree at public expense a state funeral
offensive to most of the United Kingdom, particularly
Scotland? It certainly must have played a part in diminishing
Scottish sentiment for a UK expecting its citizens to bow
down before that! Thatcher had become identified with the
wilful destruction of much of Scottish society, and that
verdict hardened by her want of remorse (as judges say when
passing sentence). Her attempt to conscript God as her
junior partner at the General Assembly of the Church of
Scotland was swallowed up in contemptuous laughter, but at
her death you squandered the taxpayers' money for an
apotheosis as fraudulent and ludicrous as any divination of
a tyrannical Roman emperor.

Let us go back to Oxford in 1985–88 where the air is
cleaner. To work under Bogdanor at that time must have
been as exciting as Walter Scott's discovery of the lost Scottish
regalia in Edinburgh Castle in 1818, cobwebs torn away, arid
formulae swept aside, history brought back to life with vital
meaning for British identity (it was more Scottish than
British to judge by the oafish conduct of the courtiers who
so infuriated Scott when the relics came to light). The study
of constitutions, laws and forms of government had been
arid for much of the 20th century. Although we worry about
political cynicism in our time, with the BBC's Nick Robinson
sneering his way from one end of a politician to another, a
much deeper scholarly cynicism about political beliefs had
developed from the 1920s to the 1960s. This was no mere
Lytton Strachey mocking the pretensions of the past. The

great historiographical orthodoxies in Britain were taken over by the gospel according to Sir Lewis Namier, which denied ideological conviction in politics and painstakingly followed movements by politicians as if they were no more justifiable than the flight of crook-taloned birds mindful of food and safety whom Prometheus observed while chained to his rock. The greatest political mind of these islands in the late 18th century, Edmund Burke, was dismissed by Namier as a mere house-servant of the Marquess of Rocking-ham. The Namierites scurried into research support at his behest, and many of the rest of the profession bowed down their heads and swayed in fear of Namier's influence. It became orthodoxy among conventional historians that what people in history said could not be sincere, much less be worth puzzling out. It prompted a conviction among the general public that what politicians said could not be sincere, since their real concerns were limited to their own advance-ment, enrichment and protection. Namier was profoundly conservative with the instinctive implication that any other political complexion was artificial and immoral, but it was a conservatism which despised its own rationalisation. The Burke cult among North American conservatives is open to criticism on many levels, notably for its frequent amnesia to Burke's great work for the suffering peoples of Ireland and India, but at least it rejoices in the life of the mind. And if you were determined to be a Conservative, for whatever reasons, you were at least learning that you ought to have reasons, and that they ought to be more than animal appetites.

Having decided we ought to have minds, the 1960s across the world demanded that the minds be used for truth. The United States can actually claim to have been founded by ideology, but its latest heirs scorned the deception by which the pretensions of freedom and equality were denied to non-whites. As President Lyndon Johnson would put it in his memoirs, *The Vantage Point*, the black people wanted their fair share of American life faster than most white people were prepared to give it to them, and as a southern white breaking with his region's prevailing conventions Johnson spectacularly directed the legislative fight for their freedom. Simultaneously his indifference to foreign affairs led him to deepen an existing war against popular Communism in Vietnam, justified by US authorities in elbow-jerk chauvinism and a failure to see that Vietnamese Communists were also patriotic nationalists (which had made them valuable allies against Japan for the United States in World War II). Gladstone had described Salisbury's vociferous opposition to Irish Home Rule as 'pot-valiant'. He had reason to use the term, having been defeated in the 1874 election by the anger of publicans and their customers at his taxes on the alcohol trade. The Bullingdon was there to train you in pot-valiant Toryism. Bogdanor was fighting to have you live by your mind.

The 1960s rediscovery of the world of ideas in the North Atlantic was initially signalled by the Americans with such great works as R. R. Palmer's *The Age of the Democratic Revolution 1760–1800* (1957, 1960) which pursued the American and European revolutions as they infected one another across frontiers and oceans, and Bernard Bailyn's *The Ideological Origins of the American Revolution* (1965) which saw initial economic anger in the American colonies become self-sustaining ideological impetus. American scholarship was less Namierist than British, naturally, but from the 1920s it had variously enthroned economic, status, and psychological interpretations of human conduct, usually determinist: Bailyn drove us back to what the American pamphleteers were actually writing and how they justified the various stages of their rebellion until it took final shape in the Declaration of Independence. In the UK the parallel development was the early 20th-century desert of constitutional enquiry, whose few contributors left sand in their readers' teeth. Palmer's thesis of ideological migration could be applied readily enough to scholarship in the 1920s when a world bitterly disappointed by the world war victors' failure to deliver on the promises of making the world safe for democracy soured them on ideological justification.

World War I was the first major conflict in which the UK had to justify its mobilisation to satisfy the mass of individuals who would be required to maintain it. Propaganda thus became more vital than ever before. And because the reasons for fighting the war were as feeble, and as accidental, as they were, the product of great-power political incompetence, propaganda had to overspill, horrors had to be manufactured, ideology had to be strait-jacketed into chauvinism. The rivalry of recently invented print-abridged, camera-dominated yellow press on each side of the Atlantic crudified the public mind and cut rationalisation to the bone. It may be argued that ideology had not failed politicians but that politicians had failed ideology, finding the intoxication of the pot-valiant more agreeable than the pain of sustained thought. After the war, with the stricken fields littered with the lies and broken promises, a disgusted white world let its victors renounce idealism, to elect Stanley Baldwins and Calvin Coolidges while the losers surrendered to the loud simplifications of demagogues. The Second World War saw impressive ideological victories from the Beveridge Report and the bases of the welfare state in general while the USA under Franklin Roosevelt from 1933 at least revived its democratic beliefs and welcomed ideas whose theory was tested by New Deal practice. Yet after the war a new fear of ideology set in. Hitler's attempts at ideology did far less to Nazify Germany than Goebbels's masterly lies. The same phenomena were evident in the USA's surrender to Senator McCarthy and the great fear from which he and his fellow witch-hunters waxed fat, and in the USSR's absorption by Stalinism. In retrospect the Attlee government looks like the sanest on the planet, at least in its domestic policy, and there was much to be said for a premier who deliberately made himself look as unimportant as possible while leading a team without peer in British history through some of its worst economic days. He remains the only head of government to have written his autobiography in a limerick:

> Some thought him not much of a starter:
> There were others, they felt, who were smarter.
> But he ended MP,
> PM and PC,
> An Earl, and a Knight of the Garter.

If you want to find a reason why so many foreigners like myself love the English, that is a good one.

But the Attlee government shied away from ideology, not simply from an overestimate of Hitler's intellectual originality but more directly from growing doubts about the USA's and the UK's wartime friend Stalin, ideologically girt in Marxism/Leninism to be interpreted solely by himself. It could be argued that the Nazi-Soviet pact of 1939 had soured the British Left on Stalin, and that Orwell was a much more representative Socialist than is generally recognised. He certainly found it was the wartime Right in government and the sympathetic publishing world which proved most hostile to anti-Stalinism in *Animal Farm*. After the war the Tories made an ideological brantub grab at F. A. Hayek's *The Road to Serfdom*, but any argument that an Attlee government would take the UK to Communism implied that the Tories in the wartime coalition had played a vital part in starting off the process. Hayek was left to be rediscovered by Thatcher's mind-feeders a generation later. I doubt if Bogdanor wasted much time on it, but you would have been exposed to revived study of ideology in the history of politics at a ripe time. Moreover you were trained to witness, examine and assess ideology, not to view it from Left or Right extremes seeking to bully the world and scholarship in general into conformity with themselves. So when you encountered Scottish nationalism you would not make the mistake of thinking it what it wasn't. It was neither Tartan Tories nor Karl MacMarx, two of the more idiotic classifications with which Labour and Conservative have classified it in their time. You knew that it was real, not merely a kilt to clothe its political behaviour, and you knew that it was not easily classifiable under normal nationalism. Or if you didn't know, Bogdanor had given you the intellectual equipment by which you could. You even had the advantage over Gordon Brown that while both of you are products of an emancipated intellectualism, you seem less constrained by prejudice than he, probably because you think widely rather than deeply. And he, in what amounted for him to be the Kirk of the Labour Party, could never see Scottish Nationalism as other than a heresy.

To get some sense of what you would have learned through Bogdanor in 1985–88, my dear Mr Cameron, we may best look at his *The People and the Party System: The Referendum and Electoral Reform in British Politics* (1981). It begins with thanks to Enid Lakeman, former Director of the Electoral Reform Society, whom I remember well from the Irish Referendum of 1959 when Éamon de Valera, accepting retirement from Irish politics via the Irish Presidency offered reinsurance to his Fianna Fáil party by proposing a referendum (as required by the Irish Conſtîtution of 1937) to abolish Proportional Representation. Being a speaker againſt îts abolîtion I was deeply grateful for this profoundly serious English lady who courageously wîthſtood the possible Irish wisecracks from uninhibîted voters. Her gallantry made her popular though I suspect most of us had a secret belief that she was actually Enid Blyton, or at leaſt ought to be. She taught us a lot, wîthout condescension and wîthout complication, and above all her lesson was nationally gratifying. For once de Valera had been outfoxed on a patriotic propaganda pull. The Englishwoman was forever telling the Irish how intelli-gent we were to have PR and how foolish the UK in failing to have ît. The beſt that Fianna Fáil could produce in answer to this was Senator Margaret Pearse, sîſter of the 1916 Eaſter Week Rising leader and martyr Patrick Pearse, shouting at an eve-of-poll rally in College Green opposîte the still Unioniſt Trinity College 'This syſtem of proportional representation was foîſted on you by the British! Throw ît back in their faces!' De Valera was triumphantly elected President the following day when the same voters firmly held on to Proportional Representation. Ireland had never lacked polîtical sophiſtication, whether displayed for virtu-ous or for vicious reasons.

Bogdanor in 1981 had got down to work in typically lucid and realiſtic fashion:

> The parties have themselves come to be the arbiters of what is conſtîtutional and what is not. Far from guarding the processes of conſtîtutional government, they have diſtorted our under-ſtanding of ît. (P. 2.)

The Irish experience in 1959 clearly supported that thesis. In the 2014 Referendum the SNP made ît clear that in the event of victory Scotland was to have îts own wrîtten conſtîtution, in part at least following Professor Neil MacCormick's draft Constitution of the 1970s. A written Constitution meant that parties, to their annoyance, were restrained and (as in Ireland in 1959) the most powerful could prove unable to impose their constitutional will despite the almost supernatural reverence with which so many leaders viewed its founder-leader de Valera. Quite apart from Enid Lakeman, the Republic of Ireland was much less immune from British example than it pretended. The British electorate voting for a welfare state against a loved and revered wartime leader Winston Churchill in 1945 was an appropriate antecedent for Ireland in 1959. As Bogdanor saw it, parties however reprehensible were inevitable in a democracy. We could add that in a potentially democratic state the same was true — the USA began its career with its unsurpassed generation of brilliant founders denouncing parties while building constitutional structures automatically assuming the existence of parties. Politicians, however inferior to the American Founding Fathers, continue to denounce party usually as a form of propaganda against their opponents, well realised in A. P. Herbert's 'By statesmen I mean the members of my party, by politicians I mean the members of yours'. But Referendum 2014 has taught us something else about party, something you admitted in leaving the Referendum to Gordon Brown (who sensibly took his timing from himself, not from you) and Alistair Darling (who did as he was told by you with more or less the fidelity with which he obeyed Blair or Brown). You implied that there were different parties in Scotland from those in England apart from those in Scotland alone. The Scottish Greens really are a different party from the English Greens and everyone realises that. The English Greens seemed if anything to be unhappy about Scottish Independence which the Scottish Greens supported with its leader Patrick Harvie having the time of his life to the delight of YESpersons from all parties and none. The Scottish Tory party you presumably know better than I do and probably better than you should, given its pretensions of nominal home rule. Did it occur to you that your ecstatic commendations of the Colonel at your British (or UK?) party conference suggested faint surprise that someone in the Scottish Tories had done something commendable? And whatever we suspected before about Scottish Labour's enslavement to English Labour however Murphed has been made agonisingly clear by the departing Ms Johann Lamont. Scottish Liberals when not your most visible puppets are the zombies who strode giantlike across the island when they were alive, Charlie and Ming. Or such is the view from Westminster. But the Holyrood LibDems, Labour and Tories no longer possess even the pretence of equal status while their bonds thicken and their overseers grow harder. Even you and the charming Colonel seen in Conference and placed alongside your wife — was this not Man Friday on parade?, given that your (and Miliband's and Clegg's) incursions into Scotland resemble nothing more than Robinson Crusoe otherwise out of humanity's reach:

> The beasts that roam over the plain
>> My form with indifference see;
> They are so unacquainted with man,
>> Their tameness is shocking to me.

(Yes, that is William Cowper's 'The Solitude of Alexander Selkirk' and yes, the original Robinson Crusoe was Scottish, and quite appropriate for Daniel Defoe seeing what he did and wrote to accomplish the original Act of Union, but we have promised not to talk about that. As Professor Whatley and Lord Strathclyde would agree, Daniel Defoe was in favour of the Union he advocated (provided they paid him enough).)

The Irish independence of their master de Valera in the matter of proportional representation looks positively emancipated by comparison with the Holyrood Unionists and their London owners. The basis for the biological differences in the Unionist parties Scottish and British seems to lie in geographical vocabulary. The Home Counties signpost the outside world with an apprehensive confidence 'To the North' or 'To the West' but whatever the presumptions in its initial use there is now a very clear distinction between 'The North' and 'Scotland'. Anything from polls to TV Comprehensives mean north England by 'the North'. It is probable that psephology (save when conducted under the auspices of Professor John Curtice of Strathclyde University) blanks out Scotland so that government actions (such as yours) are often undertaken in the light of public opinion south of Scotland. Is it, for instance, your assumption that such surveys would include Scotland (thus resulting in your being misinformed) or that they would not (but nobody says that)?

This 1981 book of Bogdanor's advocated the referendum and proportional representation. We can dispose of the latter briefly. Having grown up with the Irish form of it and having seen others, I think it the fairest system on offer, and Irish political history makes nonsense of the superstition that it gives rise to minority governments as a norm. It did much to eliminate vengeance politics and discrimination against the Protestant minority in the Irish Free State (and subsequent polities), which were possibilities. The removal of proportional representation from Northern Ireland assisted its consolidation into a one-party state and banked up fires which would explode in 1970 to inaugurate a 30 years' war. No doubt you knew all this, from the breadth and cosmopolitanism of Bogdanor's scholarly vision, and from the special study of Northern Ireland in the 1970s which you had undertaken for Andrew Gailey. You then showed exceptional intelligence when luring the Liberal Democrats into coalition by permitting them to have the most useless system of proportional representation imaginable, festooned with so many objections as to make it as loathsome to constitutional reformers (if not more) than it is to stickers-in-the-mud. And having suitably wrapped it up in pseudo-ecumenical packaging, you handed it to the wretched Clegg and left him to be flattened into the aforesaid mud. From your point of view you were no doubt doing 'the right thing'. I doubt if the United Kingdom itself is constitutionally healthier. But you had certainly shown yourself an apt, if rebellious, pupil. (On his side, Professor Bogdanor holds to his faith in monarchy, coalition, referendum, and proportional representation though he still opposes Scottish Independence despite what we might call the vow that it would entail a good system of proportional representation.)

The advantage of this Machiavellianism was that it not only masqueraded as a handsome concession in your contract with the Liberal Democrats but it gave your party a sporting chance of picking up seats when their supporters deemed them unable to fulfil their own programme. It also left possible future victories for U-PUKE.

If what you learned from Bogdanor taught you the possibilities of proportional representation and how its varieties might be used to abort it, the Referendum could have a more positive meaning for you. You presumably had little awareness of Ted Heath during his premiership which ended when you were seven. He was probably a man of greater principle than any Prime Minister since Attlee, a genuine believer in European closeness primarily as a means to reduce the chances of any further European war, and a straight-forward, not to say insensitive, man. The Referendum he put into use in Northern Ireland in 1973 to reaffirm its commitment to Union, strengthened by his previous appointment of William Whitelaw who proved the best Secretary of State for Northern Ireland ever (did you ever see Conor Cruise O'Brien's weekly column when it demanded 'Is there intelligent life on Tom King?'). But the IRA largely prevented Catholic participation in the Northern Ireland Referendum of 1973 by ferocious intimidation, and Heath's entry of the UK into the European Union lacked a referendum until two years later when his successor Harold Wilson produced one, thus making the UK's status in Europe dependent on a vote that agreed that it should have done what it had done two years previously. This in-again-out-again use of referendums probably weakened the UK public confidence in the appropriateness of its European status and unsettled the UK electorate sufficiently to keep the UK an uncertain partner. The contrast with a Referendum-backed European status for Ireland is marked: the Irish, schooled by Garret Fitzgerald, showed themselves at home in Europe where most of the English MEPs seemed uneasy.

Then the contradictions of the Scottish Referendum of 1979 were probably obvious to you even at 12. (Since we agree you are bright, we will take you to have been bright at 12. Or did people not talk about Scotland in your proximity? They do it less than ever now, perhaps by your orders.) Yet once you got to Oxford you must have recognised in Bogdanor a great Referendum advocate. Moreover, while apparently not a Tory himself, he made it clear that the initial impulse for the Referendum came from 'the deeply conservative jurist Dicey' in his 'Ought the Referendum to be Introduced into England?' (*Contemporary Review* (April 1980)

— by which, of course, Dicey meant the UK but was too polite
to say so). 'He had broken with Gladstone on the issue of
Irish Home Rule' pointed out Bogdanor (*The People and the
Party System*, p. 12)

> but continued to regard himself as a Liberal, seeing no reason
> why his allegiance should be determined by this one issue. For
> he believed that not only was the electorate opposed to Home
> Rule, but that even Liberal voters were doubtful as to its
> merits. Gladstone had converted the Liberals to Home Rule
> through force of personality, and through his command over
> the party machine; but he had not won over the minds of
> Liberals, much less their Rulers, the swing of the electoral
> pendulum would be bound to bring to power a government
> claiming a mandate for a policy which the majority of the
> electorate heartily detested.

Dicey had become so passionately engaged — and enraged —
here that he lost sight of the real background, or, as you
might say, my dear Mr Cameron, the bigger picture. For the
November/December 1885 General Election, Charles Stewart
Parnell as Home Rule Party leader and President of the
Home Rule Confederation of Great Britain told the Irish in
Britain (save for Newcastle-upon-Tyne whose Liberal MPs
were fervent supporters of Irish Home Rule) to vote Tory in
view of the 1880–85 Liberal Government's coercion policy
in Ireland, and, much more formidably, he ran the popular
Irish journalist and London newspaper-proprietor T. P.
O'Connor as Irish Home Rule candidate for the Liverpool
(Scotland) division which he won. Gladstone's conversion
to Home Rule followed rapidly, preceded by hints that it was
well on its way. The Irish Home Rule Bill Gladstone introduced with Parnell's agreement on 8 April 1886 excluded
Irish MPs from Westminster in consideration of their receiv-
ing an Irish Parliament limited to domestic affairs. This

meant no further threat of alienating the Irish vote in Britain from the Liberals. Those Liberals who continued to support Gladstone – the majority of the party – in most cases followed his logic, seeing good hard pragmatic reasons to accept Home Rule. The Centre-Right defection of Liberal Unionists under Lord Hartington was probably predictable, but the exclusion of the Irish MPs from future Westminster Parliaments was disturbing to the Centre-Left Liberals known as Radicals, led by Joe Chamberlain of Birmingham who evidently saw in this a threat of clipping his own wings, since Irish MPs at Westminster in general supported Radical measures in the 1880s. So Chamberlain went Unionist, as did some young Radicals from Wales and Scotland partly because they had ideas of Welsh and Scottish devolution endangered by exclusion of the Irish (David Lloyd George was apparently one waverer, but he was back in the Gladstonian fold when first elected to the Commons in 1888).

At the time of Gladstone's Disestablishment of the (Protestant Episcopalian) Church of Ireland in 1869 to the great satisfaction of the Irish Catholics, extremist Protestant ecclesiastics had hopes of Queen Victoria refusing her consent, but Disraeli saw the dangers of upsetting that particular apple-cart: the self-secluded Queen was still in defensive mourning for her husband Albert (dead since 1861) on whom she had greatly depended to tell her how to rule, and was therefore unpopular, and defiance of a Parliamentary vote could have revolutionary consequences being revolutionary enough in itself. She came to prefer Disraeli to Gladstone, and she interfered behind the scenes right up to her choice of Rosebery for premier in 1894, but open defiance of Parliament ran counter to her training first by Lord Melbourne and then by Albert. Dicey saw that, but casting his mind around other political systems, he lit on the

Swiss use of Referendums in the belief that a UK-wide Referendum would veto Irish Home Rule if a future Gladstone government won a Commons majority for it and intimidated the House of Lords, perhaps with a threat of ennobling enough Liberals to pass it through the upper chamber. April 1890 was an ominous moment for the Liberal Unionists. Hartington had failed to take all the Whig grandees with him, Chamberlain had actually lost Radical supporters back to Gladstone, Parnell had been vindicated on forged newspaper charges of support for terrorism, Salisbury, Balfour and the Government had become fellow-conspirators with *The Times* to wriggle out of dependence on the forged letters, the Tories faced newly-winged Opposition Furies and Harpies including even their own former Chancellor of the Exchequer Lord Randolph Churchill, and Gladstone clearly intended to carry Irish Home Rule through the Commons (at least) when back in power. The verdict against Parnell in the O'Shea divorce case set those prospects back, and by the end of 1890 the Irish party had split over Parnell's leadership, but with Parnell dying in October 1891 Gladstone became even more devoted to Home Rule for principle rather than merely for possible party advantage. Gladstone had broken Parnell by threatening to drop Home Rule if he remained leader of the Irish party, a majority of whose MPs then defected from Parnell. The Second Home Rule Bill introduced in 1893 was much more carefully drafted and looked far more like a measure intended for permanent legislation instead of political manoeuvre. And although it was defeated in the Lords and Gladstone would hardly have carried Rosebery and other supporters in the Lords to the level of threatening to swamp the Lords with Liberal peers (as happened in 1910–11) and Victoria would not have been ready to underwrite such a threat (but she was old and her successors proved more malleable), Dicey feared Home Rule might prove a matter of tomorrow if not today. He now took his crusade into extreme Tory journalism, the *National Review* under Leo Maxse for March 1894 where Dicey now preached 'The Referendum' in inflammatory prose:

> In periods of revolution, like the present, men live fast. The speculative question of 1890 may, it is likely enough, be transformed into then popular demand of 1895 or 1896. The Referendum is the People's Veto; the nation is sovereign, and may well decree that the constitution shall not be changed without the direct sanction of the nation.

By 'the nation' he actually meant England, given the support for Irish Home Rule in Scotland and Wales, but the term could also be stretched to mean the entire United Kingdom. Dicey thus left himself the option of appeal to two different nationalisms while at war with three others. Down to Thatcher's time — and indeed to yours — those alternate appeals to a nationalism sympathetic to UK Unionism, now English, now UK, haunted devolution. It profited by recruiting hostility to Scottish, Welsh and Irish nationalism, and even, from time to time, to Ulster Unionism when its varieties blossomed into Protestant regional nationalism (across history it has shown itself highly anti-English when it wants, and became so again after being excluded from the Anglo-Irish Agreement of 1985). Yet it was in itself very nationalistic. Professor John Curtice (who has done so much to strengthen the professionalism of the psephology of devolution) wrote with Anthony Heath and Roger Jowell in *The Rise of New Labour* ((2001), p. 58), as they commenced their chapter 'Margaret Thatcher's Nationalism':

> While Margaret Thatcher's radical, laissez-faire approach to the economy has been her most important political legacy, she

was also distinctive for her style of British nationalism. As Peregrine Worsthorne memorably described her approach, Thatcherism meant 'bitter-tasting market economics sweetened and rendered palatable by great creamy dollops of nationalistic custard ... Did her nationalism have a popularity that compensated for the unpopularity of her economic policies ...?

The main ingredients in this nationalistic custard were strong defence, especially the retention of Britain's independent nuclear deterrent and the deployment of American cruise missiles in Britain, a willingness to take on Argentina and recover the Falklands, and the vigorous pursuit of what she took to be British interests in Europe. On the home front Margaret Thatcher's nationalism took the form of advocacy of unionism and an opposition to devolution and the possible break-up of the United Kingdom.

As on the economic front, under John Major the Conservatives largely followed the same path as Margaret Thatcher. He displayed the same nationalistic instincts, with success in the Gulf War and opposition to devolution in Scotland and Wales....

The Conservatives' brand of nationalism is what James Kellas has called the official nationalism of the British state ... It is clearly very different from the nationalism of Scottish, Welsh or Irish separatists, which aims at securing a measure of home rule for the Scottish, Welsh or Irish nations.

It has much more in common with the political vocabulary of Ulster Unionism, especially in the Unionist-Tory political mutual aid between 1922 and 1970, and Paisleyism shares common roots, yet ill-feeling before and since 1985 has induced broodings about a separate Northern Ireland identity, and if such things seem moribund today it is the result of pragmatic self-reappraisal. The Democratic Unionists were always more suspicious of Westminster and Whitehall than the more squirearchical Ulster Unionists who enjoyed what they took to be reciprocal elite culture. And Thatcher never identified with Ulster Unionism, any more than she identified with Scots or Welsh culture. However freely she used the word 'British' it never represented more than gift-wrapping for 'English'. When some question of strengthening Unionism in the peripheries came up she told her questioner, the Scots MP Michael Earl of Ancram never to forget that she was an 'English nationalist'. To purloin John Milton's equation, her 'Britain' was but old England writ large.

And of course you played a walk-on or run-off part in Thatcher nationalism after leaving Oxford when you became its intellectual gofer with research duties apparently including espionage on Labour. A little duplicity in the cause may satisfactorily blood a new votary, as the Communists frequently found, and Orwell readily ascribed to Comrade Ogilvy.

The present situation in the archipelago thus features nationalisms formally much older than Thatcher nationalism, but in their present situation sharply transformed by having to react against Thatcherism. And similarly the Referendum while a highly democratic mechanism was proposed by Dicey in 1890 and 1894 as a weapon in an earlier version of that situation. The classicists on both sides of the Home Rule debate 1885–1894 would have thought of Heracles cleaning the Augean stables by flooding them with the Tigris and the Euphrates; Irish nationalism had to be stopped in mid-career and Scottish and Welsh nationalism drowned almost at birth by the huge tide of UK nationalism. Dicey's Referendum trumpet-call was never required to await its response since Gladstone's retirement was announced on 3 March 1894 just after its publication, Rosebery as Prime Minister eased away from Irish Home Rule, and the issue for the next ten years became more academic than Dicey's tone had foretold.

Nevertheless in one respect it was a dangerous doctrine he was peddling. The Referendum was perfectly peaceful in itself, but to excite the Tories with thoughts of a Parliamentary majority being vetoed stacked up dangerous fuel for the crisis of the Third Home Rule Bill in 1912 when the Lords' veto had been reduced to a maximum two-year delay, and at the King's request the Parliament Act itself had only been passed after two General Elections in 1910 whose victories for the Liberals and Home Rulers meant that a Third Home Rule Bill was certain and its preliminaries sufficiently amounted to a Referendum since a third General Election so soon could hardly be expected. Thus the conviction that the people's Veto could only be ensured by a rebellion through force of arms in Ulster had its scholarly validity. Bogdanor as a young academic was all too respectful of Dicey's eminence, not to say his hallowed dust, but back in March 1894 Dicey had at times crossed the demagogic frontier:

'Till 1893 no statesman dreamt that a majority of from 30 to 40 warranted the attempt to dissolve the Union between Great Britain and Ireland.' (P. 66.)

'Nobody supposes that the Irish representation fairly represents the Irish people. The Protestants constitute roughly about a fourth of the population; they are represented by less than a fifth of the Irish Members.' (P. 67.)

The 'no statesman ... Nobody' repetition is the wild work of demagoguery: the eminent jurist had run away from his evidence. He was quite right that Ireland in 1894 was one-quarter Protestant, but as Gladstone frequently pointed out, the Irish Home Rulers had been successively led by three Protestants from 1873 to 1890, and included several

Protestant MPs. Ultimately Dicey was on the same intellectual level as Queen Victoria in her diary on 1 February 1886 (quoted by Conor Cruise O'Brien, *Parnell and his Party 1880–1890* (1957), p. 150):

> Mr Gladstone continued to say that one could not doubt the opinion of Ireland when eighty-six members were returned by the Irish people in favour of it [Home Rule]. I observed that these were mostly low, disreputable men, who were elected by order of Parnell, and did not genuinely represent the whole country.

In other words, representation is what you choose to determine it. Victoria's 'whole country' was more honest than Dicey's implication that Protestants would only vote for Protestants, since she probably meant what she said (whatever she meant by it) and he must have known he was talking nonsense. The proof of his contribution to the pudding being stirred in 1893–94 was that 30 years later in Northern Ireland Protestant votes indeed went almost exclusively to Protestant candidates. But very bad blood had flowed in the interval, across the world and in Ulster itself. When after the Referendum you were quoted on 'English votes for English laws' for which Bogdanor rebuked you (and Scottish Nationalists cheerily accorded you a Machiavellian approval), it made historians' blood run a little colder. You yourself might have forgotten from your days at Eton working for Dr Gailey on Northern Ireland, or only remembered subconsciously, the first Northern Ireland Premier Sir James Craig once speaking of his polity as 'a Protestant parliament for a Protestant people'. To do him justice it was his one major lapse into bigotry: his colleague and ultimate successor Sir Basil Brooke ruled his apartheid state from 1943 to 1963 with such habitual proclamations of the kind.

Bogdanor rightly gave pride of place to quotations from the Dicey articles of the 1890s. You certainly had every incentive to read and ponder them. And certainly your references to the people of the United Kingdom have the same somewhat hollow assurance with which Dicey couched his rhetoric in 1894, although not as cloyingly artificial as Thatcher's tartan monstrosities when speaking in Scotland. The last Tory Prime Minister who thought British was Bonar Law (British with Canada and Northern Ireland included); the only later Scot among the Conservative premiers was Douglas-Home who was so enmeshed in upper-class vocabulary that he quoted Kipling's 'England's on the anvil' when he meant Britain although Kipling had really meant England. You are far more austere in your allusions to the mind of the Scottish people, save understandably reading the Referendum result in terms favourable to your policy. There is an interesting echo of Gladstone here. Gladstone and Dicey seemed to face one another with claims of popular support, Gladstone confident that Scotland and Wales wanted Irish Home Rule (sometimes hinting that reflected similar hopes for themselves, sometimes not), Dicey perpetually invoking 'England' and 'the Englishman'. Dicey preached the Referendum against Irish Home Rule, with a view to a ballot across the entire archipelago. But from the very first he made it symbolically clear that his thoughts were entirely with England. His first Referendum article, that in the *Contemporary Review* in 1890, was entitled 'Ought the Referendum be Introduced into England?' He meant the United Kingdom. He opened with a quotation from his expert on Switzerland, the recently deceased Sir Francis Ottiwill Adams, beginning 'It is a question for us Englishmen ...'. It meant 'a subject of the United Kingdom'. It will be said that convention in the late Victorian era said 'Englishman' regardless of whence in the British Isles the person came, and in support we can point to an exchange in the House of Lords around 1885–86. The Earl of Limerick rather plaintively asked whether in spoken or written official communications Irish identity when relevant could be indicated, and Salisbury, as Prime Minister, had enormous, sadistic fun wanting to know whether his friend the noble Earl would prefer the use of an adjectival 'Great-Britain-and-Ireland-ish'? Lord Limerick was simply trying to give the more Unionist Irish some means of taking pride in their country and their Union, and Salisbury made it clear that it was for Ireland to keep its place in the Union but at a respectful distance from the only place that really mattered. The situation was codified in the mid-20th century when the novelist Nancy Mitford explained that truly Upper-class people ('Non-U') said 'Britain' (Ireland by this stage being beyond the Pale in every sense of the term). Scotland and Wales were irrelevant, regardless of Gladstone's attempt to seek their judgments. So the basic assumption fortified by tradition, convention and above all snobbery meant that the United Kingdom really meant England leaving it for Thatcher with her usual crudity to make it clear this is the reality. By doing so she greatly sharpened Scots interest in as much devolution as possible to get away from her and her besotted disciples, thus sending the Referendum for a Scottish Parliament from its paper-thin majority of 1979 to its 1997 landslide (74 per cent) for the Parliament with 63 per cent for its tax-raising powers. This still set aside Independence but it certainly was growing nearer.

History gives us the additional dimension: we may have length and breadth and thickness (especially the last) but our judgments on one another lack time perspective. We can better assess one another by finding comparable people and problems in the past, all the more when our subject has actually worked at the past, as you have, complicating you in some ways, simplifying you in others. We cannot know the past fully but we cannot know one another fully either and so our unknowns may cancel some of their reciprocal ignorance — or deepen it. You, my dear Mr Cameron, are not the hero of this little epic to which I am subjecting you (as with your usual intellect with no need of your usual pretence of ignorance you will have recognised), but in one respect your conduct was most emphatically heroic and farsighted, your agreement with First Minister Alex Salmond that the Referendum should happen, should be enabled from Whitehall by you, and should take place at a date in the future of Alex Salmond's choosing. You both made certain concessions and seem to have worked out your agreement with as little room for subsequent recrimination on the decisions as possible. By this heroic act you attracted abuse of a kind with which you are familiar from your more Europhobic colleagues whose utterances frequently make one wish that Darwin had heard them for the completion of his evolutionary spectrum. (I say 'Europhobic': Eurosceptic gives them dignity and intellect of which otherwise they show little evidence.) What you did — what you both did — ensured that for all of the bitterness the debate and its contests produced at the time (and, as Mr Jim Murphy at his most saintly would wish us to add, notwithstanding the egg), matters were far better humoured than they would otherwise have been. You did it with a good grace, and a thoughtful smile. Alex Salmond is more practised and more relaxed in smiling than you — it is one of his marks of government whereas Westminster will not permit so much relaxation in the slaves of its lamp, but you did your best and it well became you. In Irish history damage was done for the want of a good grace. Peel's hatred of O'Connell (how could he forgive a man who had won him immortality as 'Orange Peel'?) meant that after O'Connell had won the Clare election of 1828 defying the ban on the election of Roman Catholics to Parliament, thus forcing Wellington and Peel to grant Catholic Emancipation, O'Connell was forced to seek re-election and not permitted to be called to the Inner Bar to which his fellow-Catholics could now be admitted for the first time. It was mean in a way we don't associate with either Wellington or Peel as a rule, and it soured the grant of Catholic Emancipation, itself the belated fulfilment of Pitt's promise 30 years earlier when gaining Catholic support for the Union of Great Britain and Ireland. You are unlikely to win victories greater than Wellington, or to work harder to carry reforms than Peel, but on this you showed yourself superior to both. You were, in fact, in the spirit of Gladstone in 1886, responding to Scotland's election in 2011 of a majority of MSPs pledged to Independence by their very membership of their party, exactly as we have just noted Gladstone told Victoria when the Home Rule party mustered 86 MPs (the 86 of '86 as they were called). And you did not fool around with Victoria's and Dicey's notions of true representation by which they meant one which produced MPs pledged to what the two of them liked. You saw a fact and you faced it. You showed yourself a gentleman. Eton paid off (and God knows it had been paid enough).

You were denounced as you were bound to be denounced by your Labour Opposition whose branch office denounced Alex Salmond. The duty of an Opposition is to oppose. The duty of journalists is to appear to justify their existence. In Ireland we have the useful phrase 'the hurlers in the ditch' meaning those watching the game of hurling (or camogie or (in Scotland) shinty) without participating in it. We will leave them in the ditch for the moment. I acknowledge that the title of this book has ironic and satirical uses, but on this occasion you earned it. The Edinburgh Agreement was a good if limited insurance against future recrimination and bitterness. You will have noticed that when the Referendum recorded NO the memberships of YES parties mushroomed, partly from disappointment, but also partly because of the positive spirit which had flowed in part from the Edinburgh Agreement as well as from being YES people. As we picked ourselves off the battlefield there was never a defeated army showing greater spirit. And you deserve credit for that. Your mean little missions to run around the world bribing, bullying and blackmailing were not beautiful, but even there the results were positive, most of all when the certainty of YES banning Trident from Scotland moved you to move President Obama now entrapped by his military-industrial complex, and when he cried NO Alex Salmond gave him the perfect reply in Obama's own great slogan 'YES WE CAN!' thus making his most powerful enemies his accomplices in the Art of the Positive. But it took greatness of mind in you to conclude the Edinburgh Agreement, perhaps your finest hour.

You obviously know what you took to be at stake, what you sacrificed, and what you demanded, better than I do. To me it turned on a choice between words and time, you won on words, he won on time, as far as the actual negotiations were concerned. We may not know which of you made the better bargain until we are all dead (that is an Irish bull for you, unless we do discover it after we are dead). Much of the public arguments which then ensued featuring your forces and his turned on prophesies about effects of Independence and of effects of the prophesies of the effects — you could instruct Osborne and Osborne could command Danny Alexander and recruit Ed Balls to tell you you wouldn't get a currency union and the YES people could reply that you wouldn't be able to hold to that and you thought ît would frighten the YES voters and in fact ît seems to have made up the minds of waverers that they were not going to be frightened by a crowd of dirty bullies with snob accents (Danny Alexander's snob accent pending) and so forth. Although the effects of this fortune-telling were psychologically heartening for us since ît blew your bullies up on their own overkill, the real prophesy duel was over the Edinburgh Agreement since Alex Salmond decided what he needed moſt was time, and you decided what you needed moſt was limîtation of Referendum queſtions. That choice made sense, and ît was also sensible to eliminate unnecessary public argument where possible and for each of you to decide on your primacies. As I read ît, Salmond felt that the people of Scotland were in many cases more in favour of Independence than elections could show, but that for moſt ît was not high on their liſt of priorîties. On this showing much fewer of them were actually againſt Independence than Unioniſt polîticians and pollſters imagined but there were many other things they thought were more urgent. On that reading the more time they got to priorîtise the better. The very fact that the Scottish electorate in the Weſtminster elections of 2010 went dead againſt the English repudiation of Labour and inſtead confirmed Gordon Brown in every Labour seat won in the 2005 General Election, and that one year later ît had given the SNP a supposedly impossible overall majorîty in the Holyrood election of 2011, was very ſtrong evidence for such deliberation, priorîtisation and gradualism on the part of the Scottish voter. It might very well be that the optimum approach for the Independence-believers would be to accept the maximum amount of devolution on offer to be balloted in the Referendum alongside options of Independence and Status Quo. Widespread polling results had strongly suggested that Devo-Max would romp home leaving the alternatives Independence and Status Quo more or less neck and neck.

Both of you knew that while both of you were genuinely interested in what was at stake – your training from Gailey and Bogdanor ensured you were brought up to be interested in such questions unlike Thatcher who apart from her hostility to devolution was bored out of her tiny mind by it – it was a lifetime's obsession to Alex Salmond and a matter to be settled once for all for you, if that could be arranged. You therefore made your primary concern the number of words on the ballot-paper while he was really – if less obviously – determined to prioritise its distance in time. Each of you were probably right. You may have believed Salmond was not really serious about Independence and personally wanted Devo-Max. This is a result of a phenomenon we noted earlier, the automatic assumption that what a politician says is probably not what he thinks. Having known Alex Salmond since he was 17, I knew perfectly well that he was as unshakeable a believer in Independence as any so-called fundamentalist, but that like his advisers Neil MacCormick and former Presiding Officer George Reid he knew the importance of diplomacy and the value of gradualism, what might be called giving Scottish Independence enough time to grow in the minds of the voters and in its own nature. But he could play fox when he wanted to, and if you and your team concluded he wanted Devo-Max rather than Independence he would not disabuse you. He allowed you to deceive yourselves.

At the time when a Bogdanor student would have been looking at most recent scholarship on devolution, the most exciting work on Gladstone's first Irish Home Rule Bill was still A. B. Cooke's and John Vincent's *The Governing Passion: Cabinet Government and Party Politics 1885–86* (1974). I remember talking about it with Gordon Brown (then still a doctoral student in History with us at Edinburgh). It was a dangerous book in its way because of its implication that the first Home Rule Bill wasn't a matter of serious political conviction at all which it certainly was in Ireland. It assumed too readily that whatever they talked about, politicians had no particular conviction other than self-interest or party discipline and prospects. It was a little too reminiscent of Namierism, about something for which men and women had genuinely struggled and died. Namierism certainly had something to teach as was shown by works as divergent as Sir Ronald Syme's *The Roman Revolution* (about Roman politics after Caesar's murder) and Conor Cruise O'Brien's *Parnell and his Party 1880–90* but these certainly did not take the mind out of history. When Vincent lectured at Edinburgh one of his hearers was the late Alfred G. Donaldson a former legal draughtsman at Stormont who pointed out from his expertise that the first Home Rule Bill was very badly and hastily drafted, in contrast to the Second Home Rule Bill, in 1893, which was drafted with great skill and clarity. I was reminded of Sherlock Holmes's deduction in 'The Norwood Builder' (*Strand*, November 1904, reprinted in *The Return of Sherlock Holmes*) that a will evidently drawn up in a moving train was not expected to be of any practical importance. But this in its way was realistic. There was never any likelihood that a Liberal Home Rule bill would survive the Tory-dominated House of Lords as then composed, whatever its fate in the Commons. It certainly sent a signal to the Irish in Britain that the Liberals were going to do their best for them and so not to vote against them or set up rival candidates for British seats. It would have been very foolish to conclude from this that devolutionary schemes arose from House of Commons manoeuvres and had no relationship to popular movements and convictions (ideological or criminal). The London media resent going outside London so they like to assume that movements and attitudes (say) in Scotland have no real bases other than passing fads. Thus without any excuse of having been influenced by Cooke and Vincent, much less by Donaldson, TV journalists like Master Nick Robinson of the BBC can smirk an implication that devolutionary questions are merely local swindles to bewilder the local hayseeds. But would you with your professional awareness of the Cooke-Vincent thesis undervalue Scottish Nationalism (however much you might dislike or oppose it)? Bogdanor had surely taught you too well for you to imagine Salmond must be a fraud because he had a sense of humour. The London media might dismiss him as a chancer who did not really want Scottish Independence, partly because from Thames boat houses and public houses, flats and sharps, they could not imagine how anyone could want it. Many of them who had invaded Scotland during previous eruptions or epiphanies of Scottish Nationalism showed qualities in common with the great H. L. Mencken whose apparent cynicism and iconoclasm covered a passionate idealism inducing such crusades as his admiration for the old Progressive Senator Robert LaFollette, third-party candidate for the US Presidency in 1924. Neal Ascherson who found Scottish nationalism the exception to the nationalism he had disliked so much across the globe, Tom Nairn who returned to Scotland to demolish Scottish nationalism and stayed to become its greatest theorist — these were neither dupes nor cynics. You, my dear Mr Cameron, might not have had time to ponder these things and to choose between the iconoclasts and the idealists but if you had been led to imagine Alex Salmond was merely a devolutionist enthroned by an innocent mob, and thus thought he really wanted nothing more than Devo-Max, I dare say you were disillusioned much more rapidly than Little Pig Robinson. There was the further considera-tion that many nationalists were quite critical of Alex Salmond although almost none were SNP MSPs, and if anything he encouraged journalists to talk to his enemies. Perhaps he believed like Ralph Waldo Emerson and Oscar Wilde that to be great is to be misunderstood. But at some point (I wonder when) you must have realised that Alex Salmond's Scottish Nationalism was as unyielding a patriotism as Winston Churchill's. And both of them had senses of humour, in some respects quite similar. (He told our Book Festival this summer that his mother worshipped Winston Churchill and his father abominated him, so the similarity may be more fortunate than fortuitous.) As we will see you must have known about Scotland not to feel enraged when it no longer appeared as the Orwellian prep-school desideratum or the untroubled Utopia for which the London media might harvest retirement hopes:

> A stream of boiling water flowed down the silvery strand. The shore was covered with oysters. Acid-drops and sweets grew upon the trees. Yams, which are a sort of sweet potato, abounded ready cooked. The breadfruit tree grew iced cakes and muffins ready baked.
>
> Beatrix Potter, *Little Pig Robinson* (1930)

Your yourself readily assume that gross simplification is required for the media as well as great discretion. Your list of Tories who became great premiers did not include Gladstone, partly because he did not remain a Tory and it might (if we all live long enough) prompt the thought that you may end up a long way from where you are at the moment. Bogdanor and his books taught you about that:

Many of the great party leaders of the past had switched party allegiance. Gladstone had begun his political career as, in Macaulay's famous phrase, 'the rising hope of the stern unbending Tories'; but he ended it on the radical wing of the Liberal Party.

BOGDANOR, Power and the People: A Guide to Constitutional Reform
(1997), p. 19

But if there is one former Prime Minister appropriate for your situation in 2014 it may have been Gladstone. We would have trouble working out to which year we should dock our time machine to make the most of him. He probably consulted very few people: he does not seem to have talked much with Parnell about the 1886 Home Rule Bill in advance though they did talk at length in 1889 when Parnell was a guest in Gladstone's house and pretended he knew no Irish history (on which he had lectured in Cork in 1885) presumably to have the fun of having the greatest English statesman of the day lecture the foremost Irish national leader on the Hibernian past. 1893 would be better, since clearly Irish Home Rule meant more to him then, but he was now very deaf. Still, Bogdanor knows his Gladstone and writing in 1997 brought clear realism to the making — or remaking — of the Scottish parliament and these may help to fix your base in 2014 as clearly as anything:

> The Union with Scotland, after all, is not an end in itself but a means to the effective government of different parts of the country. If it becomes evident that the Union is caught in a logical straitjacket such that it is no longer possible to improve Scottish government within the framework of the United Kingdom, then the framework itself will come under threat. … Conservatives, together with the Liberal splinter group which opposed Gladstone's Irish home rule proposals, also called themselves Unionists. They too argued that there was no half-way house between the unitary state and separation. Yet, by

defeating home rule, they eventually brought about the very consequence which they moſt abhorred – the collapse of the Union. In other words, if there was one objective which the Unionists failed to achieve, ît was preservation of the Union wîth Ireland. Thus, those who argue that devolution to Scotland alone is impossible, and that the only choice is between the unîtary ſtate and separation, ignore the lessons of practical experience. Moreover, they endanger the very kingdom whose unîty they seek to preserve.

BOGDANOR, *Power and the People*, pp. 39–40

Bogdanor would have had no expectation of the ultimate relevance of this to you: while his book was passing through the press you were failing to win what had been a good seat for the Tories in Stafford. Your defeat naturally filled moſt of the General Election horizon for you in 1997, but Scotland rudely recalled îtself to your attention by blotting out the entire Tory party north of the Tweed. If you saw that book of Bogdanor's you may have been a lîttle shaken by îts cold anger. Since the 2014 Referendum many YES people have told me they felt angry at the result, but that their anger was brief and their hope quick to return. Bogdanor's anger came nearly 90 years after the beginning of the Tory adventure which as he says wrecked the Union of Great Brîtain and Ireland, and he turned ît on Thatcher and her merry men who slammed the door on Scottish devolution, reneged on a promise of ît, and ate dinners in the capîtal and the rejected capîtal to congratulate themselves on their mayhem. In fact he warned you and your maſters that you were risking the end of the Union of Great Brîtain and Northern Ireland. That was the burden you bore when you recognised what would be the conſtitutional result of the SNP Holyrood majorîty in 2011 and realised that intransigence in responding to that implication would ultimately make a separation far more likely and far more ugly. Whatever you would say of

Thatcher in church or state, your journey to Edinburgh in 2012 was to do the best you could to save the UK from the effects of her Scottish folly. Your wisdom in healing what harms you could, turned your back on Tories from Bonar Law to Thatcher and Major, and from the holders of Scottish Toryism in electoral bankruptcy from 1999. From the midst of their valley of humiliation which they so richly deserved, the once-great Tory names fled from Scotland with all of the grace of Edward II after Bannockburn, and the raggle-taggle remaining courted the electorate with assurances that even if they accepted the Scottish Parliament (the one place in the country where safety-nets for minorities gave Scottish Toryism a handful of seats) they would require it to be diminished, or the Scottish representation at Westminster to be diminished. They may have sought to keep warm when the *Scotsman*, catastrophically turned against the Scottish Parliament, tried to put stuffing in the Tory demand for its abolition, and well-positioned Tory former politicians and camp followers nursed their shame by compounding its causes. You ultimately had the consolation of your chosen head of your outback station, the gallant Colonel, denouncing her party's policy on the Scottish Parliament for the previous 10, 20 or 30 years, and probably did so on your instructions. You met Alex Salmond gallantly, but you faced a leader at the head of his nation in which your party's credibility scarcely existed. And the worst enemy from whose wounds your beloved Union was still bleeding, perhaps mortally, was your canonised Thatcher.

Bogdanor's indictment was not limited to Thatcher and her Tory brood. One of the wounds of devolution from the first had been its pretended friends. James Callaghan's government brought in the first legislative experiment in Scottish devolution but Callaghan himself disliked it from the firſt. Michael Foot and John Smîth (and in Scotland the as yet unelected Gordon Brown) worked endlessly to advance the cause but were thwarted time and again by devious colleagues and outright opponents in the Labour party. In the 1990s John Smîth, Gordon Brown and Donald Dewar did what they could but when Smith was dead Blair's nominal acceptance of Smîth's devolution legacy actually masked further hoſtilîty. On the other hand, if parties were divided and polîticians sluggish, the people were showing greater and greater support for devolution. Above all the Church of Scotland's opening of the doors of îts General Assembly to a Conſtîtutional Convention was a call to action as well as prayer. Determined to repudiate any suggeſtion that ît might have accepted Thatcher's sermon at the General Assembly, the Church inspired far beyond îts doors, wîth the moral authorîty to call the people together irrespective of their theological persuasion. Intellectually ît raises a fascinating point. It meant that people who were not communicants of that Church, and recognised the Church made no preten- tions of demanding their allegiance, were proud and happy to answer îts call. It was partly spirîtual, and partly polîtical, and indeed social. But îts greateſt claim of all was hiſtorical. To those persons like myself who live in a faith once perse- cuted by the Church of Scotland, ît meant that the ecumen- ical summons was worthy and fîtting where we would never have obeyed a conſtraint. And we were proud to have ît call us. It might not be our church, but ît could ſtill demand a response from our heads and win a place in our hearts. The proceedings in the Convention commîtted the several polîti- cal parties (apart from the Government Tories' boycott) and when the General Election of 1997 loomed, Blair had no wriggle room left. The progress from the General Assembly Hall to the Independence Referendum was clear enough, all the more when the Church gave over its hall once again to the first proceedings of the Scottish Parliament before its building was ready. It has all been done without the slightest legitimisation of violence. But despite the Referendum defeat, the resources of constitutionalism continue, and the iron door against violence remains permanently closed.

The Act of Union was passed by a simple majority in the Scottish and the English Parliaments and was ratified by Queen Anne. The Scottish Parliament adjourned itself, as Winifred Ewing so inspirationally pointed out, and never in fact declared that particular term to have ended. That particular Parliament was dissolved by Royal decree after the institution itself had formally voted to be united to the English Parliament. The ensuing Westminster Parliament frequently forgot that it was a new body and generally behaved as if simply the English Parliament, augmented by the Scots, the Irish, the lower classes, women over 30, women over 21, &c., and decreased by the inhabitants of 26 of Ireland's 32 counties. But having passed its amalgamation with the Scottish Parliament, and having thereby inherited Scottish parliamentary history, the Act of Union may be repealed by the Westminster Parliament as it was enacted by its parents before their Union. Within six years, one of the most effective enablers of the passing of the Act of Union in the Scottish Parliament, James Ogilvy first Earl of Seafield, moved abolition of the Union in the House of Lords at Westminster, and lost by a paper-thin margin. Had Seafield's motion been carried in 1713 that particular House of Commons would have been most unlikely to ratify it when its verdict was required. But it was accepted that if the Lords and Commons voted the end of the Union, it was dissolved. SNP policy in the 1960s and thereafter was that a majority of Scottish members in the House of Commons would be sufficient constitutional warrant for the end of the Union, since the House of Lords can no longer be held to fulfil its functions under the Acts of Union of 1707 once it has lost veto power since 1911. So the SNP sought Independence via conquest of Scottish Westminster constituencies. The establishment of the new Scottish Parliament changed this, and the realisation that a parliamentary majority of Scottish seats was far more probable in Holyrood than in Westminster changed SNP targets and focus. But the constitutional doctrine remains that a majority of the YES people (whether SNP or not) in the Scottish electoral representation in the Westminster Commons would give Scotland Independence with no further referendum whatsoever. The General Election in May could in theory create that situation. It is a species of Nemesis for the tricks Westminster legislation has played with the Acts of Union over the last 300 years.

Bogdanor's ways are the ways of peace and his anger against those who endanger it. Hence he drew your attention to the Odyssey of Home Rule for Ireland where different advocates argued their cases albeit coming perilously close to violence in 1914 with gun-running, army mutiny, a rebel provisional government awaiting summons to action, and a Tory party ready to back the relevant acts of treason. Precedents do not include the Treaty of 1921 between Sinn Féin delegates and UK government representatives since its antecedents had been violent. Apart from the 1916 Easter Rising itself there was a possibility that the Sinn Féin MPs elected in the election of 1918 might go into non-violent protest, but ex-soldiers in arms against the UK from Spring 1919 ended that possibility. Thanks to the Scottish National Party (and they deserve the thanks of all Scotland and the rest of the UK for it), nationalism in Scotland scorned violence from the first, whereas Ireland tragically succumbed to an infection from the Great War. It was Scotland, not Ireland, which fulfilled Daniel O'Connell's prescription that freedom is not worth the blood of a single person. But while abhorring the violence of Sinn Féin supporters and the brutality of the UK government repression, we may notice the Treaty diplomacy for a moment in contrast to you. The effect of the Treaty negotiations was that Sinn Féin in Dáil Éireann split almost in halves leading to a civil war among the Irish nationalists. Lloyd George had settled the Irish question — so that it stayed calm for 50 years until it erupted into the 30 years' war in Northern Ireland killing God knows how many civilians, guerrillas and members of the armed forces. What Gladstone was trying to do was to bring peace to Ireland, ending its agrarian wars and its attractiveness to assassins from secret societies, and the older he got the more genuine he became. I think we can say you tried Gladstone's way with the improvement that you worked out your solution and then negotiated. And you played your tricks on your allies when you realised Alex Salmond kept his eyes open.

While we are thinking kindly of the Grand Old Man as a great ex-Tory, it's noteworthy that he saw Scottish Home Rule as a decided possibility in the future. Writing in 1886 (though not publishing until 1892 in his *Special Aspects of the Irish Question*, pp. 2–3) his essay 'The Irish Question, 1886' declared: 'Nor is it, in my view, allowable to deal with Ireland upon any principle, the benefit of which could not be allowed to Scotland in circumstances of equal and equally clear desire'. So he really was your model, under Bogdanor's guidance. You discovered your ideal Tory premier when he was a Liberal. That should give some solace to your coalition partners. They may even reverse Gladstone (in some cases) by becoming Tories. Gladstone's awareness of Scotland's potential for Home Rule derived partly from his Scottish parents, no doubt, but more directly from his having taken Midlothian after the most intensive personal electoral campaign British (though not Irish) politics had ever known, and his political organiser here was Archibald Philip fifth Earl of Rosebery who was the centre of very strong sentiment for Scottish celebration of identity among young Liberals and university students, who had elected him Rector of the University of Aberdeen in 1878 and of Edinburgh in 1880, with resultant Rectorials from him on Scottish identity and history.

Had you seen 'The Irish Question, 1886' or merely understood its message through Bogdanor's guidance? Gladstone wrote 'it appeared to me an evident duty to avoid, as long as possible, all steps which would bring this great settlement into the category of party measures'. We don't know how far Gladstone seriously tried to get agreement from his fellow Etonian Salisbury (never mind Hartington and Chamberlain whose objections, being those of members of Gladstone's party were not party measures). Or did he simply want to make it appear that he had thought to give Salisbury a generous offer of credit for carrying Home Rule. Anyhow 'the Buffalo' aka Uncle Robert declined with very little thanks, although shrewd enough to see where making Irish Home Rule a Liberal party measure might benefit the Tories in the long run. By May 1886 following Gladstone's conversion to Home Rule in late 1885, Salisbury was announcing the Irish were no more fit for self-government than the Hottentots, a finding in which the Irish should have taken more pride than they did. His anti-democratic lordship had already shown how little he thought most Englishmen fit to govern themselves, but his brazen frankness exhibited a mentality still at the heart of British Unionism (Irish Unionism has of course become a proud crusade in favour of its own self-government).

But you succeeded where Gladstone (and Salisbury) failed. You did it with the least trouble and expense for your party while Labour tore itself asunder and discredited itself with its more Scottish Scots, and the Liberal Democrats 'The little dogs and all', as King Lear says, 'Tray, Blanch, and Sweetheart', all ready to bark for you, licensed to growl. And even when one Sweetheart would be whistled off duty for services above and beyond its call, you had another Sweetheart to yap in its place. And in what you did you repudiated the great Tory Mummy herself, co-ordinating a policy flatly profaning the heart of her beliefs, and none dare say a word in rebuke of you, not a curse to be heard even from the Stygian darkness which shrouds my Lord Tebbit, still choking with hate and rage.

Gladstone lived in Wales as well as being son and parliamentarian for Scotland, and his awareness of them is instructive for us. He would not take them for granted although to the other Ireland (the one then gestating into existence with its linen factories and hardworking slums and sectarian riots in murderous chorus spitting on his Home Rule Bills of 1886 and 1893 and marching and drilling to the very lips of treason before World War I to be born in 1920 as Northern Ireland) he closed his mind. He ignored Thomas MacKnight, Durham-born author of the invaluable *Ulster As it Is* (1896) and editor of the *Northern Whig* whose witness (and presumably whose readers) converted their editor to Ulster Unionism and led to his assailing Gladstone with his very different interpretations of Edmund Burke whose biography he wrote. Just as Irish Catholicism in the early 19th century spun itself into a dawn of democracy under the magic of Daniel O'Connell, Ulster Presbyterianism and Protestant evangelism marched and talked and rioted its way into a voice of the people defying London authority in greater solidarity than the archipelago and perhaps the world had ever seen. I dare say it's a pity we don't have MacKnight on Ulster before he took up his editorial duties although he tries and I suppose fakes, a conversation between a native (Protestant) and himself at the outset of his Ulster career, certainly starting the book's two volumes engagingly enough. Dr Gailey may have put you on to it. Wealth, prosperity and authority developed in the south-east of our archipelago but its democratisation takes its different forms on the periphery, climaxed by Gladstone in 1879–80 who stormed the bourgeois heights of Midlothian respectability with a Himalayan succession of orations complex and coherent enough to put politics into the hands of a people entranced far beyond the limits of their own franchise.

And while we're being bibliographical do you know Christopher Harvie's *Scotland and Nationalism* (1977, 1994, 1998, 2004)? It's a fascinating case of a man converted by his own book, the first edition being a decidedly critical investigation carried out by a Labour party intellectual. He co-authored *A Voter's Guide to the Scottish Assembly* with Gordon Brown around 1979. The nationalism book is particularly rich on cultural history of which Harvie is one of the finest practitioners of our time. Any edition of the book is worth reading. He quotes what he calls Gladstone's 'gnomic endorsement' of the efforts of Liberals contemplating home rule for Scotland in 1886:

> Scotland, which for a century and a quarter after her Union was refused all taste of a real representative system, may begin to ask herself whether, if at the first she may not latterly have drifted into a superstitious worship or at least an irreflective acquiescence.

Chris Harvie continued correctly if sardonically:

He followed it with an equally gnomic disclaimer in 1889, to the relief of most of the front bench. But the Scottish Liberal Association adopted home rule in 1888. After swallowing an Irish policy they had campaigned fiercely against before 1886, anything was possible.

It must also have been a seismic shift in ethnic relations in Scotland, exacerbated by the vast extension of the male vote in 1884. Ireland presented Britain with its first incursion of mass pauper immigration most of all in the 1840s and 1850s when fugitives from Famine, some speaking no English at all (the one major Irish emigration where that seems to have been true), overwhelmed British culture and confronted British Protestantism with Irish Catholicism. In his *Immigration and Race in British Politics,* Paul Foot pointed out that they constituted the first known occasion of mass hostility to immigrants (however much the smaller incursions of Irish got themselves disliked in Britain in previous centuries) and the travail and occasional agony of the mid-19th century prefigured what would emerge later against Russian and other Slavic Jews fleeing from persecution in 1885–1914, and after World War II the immigrants from what was then called the Third World. The Irish incursion wasn't immigration in any political sense: they were migrating within the frontiers of your beloved Union, albeit a larger one than the present. But islanders are self-conscious about their differences from one island to another, and the Irish seem to have thought as migrants, often assuming (usually incorrectly) that they would return to their native shores. So the Scottish Liberal identification with Irish Home Rule (when it wasn't the Scottish Liberal identification with the other, Unionist, Ireland) must have advanced Irish Catholic assimilation in Scotland (less so in England where in the 19th century the Irish-born would have been a lower percentage of the overall population with individual high totals in different places from Liverpool to Newcastle and to the hop-fields of Kent). So while few of the Irish in Scotland as yet identified with Scottish nationalism, the conversion of Liberals (already pledged to Irish Home Rule) to some form of Scottish Home Rule must have seemed proof of the seriousness of their political change. So Irish and Scottish nationalism must have played a valuable part in the integration of the Irish into Scottish society, and, less obviously, into British society. Your UK greatly benefitted from Irish and Scottish nationalism (and Welsh nationalism produced a great UK wartime leader in David Lloyd George). Irish constitutional nationalism built political awareness in Ireland and then in Britain, greatly enlarging the popular sense of the utility of democracy. The most obvious 19th-century political leaders to enlarge British political life were O'Connell and Parnell, opponents of Union yet its builders and modernisers. Bogdanor will have taught you much of this, bless him.

Gladstone may have been vague in and out of endorsement of Liberal variations on Scottish Home Rule but he was certainly aware of Scottish democratising around the Home Rule cause. He began a speech in Edinburgh on 18 June 1886:

> It was said after the battle of Inkerman by Mr Sidney Herbert during the Crimean War, that the battle of Inkerman was the soldiers' battle. It was not won by the tactics or by the ability of the generals, but by the valour and determination of the Soldiers.

(And well might the soldiers need to take control since the incompetence of their generals two weeks earlier had caused the charge of the Light Brigade at Balaclava into suicidal slaughter.) Gladstone continued:

> You may anticipate that I mean to say to you that the present dissolution is the people's dissolution, and the present election is the people's election.

After the result of the 1886 General Elections (when England voted against Home Rule so that Gladstone lost), he might have been less rapid about identifying with popular control, but democracy doesn't always mean universal philanthropy, and some Unionists also had radical credentials. This phenomenon was also visible in the Referendum fight in 1979 and its election sequel, when the leading Labour NO-man Tam Dalyell had an enviable record as a courageous radical, as did Norman Buchan. It was much less evident in election and Referendum of 1997. By 2014 it became a matter of debate as to whether YES or NO had the real Radical credentials in themselves. Many Labour party members declared publicly for YES but MPs did not and Labour no less than the coalition government parties seem to have enforced conformity. Whether Devo-Max on the ballot paper would have induced Unionist party defections we cannot say, but many of its Left-wing supporters became among the most vociferous YES-men when you removed that choice. As far as quality of converts were concerned it looks to me as if you did YES a considerable service in eliminating Devo-Max, and radicalism (while no longer in itself a conventional label for MPs) becomes a useful term for an investigative, courageous and outspoken cast of mind meaning particularly voters whose initial loyalties to Devo-Max went to YES when reduced to two alternatives. In certain respects Thatcher may have been a major determinant. As the polls

narrowed and the Thatcherism of the Unionist establishment in all parties seemed more evident, Scottish veterans
long skilled in self-determination from anti-Thatcher
attitudes decided on YES after much mind-searching, heart-
searching and soul-searching. Devo-Max after all had been
fully compatible with anti-Thatcher attitudes since she had
made herself the English nationalist supreme inflated into
100 per cent Unionism. By 18 September 2014, Unionists
and Nationalists were united in their desire to turn out the
largest possible vote, and subsequently in their elation at
having done so. If they had done nothing else, they had
made Scotland a world leader in voter activity and both took
post-Referendum pride in that, and the pride was incom-
patible with true Thatcherism. Yet however much the new
exhilaration which followed conversion to YES asserted the
democratic intellect coming home to roost, some of the
most democratic souls in Scotland voted NO, several of
which souls I would regard as far nobler than my own. A
particularly important category in this latter group would be
English people of long residence here who had made great
contributions to Scottish radicalism and felt alienated – and
indeed hurt – by the threat of Independence.

You were very clever as usual in staying so much out of the
Referendum public eye that you gave little fodder to anti-
Thatcher attitudes. Younger voters who had not known
Thatcher save for her Voodoo resurrections could have sufficiently disliked your public school manner and (not having
known Grade A patronising of the Thatcher variety) found
it condescending. But there was little visible anti-Cameron
sentiment as unadorned motivation for voting YES. If YES
voters wished a hate figure from the ranks of NO, George
Osborne was the choice, frequently with the support of his
friends Ed Balls and Danny Alexander. These were not

moving targets, as, say Norman Buchan was in 1979 (he was ferociously critical of YES chiefly because it would make Edinburgh once more the capital rather than his beloved Glasgow, but he could well have voted YES if only for his affection and admiration for Michael Foot). Journalists were in some cases really worth following. Kevin McKenna of the *Observer* began the campaign with powerfully expressed orthodox Labour party loyalties and the back of his hand for the SNP Holyrood government, whom he particularly condemned for their concessions to cyclists. I know you were a more prominent cyclist than any other leader in London or Edinburgh, but I don't think that determined McKenna's move YESward, which produced in the end some of the finest writing of the battle. For that matter your enthusiasm for tennis didn't bring Andy Murray, the restorer of Wimbledon's honour, to your side. His declaration YES on 18 September 2014 was one of its brightest moments. J. K. Rowling's million-pound support for NO if influenced by any of the leaders of public opinion honoured Gordon Brown more than anyone else. That was the democratic intellect loud and strong: her Harry Potter books preached democratic values with supreme wit and imagination.

Radical NO-men had their instructive origin in the 1886 struggle when the great anti-war agitator John Bright and the highly promising Joe Chamberlain led Radical Unionist forces, with some Scots among them including John Boyd Kinnear, MP for East Fyfe 'whose election in 1885 was looked on by Whigs as tantamount to the implementation of the Communist Manifesto' wrote Dr I. G. C. Hutchison (*A Political History of Scotland 1832–1924* (1986) p. 163. Boyd Kinnear was no Orange Radical as were some of the Unionist Left. He had spoken in sympathy with Irish Home Rulers in the Commons although not with Irish Home Rule. His pamphlet *The Urgent Needs of Ireland* was dated 31 May 1886, the day on which Chamberlain and the Radical Unionists agreed to vote against Gladstone's First Home Rule Bill, which they helped to defeat a week later. Boyd Kinnear was much more genuinely concerned about Ireland than was Chamberlain, and *The Urgent Needs of Ireland* argued that 'some very practical grievances form which the Irish suffer' were being side-stepped by the Home Rule Bill:

> Mr Gladstone, instead of attempting to deal with the griev-
> ances which are the real and substantial causes of the discon-
> tent, amuses the nation with the offer of a bogus Parliament in
> Dublin, as a satisfaction to the sentiment of Nationality.
>
> P. 4

He credited the Irish Home Rule party with much more integrity than most Unionists would concede it and implied that it was prisoner rather than jailer of the Gladstonian Liberals:

> This the Nationalist leaders accept (under protest as to material
> points) firstly as a formal recognition of their claims for Home
> Rule, and secondly, because they honestly believe it is the only
> way of getting the legislation which their country really needs.

Boyd Kinnear's argument recalls those of the official head of the Scottish Labour party during the Referendum debate, Ms Johann Lamont, MSP for Glasgow Pollok. She insisted that the SNP Scottish Government was failing to legislate against real Scottish social and economic grievances and wasting time and money on constitutional nonsense. The grievances in question lost some of their urgency when in accord with Westminster Labour's 'me-too' forms of opposit-ion she denounced what she saw as social freeloaders who want something for nothing, a version of welfare abuse which you have heard so often from your colleagues that its

repetition in your ears must by now bore to the point of
excruciation. But as Kevin McKenna came to advocate
during the 2012–14 struggle, the YES campaign was forced
to show it knew the horrific social deprivation and administrative neglect in Glasgow must lie at the heart of its
demand for self-government. To have a Scottish Labour
leader from Glasgow working-class Gaelic-speaking origins
had been an impressive choice, but working-class Glasgow
proved the most impressive casualty of the Referendum
battle – it's YES telling you that, rejoice as you may in best
Thatcherite manner in your victory, the former second city
of the Empire is a UK black hole. Lamont's resignation a
month after the Referendum result was a bitter acknowledg-
ment that the NO-men had failed her as well as her city.

CHAPTER FIVE

THE SCOTTISH EDUCATION OF A PRIME MINISTER

He would not allow Scotland to derive any credit from Lord Mansfield; for he was educated in England. 'Much (said he) may be made of a Scotchman, if he be caught young.'

— JAMES BOSWELL, *The Life of Samuel Johnson LLD*

We now approach a more curious aspect of your credentials for masterminding the future of Scotland, my dear Mr Cameron. We agree that you must have had a first-class historical education from Andrew Gailey, and a first-class elucidation in the historical bases of politics and government from Vernon Bogdanor, offering so many tangents for reflection. We have played with your descent from William IV and the royal ancestors it gives you. But when we look closer at your immediate ancestors we find that your Scottish identity is both deeper and more complex than we might have guessed, but one which in its way is far more illustrious than poor old William IV at least until your descent from George I brings you back to his great-grandfather James VI and I, and the Scottish kings back to Robert Bruce and his complex antecedents.

Your surname betokens descent from one of the greatest and most romantic Scottish clans, and it is no vague coincidence. You have three Cameron descents, one of them from the old hero himself, Sir Ewen Cameron of Lochiel (1629–

1719), 17th chief of the Clan Cameron. Are you familiar with that wonderful introduction to England, invaluable to us foreigners, A. G. Macdonnell's *England, Their England* (1933)? (It is particularly famous for its classic narrative of the cricket match between the village team and the London men of letters.) The innocent around whose head so many disconcerting adventures will fall (Walter Scott's usual method) is indeed a Cameron, Donald Cameron, like your paternal grandfather. The cherished moment when our modest hero shows his steel happens early on when a London editor Mr Ogilvy (I wonder who was the original?) asks:

'Erracht, Mamore, or Fassifern?' he barked.

...

'I am asking you', said Mr Ogilvy, in a very broad Lanarkshire accent, to what branch of the Clan Cameron you belonged?'

'I — I don't know exactly', stammered Donald. Mr Ogilvy's kindly expression vanished and the Austerlitz manner reasserted itself.

'It's a poor Highlander who doesn't know his own chieftain', he observed coldly.

The blood ran to Donald's forehead at this, and he astonished himself by replying sharply, 'we have no chieftain. Lochiel's our chief.'

I read that well before I encountered either England or Scotland, and the passage stayed with me as one of my first images of Scotland after Burns, Scott and Stevenson. Lochiel I encountered in person in Thomas Babington Macaulay's *History of England* where, regardless of his Jacobitism and Macaulay's Whiggery, he is one of the subsidiary heroes.

Your great-great-grandfather was Sir Ewen Cameron

(1841–1908) Head of the London house of the Hong Kong and Shanghai Bank in the first years of the 20th century when his possibly most incompetent clerk was P. G. Wodehouse, who fictionalised that experience in *Psmith in the City* (1910, additionally garnished by an introduction to its omnibus appearance in *The World of Psmith* (1974)). The Bank Manager Mr Bickersdyke was not based on your great-great-grandfather, although conceivably the short-tempered Mr Gregory, veteran of long domicile in Asia, could have been; the other department managers weren't, unless your ancestor was a fanatical follower of Manchester United, or was a Socialist facing rough mobs during weekend evangelising on Clapham Common. Bickersdyke himself, the villain of the book and in some respects the nastiest Wodehouse ever drew, was an ex-Socialist Tory elected MP during the book: it doesn't say much for Tory MPs but your great-grandfather wasn't one, and seems to have been in declining health in the early Edwardian era when Wodehouse served his miserable year.

Sir Ewen of the Hong Kong and Shanghai (the New Asiatic Bank in Wodehouse) was the son of two Camerons, William of Upper Makovie near Culloden, and Catherine (whom he married in 1840) daughter of Ewen Cameron (1775–1842) and Helen McDonell or McDonnell (1776–1871) whose surname was almost certainly first known to herself in Gaelic (the spelling indicating some official scribe more familiar with the Irish usage). That Ewen's father was Alexander, his mother was born Kathleen Fraser and I have found no parents for them. Helen McDonell was the daughter of Donald MacDonald (Anglophone scribes translating nearer the customary Scottish usage) and her mother was Helen Grant (c. 1749–1827), whose father was Duncan Grant and mother was another Helen Grant. The repetition of these Christian names may confuse genealogical investigators but it clearly marked psychologically reinforcing sense of identity. These names persist to recent times, sometimes having lost the genealogical origin of the great forebear. The modernist painter Duncan Grant was Paris and Bloomsbury rather than Invernessshire, though his name lives on in Hugh MacDiarmid's eighth verse of 'A Drunk Man Looks at the Thistle' (1926):

> Whaur's Isadora Duncan dancin' noo?
> Is Mary Garden in Chicago still
> And Duncan Grant in Paris – and me foo'?

Alexander was of course a Cameron family name, as your parents showed in naming your elder brother. They were at least conscious of its immediate family piety, since it was borne by your paternal grandfather Donald's brother. Catherine Cameron's grandfather Alexander is counterpointed by her husband's grandfather Alexander married to Elizabeth Ferguson. But it is through the Grants, not these Camerons, that your glorious namesake is known to have begat you. Eighteenth-century Duncan Grant was the son of John Grant and Janet Cameron (1677–1754), her parents were Isabel Maclean and Sir Ewen Cameron of Lochiel the 17th chief. That Lochiel's mother was Margaret Campbell of Glenorchy who was directly descended from the King-Emperor James IV (1473–1513) afterwards killed at Flodden.

But let us pause upon Lochiel, immortalised by Macaulay's pen in the mid-1850s. You once remarked that an anagram for 'Cameron' was 'romance' which was accurate if somewhat tepid for one of your ancestry. The time was 1688–89, James VII and II had been eased off the English throne. He might have been permitted to live and die an unpopular Roman Catholic king whose progeny were safely

Protestant. But they were daughters, and male chauvinism in England and Scotland permitted female succession to the throne but only when all the ruler's sons were dead without issue. When James's second Queen presented him with a male heir, the Glorious Revolution was on the way and James's nephew and son-in-law William of Orange sailed from his beloved Netherlands to England, a desirable pawn in his mighty struggle against Louis XIV, the would-be conqueror of the Dutch. James lost his nerve and fled, though heroic enough in his days as Duke of York when he had led the force making New Amsterdam and New Holland into New York (city) and New York (state). William and his wife, James's daughter Mary, became rulers of England. But the Revolution in Scotland was bloodier, the Presbyterians would only accept their fellow-Calvinist William with the Church of Scotland becoming firmly Presbyterian, and the ousted James's Scottish supporters led by John Graham of Claverhouse Viscount Dundee now raised what support could be found in the Highlands. Macaulay demonised Dundee, but this, from the thirteenth chapter of his History of England, is his Lochiel:

> [The Camerons'] ruler, Sir Ewan Cameron, of Lochiel, surnamed the Black, was in personal qualities unrivalled among the Celtic princes. He was a gracious master, a trusty ally, a terrible enemy. His countenance and bearing were singularly noble. Some persons who had been at Versailles, and among them the shrewd and observant Simon Lord Lovat, said that there was, in person and manner, a most striking resemblance between Lewis the Fourteenth and Lochiel; and whoever compares the portraits of the two will perceive that there really was some likeness. In stature the difference was great. Lewis, in spite of high-heeled shoes, and a towering wig, hardly reached the middle size. Lochiel was tall and strongly built. In agility and skill of his weapons he had few equals

among the inhabitants of the hills... He had repeatedly been victorious in single combat. He was a hunter of great fame. He made vigorous war on the wolves which, down to his time, preyed on the red deer of the Grampians; and by his hand perished the last of the ferocious breed which is known to have wandered at large in our island. Nor was Lochiel less distinguished by intellectual than by bodily vigour. He might indeed have seemed ignorant to educated and travelled Englishmen, who had studied the classics under Busby at Westminster and under Aldrich at Oxford, who had learned something about the sciences among Fellows of the Royal Society, and something about the fine arts in the galleries of Florence and Rome. But though Lochiel had very little knowledge of books, he was eminently wise in counsel, eloquent in debate, ready in devising expedients, and skilful in managing the minds of men. His understanding preserved him from those follies into which pride and anger frequently hurried his brother chieftains. Many, therefore, who regarded his brother chieftains as mere barbarians, mentioned him with respect. Even at the Dutch Embassy in St James's Square he was spoken of as a man of such capacity and courage that it would not be easy to find his equal. As a patron of literature he ranks with the magnificent Dorset. If Dorset out of his own purse allowed Dryden a pension equal to the profits of his Laureateship, Lochiel is said to have bestowed on a celebrated bard, who had been plundered by marauders, and who implored alms in a pathetic Gaelic ode, three cows and the almost incredible sum of fifteen pounds sterling. In truth, the character of this great chief was depicted two thousand five hundred years before his birth. He was the Ulysses of the Highlands.

I would cheerfully lose any of your royal ancestors (apart from Alfred the Great and Robert Bruce) to be descended from that Lochiel. This is where you come from, and all you will admit to its reverence is your eight-year-old son having worn tartan pyjamas on the night the Referendum was

counted. I am glad the boy likes the thought of being
Scottish, but I hope it will mean more to him rapidly. That
extraordinary passage in Macaulay is exceedingly relevant to
you, because it is the cry of a great Angliciser, Unioniser and
(as he saw it) civiliser. (It is always agreeable to remember
Gandhi's rely to the person who asked him what he thought
of Western Civilisation 'I think it would be an excellent
idea'.) The whole purpose of Macaulay's book was to draw all
parts of the British Isles into acceptance of their united
destiny. He meant it genuinely. He wanted the Hindu and
the Hibernian, the Gael and the Gurkha, the Sawney and the
Saxon to be equal before the law and the opportunities
offered by Empire. But they had to be unencumbered by
their archaic learning, lifestyles and loyalties. He had fought
for the self-respect of Catholics and Jews that they be
permitted to take their places in the Westminster Parliament, but while he would fight for Daniel O'Connell's right
to sit and speak in the House of Common if elected, he
would not fight for O'Connell to address it in his first
language, Gaelic (not that O'Connell would want to). As the
son of a Highland-born Gaelic-speaker Macaulay knew he
symbolised assimilation, that it was by no means certain that
he would be able to ensure it, and that he could suspect his
critics were vigilant for the signs of the cloven Celtic foot.
But some part of Macaulay's mind struggled against the idea
of conformity to the forces of what he otherwise thought
progress. His *The Lays of Ancient Rome* are a very clever attempt
to guess what had been lost in growing Roman sophistication, not to say civilisation. He laughs at his imaginary bard's
lament in 'Horatius' for the loss of 'the brave days of old',
and denies in his introduction that they ever existed, but he
would not deny in his heart that the line is best delivered
with a slight choke in the throat. Here his belief in the need

for the Glorious Revolution is suddenly stopped in its tracks. He even greatly mocks the magnificent majesty of monarchy as performed by Louis XIV whom he would otherwise stress performed it peerlessly, and he downgrades the cultural accomplishments of the young polished figures of capital and courts. Lochiel dwarfs them all, literally in Louis's case, intellectually in the young hopefuls'. Macaulay finally takes refuge in his beloved Homer, having no faith in progress for poetry. He virtually throws down his pen saying that Homer alone could bring Lochiel to life.

How could you talk about your love for the United Kingdom without rejoicing in Lochiel? Lochiel was certainly no friend of the Union, enacted when he was 78, and drew his sword although with little chance to use it in 1715 in the cause of the ousted James VII's son whom Lochiel now revered as the true King, James VIII. You would not have to apologise for your ancestor regardless of your differences over the Union. Your favourite history book *Our Island Story* very shrewdly won its young readers' loyalties for the Puritans and for Charles I, for the besieged in (London) derry and for the martyrs in Glencoe, for the Union Jack and for Bonnie Prince Charlie. It wasn't simply H. E. Marshall forgetting what side she was on, which is what does happen to Macaulay at Killiecrankie:

> It was past seven o'clock. Dundee gave the word. The Highlanders dropped their plaids. The few who were so luxurious as to wear rude socks of untanned hide spurned them away. It was long remembered at Lochaber that Lochiel took off what was probably the only pair of shoes in his clan, and charged barefoot at the head of his men. The whole line advanced firing. The enemy returned the fire and did much execution. When only a small space was left between the armies, the Highlanders suddenly flung away their firelocks, drew their

broadswords, and rushed forward with a fearful yell. The Lowlanders prepared to receive the shock; but this was then a long and awkward process; and the soldiers were still fumbling with the muzzles of their guns and the handles of their bayonets when the whole flood of Macleans, Macdonalds and Camerons came down. In two minutes the battle was lost and won.

But read it yourself (and try it on your tartan-clad son) down to the end of the paragraph:

… all was over; and the mingled torrent of redcoats and tartans went raving down the valley to the gorge of Killiecrankie.

In his excitement Macaulay sounds almost the same notes with which in his *Lays of Ancient Rome* he sang of the Romans' ultimate victory in 'The Battle of Lake Regillus':

And fliers and pursuers
Were mingled in a mass;
And far away the battle
Went roaring through the pass.

Our Island Story (like Macaulay most of the time) is for William III of England, II of Scotland), but it knows perfectly well that heartthrobs for Jacobites are a most useful part of the Unionist heritage. G. A. Henty pitching boy protagonists alongside any derring-do hero in history from anywhere in anytime could be historically ecumenical — his Glorious Revolution volume put boy protagonists on both sides of Orange and Green — and Bonnie Prince Charlie found his volume. The late Victorian and Edwardian children's monthly *Little Folks* was usually Royalist and hence often Jacobite. The *Adventure* comic in the 1940s had a Hentyesque romance of the days of Mary Queen of Scots 'Vengeance Stalks the Traitor Earl' in which the protagonist was a nephew of the Regent Moray's assassin James Hamilton of Bothwellhaugh the hero of the tale, as well as innumerable Jacobite tales.

The same principle which recruited former Jacobites for Seven Years War and American Independence War seemed assured that the better the rebel the better the loyalist, especially when reading. This differed from my Irish juvenile reading matter in which the hero had to be an Irish patriot, but it would be silently if cynically felt by Authority that Irish boys would read so many British stories anyway that they were bound to get a balanced diet. The real contrast was that while many stories featured brave young Irish Jacobites with Patrick Sarsfield as a hero when he could be included (he too was one of Macaulay's Jacobite secondary heroes), but they frequently made fun of the Stuarts. Latter-day allegiance to the Stuarts over the water was not felt to be a desirable cult. As Catholics we were encouraged to admire James VII and II but as Irish we were invited to laugh at his inability to swat a fly, ably described in *Brian Óg* (1920), a Gaelic Jacobite story prescribed for use in schools. We would also have studied much Gaelic Jacobite poetry yearning for the return of whatever exiled Stuart was chronologically appropriate. One odd point for little neo-Jacobites arose from the Union. It was little talked about in itself – I know of no With Defoe for the Union volume and in any case any attempt at accuracy would include company of dubious ethics for the growing boy – but while Jacobites were opposed to it, and hoped to prosper from local anger with it, it was actually in the Jacobite interest. A successful Jacobite rising would have to conquer England or else Whig Hanoverians would conquer Scotland and Ireland as they had done before. It harmonised with the last Stuart claimant, Henry IX Cardinal of York leaving the family records and regalia to his Hanoverian cousins who had rescued him when revolutionary and Napoleonic disturbances threatened his existence. So in fact, my dear Mr Cameron, it would be traditionally British to have your son a Jacobîte and a Unionîst. On the whole you had better leave Ulster out of discussion – the past is a little more immediate there.

And the Jacobîtes were almost noiselessly moved into the Union apart from the noise of their tragic evictions from territories they had held under the rule of their chieftains. You don't have to go far afield for that story: try Walter Scott's introduction to his *A Legend of Montrose*. But Scott himself, for all of his historical Cavalier and Jacobîte sympathies, saw the immediate needs for Scotland to make the most of 'our fat friend' as he privately called George IV. His novels began with *Waverley*, an incredible achievement bringing to life not only the insurrection of 1745 but the symbolic death of the great Highland Gaelic civilisation over whose destruction good little Unionîsts could weep with no current disloyalty to Hanoverian rulers. Robert Louis Stevenson refined the trick in *Kidnapped* and *Catriona* so that the reader could identify wîth a Whig Presbyterian narrator whose own personal loyalties become identified wîth the saving of a Jacobîte agent and fugîtive. Whatever else may have been beyond the Union, ît brought to a fine art the gastronomic pleasures of devouring îts enemies' myths. Kipling – who better? – declared the principle of Jacobîte enlîstment in the cause of the UK when he wrote war verse for the many Irish Catholics serving for George V in World War I. (And there were far more of them than the rebels in brief alliance wîth Germany in 1916. World War I memorial tributes should speak of the soldiers, sailors and airmen fighting for the Unîted Kingdom, not just for Brîtain. The word Brîtain here as elsewhere is in fact treacherous to the UK since ît dispenses wîth the sacrifices of the Irish from the future Northern Ireland and from the future Republic.)

Now, my dear Mr Cameron, why do you throw away your faithful Jacobite ancestors? What would the great Lochiel call you for that repudiation? Nobody expects you to bare your shanks under the present anachronistic kilt, much less bare your posterior as in the kitsch film *Braveheart*. But whatever side of the Union you may endorse, the basis of Scots identity today is that you are welcome, and I am welcome, so long as we admit that we are Scots, with or without Scottish birth or ancestry. But the credential of descent from Lochiel should have given you a sense of identity proud in itself without having to shelter behind Darlings and Carmichaels.

I have been concentrating on Lochiel, but it is not solely your three lines of descent from Camerons that should reproach you for this dismissal of your ancestral glory. I mentioned Errol in the '45. And very recently your forebears include some of the modern stuff with which Union Scotsmanship is made. Your great-grandfather Alexander Geddes (1843–1902) was a fascinating case of what we Irish called a 'returned Yank', who had cornered grain in the American Midwest only to see much of his fortune literally go up in flames in the terrible Chicago fire caused by Mrs O'Leary's cow. (Interesting how folk history makes so much of the minimal origins of these horrifying modern disasters. The great fire of London in 1666 began in the baker's shop in Pudding Lane and finally ended in Pie Corner.) Your Cameron antecedents are almost all from Inverness, but Great-grandfather Geddes returned to build his dream house near Huntly, Aberdeenshire. Beyond vaguely announcing that your blood is Scots and English you make no attempt to show your exact roots which mean so much.

Did you want to lose the Referendum?

You will deny any such thing but you had motive to lose it, and still do. Is your Caledonian gerontophagy proof of such intent? You may point to Blair, and even Thatcher, carefully disappearing their Scottish antecedents. But nobody would seriously suggest that either of them thought of Scotland with any sense of inheritance. Blair seemed as anxious to deny Scotland as by 2005 his nominal followers in Scotland were to deny him. His first Scottish General Election was won by the dead John Smith, his third by the living Gordon Brown. Thatcher's remote Scottish connection was presumably through her mother, born a Stephenson, but Thatcher for whatever reason airbrushed her mother out of her discourse, let alone Scotland. And you have an immediate precedent in Gordon Brown whose desperate efforts to integrate his Scottishness and his Britishness are heart-rending.

You might have underestimated Gordon Brown, and thus assumed that his openly Scottish identity was a strategic mistake best avoided by you. In particular, since you seem to have done very little to pursue your Scottish identity, you may have confused what you saw as Dr Brown's mistakes about England, with his performance on Scotland, and, knowing too little about Scotland, you failed to realise that he was far more successful in Scotland than in England in spite of (or perhaps even partly because of) his palpable yearning for English approval. You may have concluded with the aid of some of your Downing Street Irregulars that Dr Brown was unpopular in England because he was Scots, and thus obliterated your own Scottishness to keep the English sweet, a fairly melancholy comment on your love for the UK. Shall we think of you as some latter-day Mr Rochester, in apparent monogamy devoted to your beloved sane England but with your mad wife Scotland in the northern fastnesses of your UK mansion, guilt hanging over your perpetual listening for the sound of her breaking her prison bonds, and revealing her presence by setting the house on fire? Is Dr Brown the first Mrs Rochester, mad in England, sane (as you become increasingly disturbed to realise) in Scotland, brandishing in spite of himself the deadly secret that the Kingdom can never be united with himself as the proof? It is my thesis that you are extremely intelligent, but you might be so, and still undervalue Dr Brown because you had been hypnotising yourself while boring everyone else with your whines about his supposed inadequacies when you were Leader of the Opposition. It is difficult to see how your Billingsgate at Prime Minister's Questions in those years could have convinced anyone, but we have to allow for the occasional exception proving the rule that your abuse was self-destruct. If your would-be Ciceronian diatribes had convinced only one person it is most likely that that person was you. This would mean not only have you ignored his example in celebrating his Scottish forebears, but that you thought him a good person to whom to entrust management of the Referendum in confident hopes that he would lose it, or convince his fellow Scots of the worthlessness of the Union he was defending. If so, it really was a blunder, since he was the only public supporter of Union who may really have rescued its cause from the advocates whose combined efforts were doing so little.

In thus paying tribute to Dr Brown's success in defending the Union and doing so as a Scot among Scots, I do not neglect the flowers of finance that blushed unseen and reserved their sweetness to inform their employees that if Scotland voted YES everyone would lose their jobs by being fired as management took its merry way southward. I was poll-watching (oddly enough in front of a polling station called Cameron House) and found my NO counterpart was a really likeable youth from such a financial establishment whose wife and two little children looked in during the day. He told me of what they had been informed to expect if Scotland voted YES. This was the logical outcome of the pressures exerted on the electorate by Messrs Osborne, Balls and Danny Alexander. It may be that their actions have rendered them justiciable for improper interference with the conduct of an election. The history of elections declared void includes one in Meath in 1892 where a priest was said to have told a man he would be turned into a goat if he voted for a Parnellite candidates. (I have little wish to be kind to the memory of that priest, but what he probably said was that Christ would separate the sheep from the goats on the last day and Parnellite voters would be goats.) Surely pressurising finance houses so that employees were threatened with loss of jobs if Scotland voted YES was as bad as threatening to turn a voter into a goat? It would give me great pleasure to watch Messrs Osborne, Balls and Alexander keeping one another company in the dock under the laws of Scotland which Osborne and Balls would not know, and Alexander would have forgotten. It would be good to feel them suffering a little of the anxiety they set in train for fathers of little families, and indeed big ones. You yourself are fond of telling us how nasty terrorists are. What is this behaviour but terrorism?

As for you, I still have faint midnight uncertainties as to which side you were really on. We will let the thought of your intent of Unionicide linger for a little, that hope that with Scotland's departure Labour would have to face election with a vital loss of seats. We will agree you would have to be subtle about it, not open murder but in accord with Arthur Hugh Clough's 'A Modern Decalogue':

> Thou shalt not kill, but needs not ſtrive
> Officiously to keep alive.

Certainly anyone who deliberately let Lord Robertson of Fort Ellen loose on the Scottish electorate muſt have realised his inevitable toxic effects on whatever cause he might inflict himself. You will plead guiltlessness but you are far too intelligent not to have been able to get him into orbît had you wished, whatever the official explanation. He was frenziedly informing the public that Scottish Independence would Balkanise Europe. Where does the wretched man think the Balkans are sîtuated at the present time? And that other solipsiſt Secretary of State for Scotland Carmichael — surely if you wanted to preserve the Union you would know better than to let him near ît? Oh, you ſtill insiſt you left that jobbery to Unterhaupt Clegg, do you? And you can't save a Union wîthout breaking Cleggs.

I will acknowledge that the greater probabilîty is that you wîth your siniſter intellect contrived from the firſt that Scottish Labour's canine support for your NO-men would coſt ît a bonfire of îts vanîties come May 2015, so that you didn't need to lose Scotland from the UK in order to ensure that Labour would lose ît from the General Election.

Unable as I am to ponder the alternative probabilîties of your possible contrivances, ît is genuinely much more pleasant to get back to your Scottish education. And we have to look at ît with the realisation that Scotland as a subject was changing in your time with a speed hard to match elsewhere. It meant that whether to save the Union or to lose ît, you would always be in danger of obsolescence. Your imîtations of Bertie Wooſter are frequently charming to me, as an old Wodehousian, but to the average Scot they offer dangerous memories of Tory representation as the Scots used to suffer

ît. You may recall that when we were visiting Mr Gladstone
he talked somewhat opaquely about a long period of the
Union when the Scots were scarcely represented at all.
Macaulay made the same observation. The rule of Pitt's
beloved Henry Dundas supplied the deficiency, or so anyone
who cared was encouraged to think. Then we saw the arousal
of Scottish democratic aspiration climax in Gladstone's
Midlothian campaigns. We should realise that if the phrase
'democratic intellect' popularised by the late great philoso-
pher George Davie has sometimes been overstretched in its
presumed application, there was a groundswell in political
education from various directions. Some of ît came from,
or at least via, the Scottish Universities, as for instance the
famous John Stuart Blackie, Professor of Greek at
Edinburgh who endowed a new Chair of Gaelic here, and
whose scholarly questionings of the law of landownership
made him a famous name among revolutionary Irish-Amer-
ican workmen as well as radicals of different kinds in our
archipelago itself. It harmonised with the agrarian crusades
led by Henry George of San Francisco who successfully
duelled in lectures and pamphlets with the Duke of Argyll,
and by his friend Michael Davîtt who evangelised the idea
and achievements of the Irish Land League both in Scotland
and Wales. Davîtt would have a major impact on the Labour
movement then struggling to be born – Michael Foot told
me he was called after him – and the Irish influx to Scotland
became identified with proletarian revolt than merely with
acceptance of starvation wages undercutting native workers.
That would have to wait until 1922 to see fruîtion in the
brilliant Catholic Socialist John Wheatley's election as MP
for Glasgow Shettleston, but the Irish Land League era,
1877–82, saw a very different audience responding in the
shape of the young Rosebery's Rectorials preaching the need

for Scottish history and Scottish pride, putting enough pressure on his successful parliamentary nominee Gladstone to start what eventually became a Scottish Secretariate of State, in all probability fired by the dynamic example of Parnell in Ireland. It didn't eventuate in the creation of a Scottish party, but some Scottish Liberal MPs (one of them Charles Cameron) allied with the Irish Home Rulers. One effect of the growth of Scottish Liberal popularity and sophistication of electoral machinery was that Scotland became a good place for prominent Scottish Liberals, Sir Henry Campbell-Bannerman becoming Prime Minister in 1905 — the obverse perhaps was perhaps shown when H. H. Asquith, Richard Burdon Haldane, and Augustine Birrell climbed a hill in Fife whence they could look at their three constituencies and remark that there was not an acre they could see which was not represented in Parliament by a London barrister. The breakup of the Liberals in 1916 and the Irish revulsion from them when in 1920 Lloyd George sent to Ireland the Black and Tans (and the far more horrific Auxiliaries, public school thugs as shameless as could be found), helped build up the Labour party thanks to Wheatley but also led many Scots into Tory ranks or into what often seemed its equivalent, apathy. And the foundation of both the Independent Labour Party and the Labour party itself were Scottish created by figures as various as Keir Hardie, James Ramsay MacDonald and R.B. Cunninghame Graham, the last of whom would ultimately also co-found the National Party of Scotland, parent of the SNP. It is tempting to see Tory Scotland in the persons of such MPs as the do-nothing Michael Clark Hutchison of Edinburgh South, or his father and brother both also MPs, or Anstruther Gray of Berwick and East Lothian who when asked on TV if he knew his constituency indignantly replied 'Certainly. Hunted over it several times.' He was defeated in the end by John P. Mackintosh who as academic and parliamentarian played a crucial role in fostering Scottish thought on devolution. TV may be the operative word there: television transformed popular representation in many constituencies in these islands as viewers were confronted by the self-indulgence of their MPs or the abuses they had condoned or fostered (Northern Ireland and the privileged elite of its apartheid state being the classic case). But the various phenomena we have been noting offer illumination on democratic moments, suggesting that if Scottish democracy would slumber it could also erupt very educationally, and the intensity of feeling and height of voter participation in the Referendum assert their place in Scottish democratic epiphany. What the Referendum was about was central, but its existence and the form its expression took had its own essence. For years the SNP had been chewing the cud of paradox that Scots voting Labour in elections bringing Tories back into power proved the Nationalist case that the countries were ideologically different, a proposition Labour itself cold-shouldered as frigidly as it knew. But 2014 left a deeper paradox: in the process resulting in saying NO the Scots showed a faith in democracy that now differed from England in kind as well as in number.

It is necessary to be aware of that Referendum as something different from the rise of Nationalism all the more since it voted against YES, but YES itself produced remarkable varieties of Scottish nationalism in addition to the party, and if to you, my dear Mr Cameron, and to most NO-men, all YES were Nats, many YES persons would have repudiated a nationalist label. There were many who would have voted for Independence regardless of the existence of the SNP, and there were Devo-Max people who ended passionately in favour of Independence but were driven there by you and your restriction of questions. Most of them, I suspect, are grateful to you for enabling them to discover themselves, but some are not. We have to assume many Devo-Max people turned against Independence on the basis of your Vow, shared with significant difference in detail by Labour and the LibDems, the whole orchestrated by Dr Gordon Brown more commanding than he has ever been in or out of the premiership.

The strange birth of Nationalist Scotland had many causes. It was highly intellectual, for one thing, reacting against metropolitan culture relapse into cynicism, post-war disillusion turning cosmopolitan idealists into patriotic introverts. It was engaged with rebuilding Scottish culture through languages waning and dying, finding frontiers with Ezra Pound and James Joyce in the process.

It wrote endlessly about itself, but much more critically than nationalism normally likes to do. It was polemic drenched in satire, and while denouncing the morbidity of morons stifling Scotland in its cloying orthodoxies it was perpetually on the watch for its own surrender to convention. Such works as Hugh MacDiarmid's 'A Drunk Man Looks at the Thistle' (1926) and Eric Linklater's *Magnus Merriman* (1934) were both proclaiming a new dawn and sending it up rotten. Their biggest gripe against England was its parochialism, significantly the very word with which chatter would mindlessly strive to label Scottish nationalism. And they had the perspective. MacDiarmid in his birth-given identity as Christopher Murray Grieve had begun his poetic career in French locations and attitudes. Linklater had produced the most perceptive English novel about America of the 1920s and maybe of the century. Compton

Mackenzie had been prosecuted by the secret service for his wartime memories of Greece. Cunninghame Graham brought Latin America within the British imagination. The environment became a Scottish nationalist priority preached by writers as diverse as Neil Gunn and Malcolm Slessor. Rosebery would certainly not have approved of them, especially in his embittered later life, but he would have recognised a return to Scottish self-discovery as a basis for national regeneration.

The trouble about Macaulayesque egalitarianism was it meant transfer of identities to competing and increasingly undifferentiated metropolitans, with what distinguished them boiled away in finishing schools. The nationalist agenda may have been formulated initially by small groups, but it demanded national histories and literatures, and opposing attitudes were paper-thin. In Ireland professional historiography had to fight its way against an official style of historiography tailored to vindication of Irish nationalist victors and demands for Irish unification indifferently to the desires of a million Protestant Unionists. The newly-trained professionals had to take prisoners and good ones many proved, using their energies to work out ideas in search of reputable historical authenticity. But the Scottish historiographical battleground was greatly enhanced by the growth of Scottish nationalism. It led to some ugly moments as nationalist piety collided with historical veracity. There was for instance the matter of the great opponent of the Union, Andrew Fletcher of Saltoun, whose edited writings newly inspired late 20th-century nationalists. Macaulay had noted his having once opined that unemployed beggars should be put into serfdom, Oxford Professor Hugh Trevor-Roper ennobled by Thatcher as Lord Dacre (as acidly English nationalist on Scottish history as could be found) parroted this after abridging Macaulay for Penguin Books, Robin Cook (in his day the foremost debater in the Commons) joyfully quoted this from Labour ranks against his nationalist enemies who assailed him with all the indignation of insulted votaries at sacred shrines. But in general the controversies were constructive, syntheses emerged from embittered controversies, and if Trevor-Roper was rude, his masochistic incitement of nationalist pursuit livened up literary and academic life. One wonders how many Scottish nationalists he made.

If you will not give us much sense of what Scotland-in-the-UK you thought you had inherited from your ancestors Cameron and otherwise, we had better go back to Bogdanor, to show us what you could have learned from him about Scotland, if you were prepared to learn it. To put it another way, if you saved Scotland, what Scotland did you decide you were saving? The obvious thought is that you were saving the last drop of marketable oil, or the last drop of water in which your weapons of mass destruction could float. When you did break your silence in the Referendum on Scottish Independence you did so with dignity, though never quite losing the pride of the Sunday school prizewinner. (It gives you a slightly eerie similarity to Gordon Wilson, leader of the SNP in the 1980s who expelled Alex Salmond, was ultimately succeeded by him, and after the Referendum called Salmond the best leader the SNP had ever had. You share the pomposity and the generosity with him, and it's possible that you also share the spectrum of judgments on Salmond.) But your allusions to Scotland were remote and your reverence for the UK somewhat reminiscent of the self-image of the House of Lords, on the eve of its loss of veto, as described in George Dangerfield's *The Strange Death of Liberal England* (1936):

But the unhappy comic spirit which took possession of this last desperate sally... was due to the fact that... they were instinctively horrified by reality. In their minds, to attack the House of Lords was to attack an ancient and virtuous talisman. There was a certain magic in the hereditary principle. That most peerages sprang from the curious powers of survival in some obscure medieval family, or from a dishonest bargain struck in the eighteenth century, or from a talent for guessing right on the stock exchange, or from a genius for keeping business projects on the windy side of the law – this they could not or would not recognise. To them, the House of Lords was the mysterious symbol of Breeding. They rallied to its protection, as savages rally to protect a house of an idol.

It is curious how little revision is needed to apply this analysis to you on the UK — you rather than any of your party members, or your rivals and creatures in the other Unionist parties including U-PUKE and Mr George Galloway. This partly explains the slightly frenzied round-the-mulberry-bush antics with which your minions enlisted the learned services of Professor Christopher Whatley to assure humanity that the Union of 1707 had been passed by many men bribed to vote for what in any case they believed. 1707 was fundamentally irrelevant to 2014, but you needed to declare the Union saved and sanctified. Therefore the Union's financial origin must be gainsaid, or at least questioned, the better that in vaguer but more satisfying terms, its aesthetic glory may be maintained. Calling oneself 'UK' is more awkward not to say grammatically suspect but far more accurate and diplomatic, calling yourself 'British' comes more naturally although more insular, calling 'English' was the most natural of all to telegraph aristocratic authenticity alongside Lord Salisbury (who would have sneered at you regardless) or Nancy Mitford (except that it really was 'non-U' to admit studying the classification).

But the very awkwardness of self-styling 'UK' could be offset by deepening its rarity of use into reverence. To return to our analogy with the unreformed House of Lords according to Dangerfield:

> The most primitive idols, even those which have been long abandoned to the jungle and the sand-drift, are landmarks in the journey of the human soul; and they represent a search for coherence in the confusions and fears of living. So this ... was not simply a constitutional relic of the great landed fortunes; it was also a fetish, it meant the ideally paternal responsibility of the noble few.

> ... those who tried to preserve it were not merely idle men or arrogant men. They saw the passing of certain values which at their best were very high and at their worst were very human; they did not realise that life consists in change, that's nothing can stand still, that today's shrines are only fit for tomorrow's cattle. Clinging to the realities of the past, they prepared to defend their dead cause with relish.

The act of venerating 'the UK' was also pragmatic. The more reverent one's manner, the farther one seemed from the need for self-justification. 'Britain' or 'British' would assert itself as the natural allusion hiding the now more secret 'England' or 'English', the last being all the more avoidable nowadays since one's very surname may suggest one is not really entitled to the full glory of its use. 'UK' became a comforting ghost of Empire in which the mother country still ruling was England but a condescending courtesy put on the awkward initials whose artificiality proclaimed their being merely uniform, or fatigues, or overalls. England was what counted, despite the exhibitionism of neurotics whose use of the St George flag merely proclaimed their failure to realise the power was still theirs. England rules – OK, UK.

If we cannot find out what you thought and said about Scotland while in the toils of education, we may as well return to your authoritative tutor, however limited your deference to him after your graduation. After the successful Scottish assertion of desire for a Scottish Parliament, in the 1997 Referendum, Bogdanor delivered the Edinburgh David Hume Institute's annual Hume Lecture, chaired by the then most distinguished Scottish Nationalist in an Edinburgh University Chair (Public Law and the Law of Nature and Nations) Neil MacCormick, son of John MacCormick who led the Scottish National Party through the 1930s. Neil MacCormick was possibly the most courteous Scottish intellectual of his time, with possibly the best sense of humour. He was a former Oxonian scholar and tutor, and while a beautifully lucid lecturer, could take the philosophy of law to a towering eminence. For all of these reasons Bogdanor in 1998 talked firmly but warily, as was evident in his title 'The Start of a New Song' counterpointing the derisive or possibly faintly mournful 'The End of an Auld Sang' uttered when the Scottish Parliament was dissolved into the Union Parliament, which itself was less a new song in 1707 than was officially assumed. The Westminster Parliament in fact behaved, and was generally regarded in England, as though it had simply enlarged itself, opening its belt, as it were. Bogdanor's title was nonetheless a frank statement of the intended new Scottish Parliament's newness. The other interpretation, which was also a rallying-cry, would be given by Winifred Ewing (MP, MEP, and now MSP) among the first MSPs to take their seats in the Scottish Parliament and signalled as much at its first session (some days before the formal opening by Queen Elizabeth (I and II); 'The Scottish Parliament, adjourned in 1707, is hereby reconvened'. The official version declared the constitutional realities in 1999,

presuming their permanence; the Ewing version offered an
open-ended creation capable of progress to full Independence. Bogdanor assumed the former, but while Ewing's
clarion-call lay in the future (and still more for the further
future) he knew that the new song was intended as still at its
preliminary stages by the charming professor chairing him,
for one.

Bogdanor's opening words merit study, as an example in
courtesy as well as in wit, and as his pupil you seem to have
learned well from him. Bogdanor was at one with his nationalist critics in the vital necessity of a sense of humour for
students of constitutionalism (or anyone else). His Hume
Lecture began:

> In thanking you for your generosity in inviting me to give this
> lecture, may I confess that my acceptance was not unmixed
> with a certain trepidation. For I remember indeed the recep-
> tion of an English MP who was added to the First Scottish
> standing committee in 1988, when it was to consider the Civil
> Evidence (Scotland) Bill. The MP, David Tredinnick, the
> Conservative member for Bosworth … was greeted by Donald
> Dewar in the following way:

> No doubt his education at Eton, the Mons Officer Cadet
> School and the business school at Cape Town University
> qualify him admirably and will give him the necessary disci-
> pline to last through a Scottish Law Reform Bill Committee.

> It is a sign of the generosity of the David Hume Institute that
> it has invited someone to deliver its annual lecture whose
> qualifications for talking about anything to do with Scotland
> are, you may think, even more exiguous than those of Mr
> Tredinnick. For I have never attended the Mons Officer Cadet
> School nor the business school at Cape Town University. I
> cannot even claim an education at Eton.

(But if he hadn't been to that school, he had met its scholars.)

> I am, however, undoubtedly English, a nation which Hume once dismissed as 'relapsing into the deepest Stupidity, Christianity & Ignorance'. At an other time he referred to the English as 'the barbarians who inhabit the Banks of the Thames'.

Thus Bogdanor won his Scottish honours, and if you lack his learned Lightness, your courtesy and deference played a good part in their time. Whatever he thought about Scotland, his publications and possibly his teaching instruct his hearers that the first essential for dealing with Scots is humour. Tony Blair lacked it, though he had occasional moments of wit (insofar as Alistair Campbell permitted him anything). Gordon Brown has it, but he has never learned how to manage it in public. You have occasionally shown signs of it, and will presumably have discarded this book by now if you don't have it. Blair or his ghostwriter used the word 'Donaldish' apparently to mean that here (wherever it might be) Donald Dewar used his sense of humour with whatever understanding Blair received it. But Blair's *A Journey* (2010) mentions Dewar so seldom that it remains unclear what was meant by 'Donaldish'. It may simply have alluded to Donald's long, lazy grin, pulling the lip back from his prominent teeth, or laughing generously. Blair seems to have thoroughly disliked Dewar, possibly because he was afraid of him. It is possible that a close reading of *A Journey* will be of most value in what it omits. Blair would have liked to wriggle out of the commitment Donald Dewar had made at the General Assembly of the Church of Scotland on behalf of the Labour party before the political parties of Scotland, its clergy and all other interested parties, David Steel of the Liberal Democrats presiding and calling his name for the delivery of that vow promising a far stronger Scottish

Parliament than had been on offer in 1979. John Smith as leader of the fight for that in the later 1970s and subsequent leader of the Labour party until his death would gladly have honoured that commitment which reaffirmed and progressed so much of his political life's work. And Blair under Dewar's cold eyes and implacable jaw would have been forced to conform to Scottish devolution with Dewar in command for the 1997 Referendum, enabling Act of Parliament, and First Ministry in the new Parliament (assuming all elections went according to (Dewar's) plan, as they did). Blair would have been forced to find new accommodation for the absurd George Robertson under whom the Shadow Secretariate for Scotland had withered before Dewar once more took it in hand. The situation appealed to Dewar's humour.

Thatcher, like Blair in so much, is acknowledged by friend and foe to have had no sense of humour whatsoever, as was finally shown in her last appearance at a Tory Conference, where she declaimed from the stage 'The Mummy has Returned' unable to realise that some unscrupulous aide conned her into involuntarily acknowledging herself to be a horror movie. Her lack of humour was probably the first nail in the coffin of her Scottish public relations. And it offers yet one more alienation of Scotland from England. Thatcher herself was a major irresistible divergence in their politics. Humour was another. The English have a sense of humour, but it sometimes seems imprisoned by superstitious belief in national character whereby it is assumed that Scots are dour, grim and humourless. As most Scots are cheerful, happy and humorous, Scottish identity becomes another fissure dividing the countries.

Gordon Brown was a victim of this notably with George W. Bush saying he wasn't a dour Scot meaning obviously that he was. Alex Salmond was another victim because people felt a Scot shouldn't have so good a sense of humour. What happens if those about to meet you take you to be a Scot because of your name? Do they then expect you to look like sour milk and blame you if you don't (you do look a bit like it sometimes)?

Let's return to the safely English pre-Cameron Bogdanor in *The People and the Party System* (pp. 36–37), where he shows the condition of post-1922 politics meant mutually adversarial economic systems as expressed by Labour and the Tories, now that Nationalist Ireland and Unionist Ulster (ignoring the ethno-religious minorities in each category) which had dominated the political debate across the archipelago for 40 years were shelved. Scotland had been represented on both sides of the pre-1922 debate, partly by ethnic migrations Catholic and Protestant sharpening Liberal-Tory confrontations, and when the Irish question became obsolete with the creation of the Irish Free State and Northern Ireland, shadows of the former duel danced provocatively over Scotland between the wars. For instance Glasgow Celtic and Glasgow Rangers had been clerically-influenced teams for amateur youth enjoying mutual respect while more snobbish support for other clubs looked down on them; it was in the 1920s that sectarianism rose to polarise them. Irish Catholic immigration to Scotland made very little additional impact after 1922 apart from seasonal migration from Donegal in harvest-time to West Scotland construction work. The Irish tramping artisan was still being hired in rural and urban piece-work as described autobiographically for immediately prewar years in Patrick MacGill's *Children of the Dead End* (1913) whose author through picturesque accidents was able to finish it in Windsor Castle. As protégé of George V's tutor (whose actual son was Hugh Dalton, later Chancellor of the

Exchequer in the Attlee Government), MacGill duly enlisted
in the King's Army in August 1914. He would survive and
continue writing, but the war must have accounted for huge
numbers of the mobile labour force. The old prewar proletarian Unionism which brought Ulster workers and aristo-
crats to the verge of armed treason under Tory auspices now
jelled in Scotland into surviving Orange lodges, a brief
growth of Protestant Action mobs, and Church of Scotland
demands for the scarcely existing Irish Catholic immigration to be cut off. The Scottish Tories gave nests for these
phenomena, while the Labour party took the Irish-born and
Irish-descended Catholics over from fragmented and feuding
Liberals. Ironically Scotland supplied two major party leaders
for a brief moment, the illegitimate intellectual Ramsay
MacDonald (Prime Minister in 1924 and from 1929) from
Lossiemouth in the far north for Labour, and Andrew Bonar
Law, Glasgow-born son of a Presbyterian minister, for the
Tories, inaugurated in 1922 as Prime Minister but dying the
same year.

Preoccupied with the Referendum Bogdanor saw its
confrontational presence in the General Elections of 1885,
1886, 1892, and 1910 in the Home Rule struggle, but
vanished from the 1920s to the 1960s. Labour was still
ideologically bound by Ramsay MacDonald's judgment that
its policies 'all fitted into one set of general progressive ideas'
and so, pointed out Bogdanor, 'most socialists were opposed
to the introduction of referendum'. Initially Scottish
Labour had believed in Scottish Home Rule, a shadowy heir
of Irish constitutional nationalism and even of the
Edinburgh-born Irish Socialist James Connolly who would
succumb to violence in the Zeitgeist of the Great War and be
shot as a leader of the Easter Rising. But as Scottish Labour
acquired really impressive practical as well ideological leaders

in Tom Johnston and John Wheatley, they thought Socialism would require the full resources of the British State, and the commitment to Scottish Home Rule disappeared from the party agenda in 1945. As one door closed another opened, but the newly-formed Scottish National Party in the 1930s did not even prohibit membership of other parties. The SNP were no electoral threat being at this time little more than 'a sect' (opined the leading modern Scottish historian Sir Thomas Devine in conversation with Alex Salmond at the Edinburgh Book Festival 2014: 'no sects, please, we're Scottish', replied the First Minister severely).

Labour was hardly wise in thus dispensing with a vital element in its inheritance. Scottish Labour made distinguished contributions to the making of the welfare state, from Tom Johnston to Jennie Lee, but the development of radio increased a Scottish sense of identity through folksong from genius to kitsch. So did the growth of folklore itself on a professional basis but led by such individualistic figures as the poet Hamish Henderson, bard of the 'Freedom Come-All-Ye' and 'Elegies for the Dead in Cyrenaica', a lament for his fellow-soldiers including enemy dead. A National Covenant organised by John MacCormick (who had broken with his party after it opposed involvement in World War II) may have attracted two million signatures for its demand 'to secure for Scotland a Parliament with adequate legislative authority in Scottish affairs' as well as a declaration of loyalty to the United Kingdom – it was coldly ignored by the new bureaucracy induced among its lesser benefits by the welfare state. The Covenant too was a shadow, albeit a very substantial one, cast 30 years before the Referendum of 1979.

Forms of Scottish Nationalism were on offer for Unionists, for whom John Buchan had offered entertaining varieties in

such works as *John Macnab* (1925), at one point even defending the idea of Scottish Independence in Parliament. Once
again, it is a reminder that belief in Independence could be
more a matter of priorities – one is reminded of the prayer
of St Augustine for continence but not yet. Quite a few Scots
examining their political consciences might be reminded of
the Israelite yearning after the fleshpots of Egypt while
knowing they ought to be struggling towards the Promised
Land. On the figures, the Scottish Tory vote reaching a peak
in the 1955 General Election might seem to have nothing to
do with the future Left-of-Centre SNP ruling Scotland for
most domestic purposes in the 21st century. But however
reactionary, it kept some nationalist phenomena alive, as
did the still reprinted works of Scottish literary genius such
as Hugh MacDiarmid, Compton Mackenzie, Eric Linklater,
Moray McLaren – even the diatribes against it such as
Josephine Tey's *The Singing Sands*. The place of Scottish nationalism in Scottish culture was in some ways akin to what the
farmer told MacDiarmid's friend W. B. Yeats when asked if
he believed in fairies – 'of course not, but they're there'.
Noisily Tory prints such as the *Scottish Daily Express* were
certainly festooned and steeped in British chauvinism but
felt the need to keep a Scottish identity coyly waving at
readers more or less with the same relaxing appeal of the
Sunday Post's comic-strip wee laddie Oor Wullie (invented
and drawn by a great English artist Dudley D. Watkins
drawing throughout his professional life for D. C. Thomson
of Dundee). The future prophet of Scottish nationalism
Tom Nairn opined in the late 1960s that Scotland would not
be free until the last Church of Scotland minister had been
strangled with the last copy of the *Sunday Post* whose prose
content and allied outlets from the anti-trade-union
Thomson sank its deep kitsch conservatism into the public

heart if not the public mind. (He later publicly retracted his commination of the Kirk when it flung its Assembly doors open to the Constitutional Convention in defiance of the state, led by the Revd Professor Willie Storrar inspired by the late charismatic Catholic priest Father Anthony Ross). And if Thomson's were Right-wing in the 20th century, their sub-Stevenson and fake-Dickens historical stories in their comics for boys and girls were startlingly progressive (for earlier centuries), and their Scottish themes were impressively authentic. And they were also Scottish international in their enthusiasm for Scots themes of frontier Canada — often authentic enough to include 'Red Indian' as well as Mountie heroes (sometimes embodiments of both).

Scotland was late in having its 1960s, but much nationalism of the Left and Right coalesced in the 1967 first election of Winifred Ewing (for conurban Hamilton). Meanwhile in the Western Isles protest had been seething at the proposed breakup of island communities to create rocket ranges and moor the nuclear weapons obtained from the USA, and in the 1970 General Election Donald Stewart, Provost of Stornoway, was elected for what proved 17 years until he retired. Labour and the SNP became bitter, sometimes foolishly bitter, rivals, but they shared common origins and stimulus in the anti-nuclear movements and marches from the 1950s, and both were excited by the non-violent civil rights crusades against racism in the USA, a legacy better enjoyed by the SNP less endangered by the proximity of election to government. In some respects the most important question to be raised and fought all the way to the Referendum, was why Scotland should waste on nuclear weapons good money better spent on the health, education and welfare of its citizens. And that is a question which neither Tory nor Labour governments nor Unionist spokes-

persons have ever been able to answer, and, certainly, my
dear Mr Cameron, you have not. Try ît now, yourself. Why
on earth should we spend a penny on the obscene uselessness
of Trident? You know we can never use ît, or that we even
have the pleasure of imagining we could use ît, since îts use
can only be allowed under orders from the USA. Weapons of
mass deſtruction are forbidden to mere suspects of being
thought new holders on pain of great power invasion. NATO
cannot demand their ownership, and if ît did ît would
logically have to invade îtself. And as you well know, the
Unîted Nations can never alter the terms of îts founder-
member the UK (from the height of World War II) remaining
on the Securîty Council wîth îts veto. Some of your minions
trotted out the lunacy that nuclear weapons are needed for
Securîty Council membership plus veto, and ît says much
for your need to keep trading on public ignorance that you
permîtted so intellectually contemptible an argument to
foſter uncauterised. It was as though NO-men had to lie
from the hip firſt, while truth being perpetually unsatisfac-
tory in îts answers is beſt avoided. What an insult to the
excellent education you have had! But demented miniſters
for education have been ſtandard Tory issue ever since
Thatcher inflicted the charming, crazy Sir Keîth Joseph on
Brîtish education. I remember a speech he gave once at an
Irish-Brîtish dinner for British academics engaged in Irish
ſtudies. It was in St Peter's College Oxford and he began by
saying how pleasant ît was to speak immediately after the
Irish Miniſter for Education who would remember that the
laſt time they met he had been cruelly insulted by the French
Miniſter for Education who had said that every child in the
Common Market or whatever ît was called nowadays ought
to speak two languages other than his own — but we English
do not speak foreign languages! These were your gods, O

Prime Minister! No wonder you permitted the eccentricities of that cute little Michael Gove for so long.

To return to Bogdanor, whose reasoning is like a spring of fresh water after the repulsive rubbish your maniacs inflict on us: *The People and the Party System* points out that the success-ful Referendum of 1975 on whether the UK should have entered the EEC two years previously or not, was followed by confused reassurances that such a thing would never happen again, apparently on the superstition evident in both major parties that a Referendum was in some respects anti-demo-cratic, or breaking unspecified rules, or something. Like Trident it was pestiferous nonsense, and inexplicable in a way that even the House of Lords in 1910–11 could not claim to be. It was as though the UK was a garment too threadbare to be sent more than once to the wash. But Ewing's and Stewart's elections had already led first the courageous Heath and then the pragmatic Wilson into devolutionary conces-sions of sorts when they were, respectively, out of power. Bogdanor recorded that the EEC Referendum of 1975 had yielded new and agreeable common purpose and mutual co-operation shared among customary foes. This sort of thing had been present in the coalitions and conspiracies of the Unionists in 1886–92, although once the Liberal Unionists voted against Home Rule few returned to their parent party. It was otherwise in 1975, although it is possible to find, within these alliances and intra-party splits, roots of the subsequent secession of Labour MPs to become Social Democrats and thence Liberal Democrats in the early 1980s. It was otherwise in the Referendums of 1979 and 1997, although 2014 may yet prove to have prompted solidifica-tion among the YES voters, above all amongst Labour YES-persons. In part an element of continued protest could be involved as today former YES-persons taunt

Labour NO-persons with their Referendum alliance with the Tories, or (if you prefer) their manipulation by you. Could it also result in a Labour-Tory Grand Unionist Coalition (with or without the rags of the Liberal Democrats, who had far fewer rebels visible in the ranks of YES than Labour)?

Mr Brian Taylor, Scottish BBC political reporter, is the master of his field, positive where so many of his London colleagues are destructive. His invaluable *The Scottish Parliament* (1999) demonstrated that in 1997 the great Unionist parties polarised on propaganda (pp. 84-86):

> Labour appeared to want to focus upon anything but the devolution project. The Tories wanted to talk of nothing else... The Tories had come to be seen, fairly or unfairly, as a party whose roots lay outside Scotland, who were not identi-fied with Scottish interests. At a time when political identifi-cation with Scottish concerns had become more important than ever, this was calamitous... Labour's Scottish news conferences began to follow a comforting ritual. Each day the party would pick a topic: education or health or employment or whatever. Each day the media would pick a topic: devolu-tion. I recall indeed being chided at the close of one such news conference by Jim Murphy, then a Labour backroom staffer, subsequently the MP for Eastwood. Why were the media obsessed with devolution? Perhaps, I replied, because Labour had placed it at the core of their message to Scotland for more than twenty years. Perhaps because it was a substantial dividing line between the biggest UK parties in an age when politics had seemingly moved into an aggregated centre.

This may suggest that Labour was much less happy about the removal of all Scottish Tory MPs than what good Socialists should have felt. The shock of what happened was the greater in that the results suddenly came in together. David Dimbleby, the London BBC's presiding genius, remarked that there were a lot of Tory defeats in Scotland, all except the Foreign Secretary, Sir Malcolm Rifkind, of course. An underling informed him stonily that the Foreign Secretary had been defeated in Edinburgh Pentlands as reported half an hour ago. And not all the victors were Labour, thanks to tactical voting for whoever might be the previous runner-up.

The Referendum struggle of 2012–14 opened on the same note, with Labour personnel denouncing the cry for Independence and attempting to dictate an alternative agenda in place of what they declared irrelevant. It became evident that the Referendum was welcome save to people whose motives were anti-Scottish. This is not to say that NO-people were anti-Scottish. On the contrary they were playing their industrious if not always glorious part in recognising and answering public expectations. From the tedious Alistair Darling to the heroic Gordon Brown, they believed in the democratic value of their campaigns. The Labour people reflecting the old, secret anti-devolutionism of Messrs Blair, Murphy, &c had to conform to the official need for a Referendum while deprecating the whole thing as a media manipulation. Theoretically, Blair was good and dead; practically, Labour was once more caught in a Blair versus Brown brawl. The underlying thesis of the Blair-Murphy persuasion was that it was in bad taste to be wasting London's time with so uncouth a topic as Scotland. The underlying thesis of the Brown crusade was that Britain was a celebration of Scotland, not an extinction. And you, my dear Mr Cameron, saw your necessities in this last round of Blair vs Brown. You saw that whatever the initial circumstances of Brown disillusion with Blair, the days of writing Scotland off as a trivial irrelevance were over. The Scottish Blairites had been indistinguishable from the Scottish Tories, save for the trifling consideration that they were still alive. But you knew if nobody else did that Scotland would no longer be conquered by being ignored. Hence you became the last Brownite, and told your foolish followers in Holyrood to maximise the virtues of devolution as far as, but not upon, the ballot paper. These things would not necessarily apply after the ball, so to speak. Or, to put it another way, how now Brown vow?

CHAPTER SIX

THE NATIONAL EDUCATION OF A PRIME MINISTER

But of all nations in the world the English are perhaps the least a nation of pure philosophers.

— WALTER BAGEHOT, *The English Constitution.*
2. *The Monarchy* (1867)

Some quarter-century ago I was getting out of a taxi at King's Cross. The driver was an upper-middle-aged Cockney, well aware of his powers of entertainment, and I was happily supplying suitable responses, and he thoroughly deserved a generous tip, and we seemed to feel we should take leave of one another with some ceremony.

'You going back to Scotland?'

'Yes.'

'Would you do one thing for me?'

'Certainly.'

'Would you mind getting Independence? Because that'll really annoy that bitch in 10 Downing Street.'

Vernon Bogdanor in his invaluable *Devolution* (p. 153) saw the foundation of Welsh and Scottish nationalist parties in the inter-war period as 'a sign not of the strength of peripheral nationalism but of its weakness' since 'both movements were founded on a recognition that neither national self-government nor even devolution were to be obtained from the other parties'. He contrasted their potential in Plaid Cymru's 'most obvious badge of Welsh identity', the Welsh language, 'for many years... to prove a deeply divisive force, tending to confine' it 'to Welsh Wales in the north-west, as opposed to the industrial south-east', whereas 'in Scotland, nationalism was a unifying and integrative force, the institutions of nationhood eliciting feelings of sympathy from nearly every Scot'. His Scottish argument is a masterly reminder that for Scotland itself, nationalism is its most natural condition, something to tell the student Cameron (if you were listening and reading) to beware. Modern politics operates on a basis of how-far-can-they-go, how-far-will-you-let-them-go, how-far-can-we-stop-them which can apply anywhere from the demolition of the welfare state to the Russians in Ukraine. Dream what you like, where you will (especially if you have the sense to dream of the Lochiels in your ancestry for sheer self-respect) but you are metropolitan and Welsh and Scottish nationalism assail you from across the frontier. If you will not listen to common chords, you are the nearer to political paralysis, because English nationalism is the nearest to omnipresent, the farthest from definition. Thatcherism gave it an unavoidable visibility and audibility. The Dutch historian G. J. Renier's *The English: Are They Human?* (1933) goes into English resistance to definition but uses as epigraph the deservedly anonymous:

> The Americans live in America
> The Romans live in Rome
> The Turkeys live in Turkey
> But the English live at home.

Students from across our archipelago would warm up their inter-university audiences with definitions in the days when Donald Dewar, John Smith and I debated: 'the Welsh keep the Sabbath and everything else they can lay their hands on, the Irish pray on their knees on Sundays and [prey] on their neighbours for the rest of the week, and the English are self-made men who worship their maker' but the origin of that last was apparently John Bright about Disraeli, and for all of Disraeli's often being called 'alien' he makes an excellent English symbol. Has any Englishman ever written so profoundly about his country? (I said ' Englishman': Jane Austen may have been more profound.) To the foreigner, English identity may be at its most moving when under attack, and even in fear of survival ('There'll always be an England' in World War II, or even the ruderies against Hitler scrawled on blitzed buildings) but even then its self-definition rejects weakness (Shakespeare's *Henry V* filmed by Olivier as a contribution to the liberation of Europe, as tactless a choice as could be made). Rudyard Kipling and G. K. Chesterton unite, rather unexpectedly, in their definitions of the English, both singling out silence.

British nationalism is nowadays far more audible but, post-Thatcher, it generally means English nationalism rounded out unconvincingly. The problem has haunted you, as when recently reaching for a historical symbol of Britishness you came up with Alfred the Great. There is a good case for calling him England's best king, but he never was British. You claim descent from him, and since you are descended from Robert Bruce who is descended from St Margaret, second Queen of Malcolm III, and she was the widow of the true heir to the English throne set aside by William the Conqueror, I take her to be descended from Alfred, but while your ancestry ducks in and out of the Scottish Royal houses Alfred remains English. It's understandable you think of Alfred, presumably your most reputable English ancestor but it leaves your Britishness hollow. In any case England=Britain has been going on for years. It particularly applies to insularisation as when Shakespeare makes characters speak of England as an island. Even your and my friend H. E. Marshall was concerned only with English history in *Our Island Story*, the other lands of the archipelago winning attention only at points of contact and impact, by no means always to English credit, certainly. Your favourite book wanted to be a fair-minded book, fair-minded but English. That the sequel was *Scotland's Story* indicates that from the English perspective the Scots were intruders, as if when they supposedly climbed Hadrian's Wall it had been built around the island. It was a great deal more honest than Edward I, with his bogus overlordship. But it does make life hard for you in having to make Britishness out of Englishness and remembering when to say 'UK'.

Bogdanor's contrast (well founded in many other analysts) between Scottish institutionalism and Welsh linguistic priorities does not always reflect perceptions of ideological superiority. You might feel as you attend criminal trials ('just visiting' as they say in 'Monopoly') that the Scottish system of opening with the evidence instead of a speech for the prosecution is fairer, but few people would cite that as a proof of Scottish nationalism's superiority. But other nationalist cultures seriously envied the Welsh emphasis on language in contrast to the vulnerability of Scots-Gaelic, the inadequate scholarship on Scots, and the failure of Irish linguistic revival. It made for a more intensely intellectual nationalism than most, and also more intense arguments on identity so long as linguistic proficiency made an acceptable yardstick. It also put a virtuous superiority on rural nationalism, akin to the hostility to cities and towns so evident in the Bible. Cardiff, like Belfast and Dublin, was an easy target for rural nationalistic derision, all the more because the rise of those cities through migration leaves their most recent arrivals with inferiority complexes about their watered-down versions of their former rural integrity. There is less of this in Scotland, where the most penetrating mockery of cities seemed to come from the other cities. Edinburgh really was a capital, not chiefly a base for invaders as Cardiff and, even more, Dublin were. Glasgow was an imperial global centre, capitalist if not capital. Above all Scotland was not a conquered country, a definition vital to classical political theory, and more loosely to national psychology. It was possible to think of the Act of Union of 1707 as a conquest, with thoughts on the potential menace from the warlord Marlborough, the economic blackmail, &c. But the Act of Union was supposed to have been voluntary, and Anglocentric interpretation of the Treaty of Union desperately tried to make it so.

Christopher Harvie and Peter Jones in *The Road to Home Rule: Images of Scotland's Cause* (2000) began with useful remarks on the dual (sometimes mutually hostile) forms of Scottish nationalism 'which… is deeply unstraightforward' (p. 2):

> Throughout the time it has been a feature of Scottish politics, it has taken on many forms – a romantic fashion, a non-sectarian movement, a with-us-or-against us political party. It has had diverse goals and has adopted diverse stratagems: an incremental bit-by-bit approach or an all-or-nothing break-through dash. It has been quixotic – at times seeming an unstoppable inevitability and then just as quickly converting into a distant fantasy. For those who have wanted to be part of it, or just to study it, it has, simultaneously, been exhilaratingly exciting and frustratingly mysterious.

Our authors distinguish its two forms, one the party existing from 1928 and its phoenix-like offspring born in 1934. The other form is Scottish nationalism with a small n, a much longer tradition first detectable perhaps a thousand years ago in the resistance to the Viking invaders, elaborated in the late Middle Ages into something of a popular movement, in the proud words of the Declaration of Arbroath of 1320:

> For as long as a hundred of us remain alive, we will never on any conditions be subjected to the lordship of the English. For we fight not for glory, or riches, or honour, but for freedom alone, which no good man gives up except with his life.

It's not the easiest thing in the world to put yourself on the enemy side from that, my dear Mr Cameron, but then so many of your ancestors must have been its friends. When I was growing up in Ireland and studying and teaching in the USA we were always told that nationalism emerged from the French Revolution with Professor Hans Kohn preceding it with some choice quotations from Machiavelli. But the Declaration of Arbroath really is nationalism, perhaps the oldest document we have expressing it. It kept up, too, in the subsequent century, to judge from its Scottish poetry and prose. It was adopted in the presence of King Robert Bruce and with his approval, and it swore that if he ever accepted a status subordinate to the English they would seek another King. His ancestral claims to the throne were flawed, so that his place as the choice of the community of the realm was vital. It meant also that we no longer had kings of Scotland, but kings and queens of the Scots: your ancestors may have been grandiloquent, notably James IV 'King-Emperor' but 'of the Scots'. When Reformation made its way in, it took as radical a form as could win a country in the 16th century. It was against the rulers Marie of Guise the regent and her daughter Mary Queen of Scots, where other Protestant peoples followed and were constrained to do what the ruler did.

But the reach of the pious nationalist clutches farther back than Bruces and Wallaces. Tacitus's *Agricola* includes a great speech from the Caledonian-chieftain he calls Calgacus, before the battle of Mons Graupius. Modern scholarship, happier to dwell in cities, usually ascribes this to Tacitus's fictional powers, whetted by his loathing for the Roman Emperor Domitian. But Tacitus was at the battle, and as son-in-law to the general Julius Agricola, he could have been present at questionings of spies, prisoners and traitors, with the assistance of interpreters. With an eye to topography he had his own good reasons to make further enquiries of enemy survivors as well as working up the speech from such fragments as its terrible indictment of the Romans concluding 'Solitudinem faciunt pacem appellant' — 'they have made a Wilderness, and call it peace'. Calgacus variously inspired successor Scots (if not Picts) down the centuries, and many cultures have strengthened themselves with transient cults of ill-fated opponents of Roman Empire from Boadicea in Britain to Civilis in the Netherlands, but it was Calgacus who made The Speech. It did not always have to be Calgacus, or even Britain. The Scottish novelist Naomi Mitchison's *The Conquered* (1922) told Caesar's Conquest of Gaul from the point of view of Vercingetorix and his fellow Gauls, and the Scottish poet Byron ('I was born half a Scot and raised a whole one') thought in *Childe Harold's Pilgrimage* of the last moments of what would now be a Romanian gladiator:

> The arena swims around him — he is gone,
> Ere ceased the inhuman shout which hail'd the wretch who won.
>
> > He heard it, but he heeded not — his eyes
> > Were with his heart, and that was far away;
> > He reck'd not of the life he lost nor prize,
> > But where his rude hut by the Danube lay,

> There were his young barbarians all at play,
> There was their Dacian mother – he, their sire,
> Butcher'd to make a Roman holiday.

Scotland was not conquered, but it suffered enough defeats to live historically among victors and vanquished. The worst defeats of all must be those its people inflicted on themselves:

> When the bold kindred, in the time long vanish'd,
> Conquered the soil and fortified the keep, –
> No seer foretold the children would be banish'd
> That a degenerate lord might boast his sheep.

That is from the 'Canadian Boat Song' of much disputed authorship, but made in Scotland or at least first published there, in *Blackwood's Magazine*'s serial causerie (usually scurrilous and certainly envenomed) Noctes Ambrosianae XLIV (September 1829). It appeared under the secret editorship of John Gibson Lockhart, who was moonlighting and supposed to be in London. He would have been staying at Abbotsford with the father-in-law whose biography he would later write, Sir Walter Scott, whom I believe its author. As Scott lived most of his life as a novelist whose works he kept anonymous, he would hardly trouble himself or get Lockhart into trouble by claiming authorship of this:

> Come foreign rage – let Discord burst in slaughter!
> O then for clansmen true, and stern claymore –
> The hearts that would have given their blood like water,
> Beat heavily beyond the Atlantic roar.

Scott had written his own impassioned denunciation of lairds evicting the tenants they should have protected, in *Guy Mannering* (1815) and in opening *A Legend of Montrose* (1819). 'Small-n nationalists include people who would be horrified to be thought of as Nationalists', murmured Harvie (who would have been one of them until he converted himself).

Scott would hardly have been horrified at being misclassified – *The Antiquary* (1816) includes a hilariously mocking self-portrait as the title-role whom he makes a Whig – and he was a Tory! He was a nationalist in the most important sense of all, a conserving Conservative, conscious of so much being lost while Scotland was enlightening itself and the world and grimly determined to keep as much of his country's culture alive before it was winnowed away into the dull norm of civilisation. A century and a half later came a troupe of actors and their director and part-author (for between them their scripts reflected the ensemble): the 7:84 company and John McGrath eminently comparable to Scott in their zeal to preserve and reaffirm a great, tragic past as Scott did in capturing the destruction of Gaelic Scotland in *Waverley* and liable to be enraged at such a coupling, as they were when called on to give a command performance before the Scottish National Party in Conference, and delighted their hosts who (officially at least) infuriated the company by their applause for the epic since they insisted nationalism was bourgeois. It is tempting to say that it that added to the thrill – nationalism flourishes above all when being denounced by clerics, prophets and saints, and while 7:84 would be even more annoyed by that description, the Highland/Island culture they portrayed and whence some came was accustomed to such spiritual impact. As for Scott, 7:84 would automatically denounce him for a Tory, a landlord, a king's man, who brought tartan trews to the king's fat legs, an inventor of bogus tradition, a Super-kitsch-man. And it was true that Scott got excited in 1819–20 and worried about a possible revolution from radicals whom he thought required repression.

Scott was a nationalist who like Robert Burns saved song, verse, tales from folk sources which would otherwise have been lost for ever, and who wove his magic to convince Highlander and Lowlander they were one people when they had lived out many centuries in a mutual hostility that often seemed the central theme of Scottish history. Whether they admitted it or not, 7:84's reliance on pan-Scottish audiences was possible because Scott had conquered Scotland, and if his *Montrose* and *Rob Roy* romanticised the Highlands it was with considerable brutality from folktale and document. And Scott was as bitter as 7:84 about the Anglified chieftains who had found sheep more docile than the kinsfolk from whom they had squeezed what funds they could. And he would have agreed with 7:84 about the economic basis to so much suffering in Highland history, as well as with the necessity to tell your historical story with as much laughter as will not blunt your satire. Characters such as Jeanie Deans in *The Heart of Midlothian*, Di Vernon in *Rob Roy*, and Rebecca in *Ivanhoe* were hard feminist critiques of male patriarchy and chauvinism. He might have made a better novel out of us all than we are making, but his eye would not have been easy for any of us to hold. Alex Salmond's laughter would have delighted him. What would be have made of you? What do you make of yourself, my dear Mr Cameron? Don't tell the world. Tell yourself. Cameron comes home, the book you refuse to think?

The Cheviot, the Stag, and the Black, Black Oil toured Scotland in the 1970s extensively playing in small village halls across Highlands and Islands, and its triumph was certainly another democratic moment, transforming public consciousness of what had been lost and sacrificed on the altar of oligarchical fortunes. It had the hard bite, the iconoclasm, the laughter and grief of the great documentary musical *Oh, What a Lovely War!* But while it humanised the four years of the Great War, the *Cheviot* captured centuries, with real genius in the mix of

mad Music Hall and stark tragedy such as when two narrators
turned misery into mockery sharpening the betrayal e.g.
'Macdonald is driving all his people down to the shores!'
'What shores?' 'Mine's a double Scotch.' It's hard to envisage
so potent a diet of anger, laughter, history, song, grief and
fear. One unforgettable *coup de theatre* featured an Anglified
laird, heir to the name of ancient chieftains – or chiefs – and
heroes, and his equally top-drawer lady-love, staggering
around the stage with their guns obviously unable to hit a
tree let alone a stag, and then with the audience almost
paralysed with laughter in front of them the two swing round
turning their guns on us, telling us in icy sobriety what to
expect if we ever tried to get out from under. It is as chasten-
ing a moment as the sound of faraway whistling three-
quarters' way though *Oh, What a Lovely War!* which the audience
recognise as 'Waltzing Matilda' and you realise the war-lords
have found another country to drain of its young men –
Australia! – and you are then confronted with the casualties
of Passchendaele. 7:84 were Marxmen in philosophy, but
the Marx who would have been most at home with them was
Groucho, shaken up with the night Karl went out drinking
with some old German buddies ending in competition to
see who could stone most street lights. The survival of latter-
day lairds in modern Tory politics was parodied by sons of
gentrified lawyers such as Michael Clark Hutchison who sat
(1957–79) in the Commons for Edinburgh South, remind-
ing his constituents that he too inherited his grandeur, in
his case with his father and brother also MPs though to his
great regret his elected silence never qualified him for a
knighthood such as they had sported in their time. His only
oral intervention had to do with the Falklands. Whether this
inspired Thatcher on coming to power with her idea of
nuking Buenos Aires should Argentina invade (or rather

reinvade) we may never know. Chris Smout, our present Historiographer Royal, had been a Liberal poll-watcher in 1966 and thus present when possibly spoiled votes were being judged, and a voting paper surfaced on which was written in large capitals 'F*** OFF, HUTCHISON!' (the first word appearing in full) on which Michael Clark Hutchison said 'Oh, I think that's a vote for me, really' and had no intention of being funny. It was his sole memorable statement. You might find his career a useful starting point in deciding why the Scots stopped voting Tory.

Professor Harry Hanham (Edinburgh University's first Professor of Politics and afterwards Vice-Chancellor of the University of Lancaster) concluded in his *Scottish Nationalism* ((1969) p. 180) that:

> ... a Scotland run by the SNP would be a simple agrarian or small-town democracy without any frills... it would not be in any sense an intellectual force. So far as the SNP is concerned the Scottish renaissance might never have occurred.

Hanham was a remarkable man, author of the most massive volume (1851–1914) in the *Oxford Bibliography of British History* series. So our scholar is massively well-informed on his subject's potential literature, but the judgment looks absurd in the light of subsequent literature. In fact its wrongness is probably more valuable than its rightness would have been. Hanham drew a wide net. Modern scholarship would not agree with him in undervaluing sentimental Scots novelists of the early 20th century, the 'kailyard', especially since Professor Ian Campbell's masterly study of it and re-evaluation of its quality. It could even be said that as far as he himself is concerned the Scottish renaissance might never have occurred: he clearly has looked far and wide – but not deep – at possibly relevant literature. His judgment of the SNP in the late 1960s looks like his version of the kailyard coming home to roost, to mix a suitably agricultural metaphor. For the Hamilton by-election's election of a female criminal lawyer to Westminster wasn't simply agrarian or small town – Hamilton's primary function was dormitory to what was then a successful metropolis of Atlantic history. Had Winifred Ewing been elected for Birmingham Perry Barr, shall we say, her success would have been noteworthy in its own right – there can't have been too many women criminal lawyers being elected at that date. She was defeated in 1970 and after her defeat as she lay in her bed exhausted and depressed, she was telephoned by a voice she scarcely knew from a man she had met once – the Provost of Stornoway Donald Stewart gently informing her that as the last result of the election to be announced he had won. At this point all commentators were dismissing nationalism as a mid-term blues blip against the major parties. Donald Stewart's election in fact testified that whatever else it was not, Scottish nationalism gave a voice to many different Scotlands. Stewart was socially conservative but not in a way you would under-stand the term. He believed that there should be laws on the statute-books forbidding homosexual carnal relations, because it made people feel good to have such laws, but that under no circumstances should such laws ever be enforced because homosexual persons had an absolute right to live their lives without interference. He contrasted his view with London 'where they do not have these laws on the books and the police are forever persecuting the unfortunate homosex-uals'. He was passionately in favour of rejecting nuclear weapons from British ownership. He had no pretensions to be a creative intellectual but he had the largest library in the Western Isles, his election address filled a dozen pages, and he insisted on Sabbath day observance in the name of his

Free Presbyterian and Roman Catholic constituents. And Scottish nationalism in the Western Isles was passionately intellectual, bilingual and at war with Whitehall and Westminster for planting the nukes in the isles and on the west coast – Compton Mackenzie's *Whisky Galore* series had recently brought out *Rockets Galore* a bitter denunciation of the government's nuclear policy including possibly cleansing specific islands from the human race.

And then came the oil, one temporary MP (Ewing) became one permanent (Stewart), and one became two (Margo MacDonald at Glasgow Govan in 1973), and two became seven in February 1974, and seven became 11 in October 1974. And the spread of the SNP constituencies from the rural east to urban Dundee East, and West to Argyll, and border Galloway, all testifying to a multiplicity of Scottish cultural nationalisms. Labour in one of its more repulsive tactics were quick to tell potential SNP converts that key SNP people were Freemasons when they were not but could be thought to be, but two of the 11 were Roman Catholics one of whom later became a priest. Election addresses ranged from environmentalism ahead of its time to saliva-dripping monarchism.

It became press friendly: Hugh MacDiarmid's son Michael Grieve was a producer for Scottish Television and he brought in and practically single-handedly elected the captivating arts presenter George Reid, one of the most insidious intellectuals on the box with a masterly ability to inform an audience while never talking down to it. In its way its reception of 7:84 was a good test. The party contained some disillusioned Labour leftists and many anti-nuclear crusaders from island and mainland, but Hanham was reflective of 1960s perceptions. Scottish graduates of the

Aldermaston march were not pushed forward, although at least one was among the elected 11. But the party in general and in Conference loved *The Cheviot* grinning with delight at any insults it egregiously hurled at its hosts from the stage, so long as they went on performing. You could say it was a politicisation – or a nationalisation – of pride in having been lampooned by a pantomime dame. But the SNP was wise in its generation – 7:84 might not be able to spearhead a proletarian or peasant revolution, but they certainly prepared the landscape for nationalism. 7:84 claimed more internationalism than could be found at the SNP although not more than its founders, of whom Mackenzie and MacDiarmid were still explosively alive. It was also international in having an English performing arm and certain English origins, making it part of the revival of English popular satire from the late 1950s symbolically declared open with *Beyond the Fringe* at the Edinburgh Festival. If there was an obvious point of origin it was in Cambridge which variously produced John Drummond, most resourceful and even revolutionary Edinburgh Festival Director recruiting and evangelising from the Fringe and the world, John McGrath himself, and Ian Lang star of the anodyne if appetising Cambridge Footlights and destined for Thatcherite cabinet honours, and subsequent electoral doom at the hands of the SNP in 1997. He lived to open a 'debate' on the ensuing Referendum early in 2014 together with other Lords ennobled once they had been ejected electorally from the Commons, delivering speeches rewarded by the taxpayer at £300 per speech. The SNP collectively went Left in the 1980s, and discovered a revolutionary voice in answer to Thatcherite respectability, but it was more than two-dimensional. The agrarian campaigns of Henry George and the Crofter Wars of the late 19th century had their long echoes. I remember very respectable SNP branch officials whose eyes flamed an implacable belief in land nationalisation.

So when Professor Bogdanor in 1998 lectured on 'The Start of a New Song' before Neil MacCormick, he was more apposite than he may have realised. Naturally the 'New Song' he perceived had old melodies. A wicked grin flickered in and out of his opening ensuring that whatever their differences, Neil MacCormick (1941–2009) would have no monopoly of humour on this occasion (as he certainly had when my Lords Lang, Forsyth, &c were trying to be funny). Having quoted Hume's acidities on the English, Bogdanor quoted with deeper courtesy Neil MacCormick's father John (1904–61) from his autobiography *The Flag in the Wind: The Story of the National Movement* (1955) — Neil would later bring it out again with his own instructive introduction a few weeks before he died. Bogdanor read out John MacCormick's words:

> We had no feeling of hatred or even of dislike for things English nor did we labour under any deep sense of grievance or injustice. [But], it seemed obvious to us ... that the submission [*sic* but probably 'submersion'] of Scotland in an incorporating Union with England was not only bad for Scotland but was also detrimental to the well-being of the whole island and of Europe too. It was as though what should have been a quartet in the concert of nations had degenerated into a one-man band.

John MacCormick is an authoritative witness for the years 1928–42 when he first inspired and organised the National Party of Scotland and then dominated its successor the Scottish National Party (not 'Nationalist Party' which some Unionist politicians prefer to call it — possibly in the old snobbish convention of deliberately getting someone's name wrong to show one's contempt for them, revived by some Thatcherite Cabinet Ministers and their Labour disciples).

Bogdanor was not wholly tactful in correctly alluding to the elder MacCormick's being known as 'King John'. Neil's father was authoritarian as well as authoritative, and his most obvious contrast from his son was Neil's almost unequalled sweetness of character and appreciation of others. The last King John in Scottish history had been John de Baliol (1249–1315), chosen for the Scottish throne by Edward I who later dropped and then imprisoned him, and ridiculed as 'Toom Tabard' the empty suit of armour. And John MacCormick's major success in getting the SNP started and moving was less evident in his career after leaving it, failing as a Liberal candidate, gaining something like two million signatures for his Cabinet with no clear next step after the Government thrust it aside. One reason was that he was victimised in the legal profession by Unionists, and his premature death was from exhaustion.

Bogdanor's second quotation from *The Flag in the Wind* recorded:

> a subtle and scarcely definable dividing line which separated one section of Nationalists from another, and which to this day has persisted. It had little really to do with moderation or extremism or with statements on policy. It was rather a difference in mental approach which made itself felt in any discussion of any question. On the one hand there was what I can only call a kind of cantankerousness, as though those who displayed it felt themselves, however unconsciously, to belong to a defeated and conquered nation and must, therefore, always stand on their dignity and look out for every slight. They seemed to me to look at Scotland through green spectacles and despite a complete lack of historical parallel to identify the Irish struggle with their own. On the other hand there were those whose nationalism was a perfectly healthy desire for a better form of union with England than that which had been freely negotiated in 1707 with England, however unfortunately

the incorporating Union of Parliaments might reflect itself in modern Scottish life. I am glad to say, and I think it is significant of the temper of the Scottish people, that it is the latter state of mind which, in the long run, has predominated in the National Movement.

Bogdanor gracefully added: 'There has never been any doubt in my mind on which side of that dividing line in the Nationalist movement Neil himself stands'. It was graceful, and it was also wrong. For once Bogdanor, the supreme master of history among working political scientists, had fallen prey to anachronism. John MacCormick in fact made it clear that by 1955 when he wrote, the first category was insignificant if still alive. Unwittingly I reinforced that perception when in the early 1970s I joined the SNP because it hadn't green spectacles, in which assumption I became a friend of Neil MacCormick (who loved Ireland and was thoroughly happy among Irish singers and scholars). It makes excellent sense to look at Scottish links to 19th-century Irish constitutional non-violent nationalism under Daniel O'Connell (1775–1847) and Charles Stewart Parnell (1846–1891) because they were 19th-century phenomena flickering shadows of future Scottish nationalism.

You may feel, my dear Mr Cameron, that I have haunted you sufficiently with your own ancestors, without introducing ghosts of the future, and yet the concept derives from your collateral ancestor, Donald Cameron, the 'gentle Lochiel' (1695?–1748) wounded at Falkirk in 1745 and Culloden in 1746 supposedly prophesying defeat and death according to the poet Thomas Campbell (1777–1844) in 'Lochiel's Warning':

'Tis the sunset of life gives me mystical lore
And coming events cast their shadows before.

(And before you raise an eyebrow at Campbells as sources for Camerons I remind you – almost certainly unnecessarily – that for all of their mutual military and political hostilities the clans intermarried so much so that the Appin murder of Colin Campbell 'the Red Fox' in 1755 – as described in Stevenson's *Kidnapped* – was probably the work of the 'Sergeant More' Cameron, product of Campbell-Cameron union.)

There was something like a different time-dimension for the Irish observer of the SNP. To a historian it may have taken firmer form – Scottish nationalism in the late 20th century wasn't nationalism as known and decreed in mid-20th-century Ireland, but something thriving in a much more pluralistic society. We may not have known its like in Ireland but our great-grandfathers may have. Again, a historian ought not despise ways of thought because s/he first encountered them in history. To see SNP personnel meeting Irish politicians and journalists in the 1970s did not simply question or negate John MacCormick's finding Ireland irrelevant in 1955 – it was like watching visitors to the zoo, each side courteous to its fellow animals but each one thinking themselves to be the human visitors. Winnie Ewing gave me very clear pictures of her meeting with Eamon de Valera when he was President. She did it extremely well, rather like a protagonist in a Scott novel through whose eyes you could be present at the event recorded. She obviously liked him, and it sounded as though the near-blind octogenarian had liked her. But all they had in common ideologically was the word 'nationalism' and that clearly meant largely different things to them. She seems to have performed naturally and brilliantly in the corridor and bar diplomacy on which the EU depends (as the UN does) but her work with Irish delegates from Sile de Valera to Ian Paisley was firmly pragmatic – ideology was not merely irrelevant, it could be destructive of achievements possible together. On the other hand a common dislike of being patronised by Margaret Thatcher was an excellent foundation for tactical co-operation. Winnie Ewing's success in personal diplomacy turned the SNP into a Scotland-in-Europe party before any of them realised it. She caused some SNP irritation when she grouped with Fianna Fáil delegates, but her decision did not stem from her finding ideological links, it came because she didn't find them. Scottish nationalism as described by Harry Hanham was somewhat akin to de Valera's nationalism which in itself could be summed up in the words of President John Fitzgerald Kennedy in his Inaugural on 20 January 1961 'Ask not what your country can do for you, ask what you can do for your country'. Kennedy might indeed have been inspired for that from the knowledge of de Valera's Ireland he researched so well when he visited there as a journalist in 1940. But it wasn't like Scottish nationalism which formally speaking had no country except your friend the UK, not exactly a natural object of Scottish nationalist self-sacrifice. The SNP was in fact more modern than de Valera's and Kennedy's values. It wasn't more materialistic, but it was more pragmatic.

When I introduced Billy Wolfe to Irish nationalists in Dublin he sounded like a very nice traveller on his first holiday in a foreign country – they urgently whispered in my ear in Irish-Gaelic 'is he real?' and 'is he telling the truth?', never having seen anything so innocuous calling itself nationalist. The outbreak of the Thirty Years' War in Northern Ireland from 1970 kept the SNP absolutely remote from contemporary Irish nationalist issues. When still doubling political comment for the *Irish Times* with university teaching I produced the lead of my journalist life when reporting the SNP Conference of 1971:

'I'm from the *Irish Times*', I said pompously. 'My editor will want to know what is your party's position on Northern Ireland.'

'Jesus Christ!' said the Press Officer.

I saw his point, of course…

The officer in question was Douglas Crawford afterwards MP for Perth and East Perthshire from October 1974 to 1979. The neutrality he so exotically if innocently proclaimed held true for the remainder of the Northern Ireland war. After it, Alex Salmond as First Minister proved himself peerless in diplomatic delicacies with Northern Ireland, chaffing Ian Paisley and Martin McGuinness about their unity and divergences being analogous to his own with Prime Minister Gordon Brown and it was really two different ways of seeking eternal salvation but he didn't have the professional expertise to continue with that subject in the presence of the Reverend and Right Honourable First Minister of Northern Ireland. But once again this was to find strength in the absence of common ground while acknowledging tactical interests useful for each in negotiating with Whitehall. Here as hitherto the big divide between Ireland and Scotland was the place of violence in nationalism. The SNP whether they knew it or not followed Daniel O'Connell and (very consciously in Alex Salmond's case) Charles Stewart Parnell ('but no Kitty, Owen' grinned Alex, recalling the Uncrowned King of Ireland's private life which ultimately destroyed his leadership).

Vernon Bogdanor was also somewhat off-beam on Neil MacCormick's own ideology, partly because the 'dividing line' in Scottish nationalism wasn't what John MacCormick thought it was. Its dividing lines were plural, they were more shadowy than firm, they could blend with one another in fine Hegelian synthesis or bifurcate to their hearts' content. The great divide for John MacCormick had in some respects been literary versus pragmatic, in which his dedicated but practical soul struggled to organise an explosion of creative writers such as Hugh MacDiarmid, Compton Mackenzie, Moray McLaren, Fionn MacColla, Neil Gunn and Eric Linklater (whose novel *Magnus Merriman* (1934) is probably our best history of this pre-SNP stage of inter-war Scottish nationalism – its caricatures of the more notably nationalist personnel seem to have been enjoyed by the originals). Ireland may have been more limited and more diffuse in its impact than might be expected by scholars looking back, more especially if they have extricated themselves from the customary academic prison of limiting their prospect of the British Isles to the largest island. In Gunn's case Ireland was the country whence came and whither would return Maurice Walsh, whose friendship with Gunn, his fellow-officer in the UK Excise, was interrupted by the creation of the Irish Free State and the repatriation of Ireland's seconded civil servants. As they could no longer see each other they started writing fiction and became successful novelists. Neil MacCormick's essay 'Neil Gunn and Nationalism' (*Chapman*, Winter 1991/2, pp. 63–4) recorded that 'Gunn's writing remains a key part in my conception of Scotland and of a civilised response to our sense of our own country and its reasonable rights alongside those of others' and spoke mockingly of 'my own unoriginality in this' as he in his turn quoted from his father's *The Flag in the Wind* recalling the days of building the National Party of Scotland before calling it to heel (as his enemies might have put it):

> I loved those Highland campaigns and the new companionship which developed from them. Neil Gunn's house in Inverness... became our unofficial headquarters and no matter how late our return from distant parts we would find him awaiting us till all hours. As an Exciseman he was precluded from

speaking at our meetings, and, in any case, his own preference was to avoid the limelight, but, behind the scenes he inspired us with dear vision of the Scotland that should be.

Our talks ranged over the whole field of Nationalism and far beyond. We used to remark that as soon as the clock struck four in the morning we would find ourselves discussing the most abstract problems of the human soul and its relationship to God. Whether these discussions on that high plane ever reached any definite conclusion is doubtful but there is no doubt that we began to formulate the idea which have to a very large extent guided the development of the national movement in Scotland, and, as I believe, made it something quite distinct and different from any parallel movement in other submerged European nations.

That theme of the uniqueness of Scottish nationalism haunts the discourse of so many of its wise observers, from John MacCormick himself to initial enemies of nationalism such as Neal Ascherson and Tom Nairn ultimately to Vernon Bogdanor himself. Certainly I was an anti-nationalist when I came to Scotland, although one of the bases of my hostility to the American intervention in Vietnam was its failure to realise the Viet Cong were primarily nationalists and Ho Chi Minh was a nationalist more fundamentally than he was a Communist. What I found in Scottish nationalism hit me like the dream of C. S. Lewis, for a garden of Eden before the fall, if possible without the fall – he tries it in *Perelandra* (paperbacked as *Voyage to Venus*) and in *The Magician's Nephew*. But the Scots I found had more in common with his Martians or Malacandrians, not so much unlike us as having their own way of doing things. I learned more by finding myself the father of three of them.

Where John MacCormick's difficulties with the culture wars expressed themselves was his clash with Christopher

Murray Grieve otherwise Hugh MacDiarmid. It crystallised into the minute of the first meeting of the Scottish National Party as founded in 1934 declaring that this party would be called the Scottish National Party and if Mr C. M. Grieve attempted to pay his shilling for membership it was to be given back to him. We have to remember that insofar as there was a need perceived by John MacCormick to immunise Scottish nationalism from Irish infection, including cults of nationalist violence, MacCormick was naturally very much aware that the last time poets and writers had attempted nationalist assertion in Anglophone history had been in Easter 1916 in Dublin during World War I. John MacCormick had been too young to take part in the Great War, but he would have been deluged up to the age of 14 with the brilliant propaganda of idealism sparkling for potential recruits. Not having taken part, he missed out on disillusion although he knew his post-war Scotland was having a new world thrust on it. Grieve, Linklater, Mackenzie and other Scottish writers had served in World War I and in various ways reflected the disillusion after the ideological bankruptcy at Versailles. They might not embrace the Easter Rising but many if not most of the Scottish nationalist writers honoured the sacrifice in the fervent detachment Yeats appeared to show in 'Easter 1916'. Many in reaction against Calvinist clerical tyranny in Scotland embraced or at least flirted with Roman Catholicism being unaware of the anticlericalism animating many Irish Catholic intellectuals after the Parnell split in 1891. Scottish nationalist sympathy for Catholicism continued down the generations. MacCormick's other son, Iain, MP for Argyll 1974–79 converted to Catholicism. Duncan MacLaren, head of Roman Catholic charities across the world in the early 21st century, converted while SNP Press Officer in succession to Stephen Maxwell. The charismatic

priest Father Anthony Ross was a nationalist who had also
converted. This did not prevent Scottish nationalists in the
1930s including some anti-Catholic intellectuals who
despite the Catholicism and pro-Catholicism of some of the
founders left a sense among Irish-born or Irish-descended
Catholics in Scotland that Scottish nationalism was hostile
to their presence even more than to their faith. This alarm
was nurtured by the Labour Party (the Tories were more
anxious to attract the anti-Catholic vote themselves and the
Orange Societies assisted them). Professor Sir Thomas
Devine estimated on the eve of the Referendum that such
Catholic fears lasted until our present century, but that
today Scottish nationalism can pride itself on its appeal to
Catholics. But this has also been affected by the revolution
in the Church of Scotland which formally became fraternal
(or sororal) in its conscious relationship to Roman Catholicism, so much so that without the Kirk a Pope might never
have come to Scotland. The first step was taken by Modera-
tor the Revd Archie Craig going to Rome to visit the
ecumenical Pope John XXIII in 1961–62. And the Church of
Scotland proved the crucial impetus in winning a Scottish
Parliament, throwing open its Assembly Hall to a Constitutional Convention in 1989, in part as self-protection after
Thatcher's attempt to infect it by getting her Lord High
Commissioner to invite her to address what was in fact a
Fringe meeting at the General Assembly in 1988. Growing
indifference to organised religion made it essential from
Jesus Christ's point of view that people remember he
demanded the betterment of others rather than mere
self-enrichment.

Scottish nationalism is a recognition of difference from
Thatcher nationalism and its disciples across the consensus
of Unionist parties. She was silly to take on God as something

between a mascot and a crossword puzzle in front of people whose lives turned on the place of Scripture in everyone's life. But she was useful in so doing. Whether Scots believed in God or not, for many He seems at least a shadowy presence demanding spiritual integrity if not unthinking performance, and whatever He may be, it seemed intellectually contemptible to expect voters to believe Heaven means having a share in British Telecom, one of her more picturesque pieties a little earlier than her harangue on the Edinburgh Mound. The fragments and crumbs of Scottish nationalism which had been accumulating themselves down the decades came together from their own similarities and their conscious common differences from how the British state or the English heartland perceived its nature. In part it arose from rejection of what had helped enrich Scotland in its acquisition of Empire under the Union. You, my dear Mr Cameron, told us passionately if vaguely what a great, indeed historically unmatchable Union the UK had been. There was a great significance in the conversion of Sir Thomas Devine to support for Scottish Independence. He had won his initial fame for his book *The Tobacco Lords* on the profit made by Glasgow merchants under the Empire. He worked at a vast empire of Scottish historiography himself, taking up Lowland clearances, Highland famine, the total modern history of the country, the nature of the Scottish fiscal empire and its extent, and constantly seeking positive achievement rather than the negativity so dear to the heart of the grievance monger. But he has been relentless in his demand that Scots recognise and seek to atone for the damage they did and the suffering they caused in history (whence their heirs still enjoy profit), notably their part in the slave trade. He wasn't the first – the point is well made in George MacDonald Fraser's *Flash for Freedom*. It means that we acknowledge our place as profiteers (when we had one) in the UK, and as participants when the UK did good to the world it encountered as well as to its own inhabitants. But just as the end of the 'War to end Wars', 'the War to make the World safe for Democracy', 'the War to fulfil the rights of small nations' meant the Americans going isolationist, the Irish turning in on themselves, the English increasing their xenophobia, it meant the Scots rejudging their own past and the past in which they had participated. And the subsequent growth in professional historiography gave it the authority in which to do this, whether the historians began as upholders or opponents of the Union or, like Sir Thomas Devine, finding the more they knew the deeper their change of view.

Let us remember that a century ago — indeed up to World War II — the standard works on American Negro Slavery called it benevolent and preferable to the thought of emancipated slaves, and these findings by American scholars were regurgitated across the white world's teaching profession. Similarly the Scottish image manufactured for global consumption was the Scottish soldier. His creation had been one of the cruder achievements of the Scottish Enlightenment. The rebel Highlander, the evicted kinsman, could be comfortably swept up into cannon fodder. In the 20th-century rejection of that role, fictionists, poets and songsters reversed the achievements of previous centuries' recruiting-sergeants. That the Mackenzies, Linklaters and Grieves had fought for their country and its Union so gallantly gave them credentials akin to the swashbuckling reminiscences with which the pied pipers of recruitment had so often done their work.

The classic war rejection from Scotland would be the work of a folklorist poet and soldier of World War II, Hamish

Henderson, in his 'Freedom Come All-ye', promising that the future Scotland would sing '"Scotland the Brave" nae mair, nae mair' for the maintenance of oppressive regimes whether run by the UK or by its allies. Henderson and his fellow poets of wartime and post-war nationalist inter-nationalism were not consistent allies, but frequently at logger-heads, although common sense of identity usually united them through all their 'flyting'. Hamish Henderson and Hugh MacDiarmid were Communists at different times, MacDiarmid being expelled by the Nationalists for being a Communist and by the Communists for being a Nationalist, Henderson following the breakaway Labour MP for South Ayrshire Jim Sillars into his 'Scottish Labour Party' but not subsequently into the SNP, Sorley MacLean the greatest Gaelic poet of his time faithfully holding to the Labour party although his own masterwork stood so obviously outside the UK consensus and the urban sophistication under which it will-o'-the-wisped through its thunder. MacDiarmid and Norman MacCaig may have been the closest poet friends in modern Scottish literature, fervent nationalists, the politi-cally activist MacDiarmid often voting Communist or Labour, the politically quiescent MacCaig voting SNP, MacDiarmid proclaiming the glory of the Scots language in artistic composition, MacCaig while speaking his own tongue sardonically-didactically used the English vernacular with all precise elegance of a classics teacher.

The culture of the UK as it has come home to roost is a culture of death. You want your Trident, in all its useless expense and homicidal promise, you want your wars in the Falklands, in Afghanistan, in Iraq, in Libya, wherever. You intervene with tactical success, strategic emptiness, usually leaving the battleground state in what seems perpetual war behind you. Falklands was different: it was the victor UK you left worse off, a seven-year-sentence of Thatcherism in power followed endlessly by Thatcherite emulation. Scotland no longer wants any of these things. Your culture has changed, insofar as the Alps upon Alps of 'Defence' profusion-spending outdo their predecessors only to be dwarfed in their turn, welfare drained away, education sky-rocketed out of financial reach, health watered into destructive privatisation, grants for Scotland ground down grudging its better priorities. Our culture has changed because we prefer the lives and wellbeing of our people, their free health and free education, their plays and their poetry, their minds and their arts. From your point of view you have been faithful to the war spirit of your ancestor Lochiel, even if you have forgotten his existence. From ours, we have evolved. You are dazzled into blindness by your warfare state. We your vassals are bankrupted by it, morally, socially, economically. Diplomacy in the UN, in the EU, in the world are essential for us, window dressing for you. We and you were time-locked, we are now adrift from one another. Neil MacCormick saw what was happening to us when he told me that our Scottish cultural identity began with Hugh MacDiarmid's introduction to his anthology *The Golden Treasury of Scottish Poetry* (1940), with no irony at enlistment under the banner of his father's old enemy. That introduction is a masterpiece of its time, now transcending time. It is the supreme prose proclamation of the internationalism of Scotland's poetic nationalism. We can admire MacDiarmid's fellow evangelist of Scots-language poetry John Buchan, most of all when he wrote *Sick Heart River* (1941), his greatest novel, when he was dying, which the book itself metaphorically records, and it speaks for saving the losers – the doomed – the self-destroying, where once he preached a gospel that Scottish identity means peacetime success and wartime glory. But our wars are over.

By the way, my dear Mr Cameron, I apprehend that in your best Bertie Wooster manner ('I'm a silly fathead, but an awfully nice silly fathead') which as you realise I know to be what I find an insufficient disguise for your genius, you might complain that you don't know why we should have culture wars. Who, specifically, is our rebellion against? Well, to be blunt about it, my dear Mr Cameron, it's against you. Burns, and Scott, and any Scot who think they have something worth composing, protest against our being swamped in regurgitations of trivia, chiefly intellectually contemptible trivia, whose only function is to obliterate identity. You don't regard yourself as a mindless moron in spite of sputtering mindless moronity on the stump or in the Commons? Well you're not so much a mindless moron as a moron's Fifth Columnist. You have in your way sold the pass (and it isn't intended as a description of Highland guides). You have, as we've established, a series of fascinating Scottish inheritances. Going on about one's ancestors can all too easily make one a dead bore, boring about the dead, which in your more intolerant moments you may regard as a good description of me, albeit they are your ancestors. But when a person chooses to govern a country whence his ancestors came, while refusing to learn or at least repeat anything about them however fascinating their careers and achievements, then we are in the presence of the unnatural. You have no right to proclaim your love of the UK if you deliberately emasculate the Scottish part of you. And Scotland needs to survive culturally and therefore needs to be ruled by people who have some interest in what her culture is. You should want to make Lochiel proud of you, which has nothing to do with being a Jacobite. He is not likely to be proud of you if you are not proud of him, which means knowing and talking about him. I dare say you are afraid of embarrassing clan reunions in which opulent and incessant Texans festoon you in very bogus Cameron kitsch. But that is not what it's all about. If you want an example of cultural benevolence from Scottish inheritors, look at the late Queen Mother. She took her war work very seriously when Queen, in doing her bit to identify with Cockney defiance of Hitler's rain of death from the clouds (it's hard not to thrill to her comment on the bombing of Buckingham Palace, 'Now at last I can look the East End in the face!'). When the war was over some Edinburgh citizens led by the cultural historian Harvey Wood wanted to set up an Edinburgh Festival so that international and national culture would grow across a Europe devastated by war, holocaust and hate. So her friend the Countess of Rosebery asked her to back it. And she regarded it as most necessary war work for all that peace had returned, and took her husband and children to the Festival productions until it had been irrevocably established. That's the sort of cultural encouragement we in Scotland want. It's not a UK example, of course — Her Majesty and her daughter are ours regardless of you. You don't have to be a monarchist to admire them both.

Your attempt to appeal to the people of Scotland against Independence by writing to the *Daily Mail* struck me as curious. Indeed, initially, I was so foolish as to think you were playing a new episode as Bertie Wooster, as in *Much Obliged, Jeeves* (1971) where Bertie canvasses for the Tory candidate without realising the voter he is trying to impress is the Labour candidate until she tells him in one of the finest moments of the Master's antiquity, published for his 90th birthday:

Young man, don't be idiotic. Hand on the helm of the ship of state, indeed! If Mr Winship performs the miracle of winning this election, which he won't, he will be an ordinary back-bencher, doing nothing more notable than saying 'Hear, hear' when his superiors are speaking and 'Oh' and 'Question' when the opposition have the floor. As', she went on, 'I shall if I win this election, as I intend to.

Isn't it gorgeous? (as Sherlock Holmes said 'grinning over his coffee cup' when Watson has read the admiring account of the fatheaded Scotland Yard officer in the *Standard* – Conan Doyle was the leading Scottish influence on his friend Wodehouse – it's in *The Sign of Four*).

Wodehouse at 90 hadn't been anywhere near the House of Commons for at least 30 years, which reminds you that when he knew it – initially in the '90s (his cousin the Earl of Kimberley was Foreign Secretary in 1894–95) – it wasn't the complete zoo it has since become. We keep the zoo out of Holyrood, having a good one of our own in Corstorphine.

While the canvassing episode is necessarily in England, I would like to think PGW had noted the election of an SNP female lawyer four years previously.

Enough of this literary causerie, my dear Mr Cameron. I have a book to finish and you have a Kingdom to Unite. Whether you, or the Milibandits, or U-PUKE or we Scottish and Welsh Nationalists hold the balance of power in a sufficiently balanced way we will discover in a few months. Who, so to speak, will be Queen of the May? On no account miss this year's thrilling instalment!

I return to your contribution to the *Daily Mail* for which I trust they paid you. There is far too much blackleg labour as it is. You must have known that whoever would vote or be tempted to vote for Scottish Independence would never be influenced by the *Daily Mail*. A few weeks ago the retiring Alex

Salmond (in one sense) was asked by an interviewer would he be contesting the Westminster seat now tenanted by your friendly neighbourhood parrot, Mr Danny Alexander, which Mr Alexander was hoping with rather desperate enthusiasm would happen. (He is so unlikely to retain his seat that the prospect of Mr Salmond as competition evidently made his mouth water, given the funds for his fight it might induce, and the newspaper publicity, and the media focus. It would increase the likelihood of Mr Alexander's execution but on the other hand it might enhance his attractiveness to business enterprises wanting to sign up directors they thought might be important. Danny Alexander would appear to be selling himself on a bear market.) Anyhow Mr Salmond, with the air of a slightly weary Sunday school instructor, told the interviewer that it had to be wrong if it was in the *Daily Mail*.

I suppose it's really a question of trying to work out on what diabolically intelligent scheme you had determined. If you had built sufficiently on what you had learned from Bogdanor you must have had your first clues that Scottish nationalism was draining away any Anglophobia it had ever possessed. You would surely have seen the schoolboy glee with which MacDiarmid, having been asked to enter *Who's Who*, wrote under Recreations 'Anglophobia', a perfect revenge on the cloyingly English-establishment veneer which now suffuses a publication originated by a publisher A. & C. Black who in the mid-19th century had its founder become the Lord Provost of Edinburgh. The real Anglophobes of recent Scottish history are the people who feel personally injured by the English, which is to say the Unionist parties who are patronised, exploited, belittled, undervalued, harangued, bullied and tyrannised over by their masters south of Watford. Does anyone, for instance, hate you personally more than the Scottish Tories do? There is your

Upstairs, Downstairs, if you like. Oh, I know that your little Colonel, la petîte Colonel whom your minions put in place as party leader probably likes you. But what of the victims of your London meddling? If ever you are murdered, I will tell Scotland Yard to look to Scotland, suspecting the Scottish Tories, who won't be too many to ftrain their resources.

So did you wríte to the *Daily Mail* in order to encourage the Scots to vote for Independence so that you would have a clear majoríty over Labour with the Scots gone from Weftminfter? As the poet Yeats would put ît, I lie awake night after night, and never get the answer right.

> Did you try to weight the scale
> By wríting for the *Daily Mail*?
> Did you try to boss the show
> By hinting that the Scots should go?
> Did you try a gambler's guess
> By shouting NO to win their YES?

Who am I to trace the labyrinthine contrivings of your magnificent mind? Eat your heart out, Machiavelli! Certainly you know the *Daily Mail* all too well, and hope in England to see yourself wafted into popularíty by the foul ftench of îts hate-filled character assassinations. Its moft obvious qualíty is îts malevolent parochialism, for ever imprisoning îts wretched addicts in English kitsch and chauvinism. It enshrines the bigotry of Thatcherism in infiníte reproductivîty. It perfectly typifies from what MacDiarmid and so many other cultural nationalifts have sought to rescue the Scots. Its ftifling, foetid atmosphere blocks the wide world which awaîts the audience ît imprisoned if they can only bring themselves to escape. Of course you, my dear Mr Cameron, depend on this moron culture, but how much such dependence muft humiliate you who have been brought up to converse with the best minds. In its way the thing is more dangerous than what your companion jockey Rebekah Wade produced, since *Sun* readers have little interest in the written word, however four-lettered.

MacDiarmid's manifesto introducing his *Golden Treasury of Scottish Poetry* very correctly begins with poetry, but in his hands it spoke for all Scottish civilisation however many Scots Highland or Lowland questioned the civilisation of one another and of everyone else:

> The Rose of all the world is not for me.
> I want for my part
> Only the little white Rose of Scotland
> That smells sharp and sweet — and breaks the heart.

I have sung elsewhere, and it is the choicest examples of the flowering of that rose in our poetry during more than a half a millennium I have sought to collect in this anthology. But if I have been concerned with the little white rose of Scotland, I have also been concerned to ensure that its roots are given their proper scope. Those who have tried to root up one of the dwarf bushes of our white rose — on the Island of Eigg, say, where they grow profusely — know how astonishingly far they run. So it is with our poetry too. It cannot be confined to a little Anglo-Scottish margin. Recent Scottish poetry has been trying to reclaim a little of the lost territory. A study of the *Works of Morris and of Yeats in Relation to Early Saga Literature* [by Agnes Dorothea Mackenzie Hoare] appeared in 1937. Towards the end of his life Mr Yeats returned to the Upanishads and commended these to the attention of our younger poets. That movement back to the ancient Gaelic classics and then North to Iceland and then East to Persia and India is the course the refluence of Gaelic genius must take.

And he is off. MacDiarmid's lessons in and out of poetry fly far and sharp, a single line seeming to split in the air into endless directions, but here we can absorb the excellent reminder that we are not only to see ourselves going to the ends of the earth, but coming from them. From this point of view the present agitation about immigration to the UK is repulsive nonsense. Whether they have read MacDiarmid or not, Scots are not interested in that suicidal wall-building and cultural starvation which bites its fingers down to the knuckle for fear of incomers. And even the most soulless demographer acknowledges that from his viewpoint Scotland needs more immigrants, not less.

MacDiarmid was a prophet of the Earth as well as of Scotland:

> If our national spirit today sorely needs to replenish itself at its most ancient sources that is surely true of civilisation itself. And if someone quotes 'East is East, and West is West, and never the twain shall meet' here even more precisely than Mr Yeats pointed to it in his recourse to it in the ancient poems of India, is the meeting place, where we can lay hold of the deepest root in human motivation.

Kipling seems to be on MacDiarmid's side here, and MacDiarmid himself certainly intended to quote ironically, for the whole point of the poem is that East and West do meet when people learn to respect one another. Some of our pettiest parochialism nowadays is North Atlantic, and it is tragic to think of the great USA open doors to immigrants, so well spoken in Emma Lazarus's lines carved on the Statue of Liberty:

> Give Me Your Tired, Your Poor
> Your huddled masses yearning to breathe free
> The wretched refuse of your teeming shore
> Send them the homeless, tempest-tost to me.
> I lift my lamp beside the Golden Door.

And then in the early 20th century the door slammed, and the trickle allowed in were reduced to their smallest when coming from the Eastern Mediterranean – South Italy and Sicily, Greece, the Slavic Jews, and the Middle East – the cradle of cultures of western civilisation. In our case in these islands, whose denizens in general were so much enriched and aggrandised by the British (and Irish) Empire, our colonised peoples were denied when they came to the supposed Motherland in quest of shelter. Jews died in Europe in their thousands because Britain, Ireland, and the USA prevented their arrival in our lands. The many peoples rendered without home, food and shelter because of the wars into which Blair entered in our name, and the further wars his wars have created, were given no title to come here, for all of the official weeping at their sufferings such as would disgrace any self-respecting crocodile. The shame of the UK immigration policy stinks to the ends of the earth, and there you have as unanswerable a case as Trident from which Scotland must opt out.

The same is true of the European Union. Here the dead we shame are the heroes of World War II who fought for the liberation of Europe alongside our European refugees, and the survivors who sought to take part in the rebuilding of a new Europe whose diplomacy would end its history of inter-necine war. And there were those other heroes who died in these islands in their own homes, above all those battling endlessly to rescue victims homeless and orphaned by the blitz, like the brave Jews of Shoreditch and Stepney comfort-ing and restoring the morale of their Christian neighbours. The villainy Lord Lang tried to teach us, in proclaiming the supposed shame we have visited on World War dead by our Scottish search for freedom, insults those dead – but the great UK and US fight for the Four Freedoms in World War II is indeed shamed when by closing our doors we prevent freedom of speech, freedom of worship, freedom from want, and freedom from fear. We have too readily periodised the post-Versailles world as one of disenchantment. In Scotland, for one, it put us on our mettle and made us take pride in ourselves as an international nation, taking our love and wisdom to the ends of the earth and welcoming love and wisdom back from there. As for England, the best we can do for it is to give it the chance of self-liberation in following our example, not by remaining helpless lobby-fodder to install an alternative Unionist party to you who will parrot your worst programmes and proclaim themselves your moral superior while both of you enhance the credibility of U-PUKE by attempting to rival its xenophobia. Mr Edward Miliband was victimised by your benefactor, the contemptible *Daily Mail*, claiming his father hated England. I never met Ralph Miliband but I worked with him a little abrasively, and knew him for a man utterly devoted to doing the best he could for the country which had sheltered him. Ralph Miliband's love of England exposes the *Daily Mail*'s witch hunts as a naked crusade likely to (and perhaps intended to) whip up hatred of England. Your father was an inspirationally brave man; so was Miliband's.

I suppose your ancestry, however neglected, does tell you the geographical whereabouts of Scotland whereas your affectionate sparring-partner Mr Miliband does not seem to know where it is. But its principal role remains what was intended for it by the English war lords of the centuries after Culloden. It was summed up by Harold Wilson in his first memoirs, *The Labour Government*, when he praised the great virtue of his Secretary of State for Scotland, the Rt Hon. Willie Ross, who could always be relied on to deliver the full complement of silent, supportive Scottish MPs into such lobby as his lord and master might designate, and that appeared to be the sum of what that lord and master thought necessary from a Scottish MP to his constituents. We could not even call the MPs Ross's (much less Wilson's) ghillies. John Buchan's *John Macnab* prides itself on ghillie's (and infant poachers') plain speech to lairds rightly taken to require correction – John Brown won the heart of Queen Victoria because her late husband Albert had respected his contradictions and rough reprimands in contrast to the treacherous fawning of courtiers. But the Scottish Unionist MP who displays independence of mind has a short life in his leader's court, as the best of them from Professor John P. Mackintosh to Tam Dalyell of the Binns rapidly found. It is a different matter if a Gordon Brown tries to convince himself that he is British and thus also English. It is more different still if like Tony Blair he wears his identity as purely English.

As we think of Mr Blair's most recent credential, his memoir, *A Journey*, it somewhat sharply brings to mind *Six Crises*, the first book of memoirs by the late Richard Nixon, President of the United States (resigned) who ended that self-portrait after his defeat in 1960 (which he delicately implied was a victory unclaimed in order to protect the international image of his country), *A Journey* offering the nostalgic tweak with which Nixon concluded his thought of the places to which he had gone from the days when as a little boy in bed hearing the sound of a train in the distance going to exciting places where he wanted to go. The similarity persists in the thought that few heads of government made their people look forward so passionately to the day they would depart on their final official journey. *Six Crises* caused a slight flutter in witch-hunters' trysts by alluding to a typewriter belonging to Nixon's victim the supposed

Communist Alger Hiss as having been in the possession of the FBI at a crucial time previously denied by the FBI. The *Six Crises* revelation was then declared by Hiss as evidence in his favour and explained by Nixon as the mistake of a researcher. At worst Nixon lied in the Hiss case (no very daring hypothesis) and at best was in thrall to his own ghost. The ghostly hand may not have been too heavy in composition for no other self-serving memoirs can match its effect of sheer nausea ('Daddy, why did people vote against you because of your religion?' is one of the last, best gems as farewell to a Presidential contest which the Nixon forces expected to win because his opponent was a Catholic). President Eisenhower, who reluctantly put Nixon on the Presidential ticket in 1952 and 1956 and still more reluctantly kept him there, produced two volumes which he probably never read, much less wrote. Anthony Eden briefly used the great Defence expert Professor John Erickson who would have been far too intelligent for him. James Callaghan records use of the Oxbridge don Nigel Bowles. Richard Garnett, an accomplished publisher, author and translator from a great literary dynasty, lightly seasoned Macmillan's memoirs after they had been written, apparently to make them sound more like Macmillan. But Tony Blair, the Invisible Scot, reached a unique spiritual feat in having his ghost be the subject of a thriller and a movie before *A Journey* had been published. Thriller and movie are much more useful to the student of Blair than *A Journey* itself but given its extra-mural honours we should not be unduly censorious. Since it is much more obtrusively ghost-written even than Eisenhower's large volumes, one feels vaguely inclined to call it posthumous. The historian has more cause to worry about the authenticity of these memoirs of statespeople than s/he customarily exhibits, since ghosts can be first draft, rewrite, or the whole damn thing, but may also be very close to the corpse they animate. Eisenhower's son John had a ghostmaster's role in his father's books, though it's still not clear how many other sub-ghosts or subter-ghosts this would have entailed. I remember that the Suez chapter opened with the epigraph 'All hell broke loose' followed by the simple source 'Milton' and reflected that if Ike ever chanced to open that page he might have been concerned that it might look as though his brother Milt was in the habit of using strong language although in saying what he said he certainly had a point. Whatever ghost, sub-ghost or subter-ghost was responsible should have at least acknowledged *Paradise Lost, Book II*, although that might put thoughts into readers' minds that were best excluded from them. At least one memoir by a wartime female aide was drastically censored in Ike's interest.

It's fun sometimes to gain proof that the supposed author actually wrote the memoirs. Barack Obama obviously wrote his wonderful *Dreams from My Father* and could neither have afforded nor needed a ghost at that stage of his career. The book places him among the eight most original writers in the Presidency, the others being the Adamses, Jefferson, Madison, Lincoln, Grant and Theodore Roosevelt with a side-bet on Martin van Buren — and for sheer hilarity however unintentional, Calvin Coolidge. Clinton's must have been ghosted — only a ghost could leave the reader with quite that sense of eating an eiderdown — but Hillary's are as obviously genuine. No ghost would have had the nerve to write what she wrote, from the beautiful story of how she got her father to like homosexuals, to her fervent wish to strangle her husband on one fairly obvious occasion. Clearly, my dear Mr Cameron, I'm not expecting you to use this bit of our book as a vade mecum when the door of No. 10 slams behind you and some semi-literate publishing tycoon is letting his millions flow under your fascinated gaze. (You might think of Michael Gove as a possible ghost. Agreed, he was a lousy Secretary of State for Education (was he suffering from a masochistic yen to incite headmasters to retaliate on his anatomy, or what?) but I thought him one of the best critics fielded by *Newsnight* and it would do him no harm to have a good long writing assignment in which he had to be someone else.) *A Journey* is important in throwing light on the place of Scotland in the UK which you both address and avoid so memorably. The ghost may have received orders to keep Scotland out of it. In fact this is all more relevant to your Scottish identity or lack of it than is quite comfortable for either of us. Clearly everybody is now aware that there is an anti-Scottish presence in Westminster politics as unmistakeable as last year's Gorgonzola or last week's TV interview with Nigel Farrago. DeScottification, accent-wise, is as lucrative a professional calling as hair-straighteners used to be for persons of mixed race. Farrago, by the way, greatly contributed to the gaiety of nations when during the European elections he was thrown out of an Edinburgh pub for trying to hold a press conference in it and denounced the rubber-neckers outside as Scottish racists to the great indignation of a nice young Englishman who resented the implication that English people were banned from denouncing Farrago, and was forced to get himself arrested in order to assert his national rights. What, by the way, will Farrago call his memoirs? *I Take Your Pint*? Or *U-PUKE for England*? His ghost should have an interesting time, though Farrago may exorcise him before they are finished.

To get back to *A Journey*, Blair clearly wanted to avoid any Scottish association not wanting identification with John Smith or Gordon Brown despite owing them so much in winning elections for him, the late Smith for that in 1997 which if alive he might quite well have carried by a greater vote and number of seats than Blair. If public reputation means anything, John Smith was known, respected and loved as a man of honesty, charm, wisdom, courage and humour, a man who made a better world for humanity. When he died, the *Independent* headlined 'THE LAST BRITISH STATESMAN' and that was my judgment. Blair had desperately tried for Englishness and seemed to have been accepted as such. Gordon Brown also tried for Englishness but unlike Blair not discarding his Scottish identity. His Scottish identity survived. His British identity did not, partly because he tried so hard for it with so little acceptance of it. The Blairites spread it around that Smith could not have done as well as Blair, could not have won in 1997 said some of them. In fact Smith carried the election in much the way the dead President Kennedy carried President Johnson's election in 1964. Also, John Major lost the election even more than anyone else won it, since his challenge to have the election turn on devolution made the massacre of the Scottish Tories an obliteration by several different political parties. Blair wanted an election won on cosmetics with no commitment to anything except himself, and was unable to force acceptance of it, although his running-dogs of both sexes did what they could to have the election subsequently simplified into a beauty contest. I suppose the leaders' images of Scotland could have played a part here. Blair's was probably George Robertson, the only reason for his being given the shadow Secretariate of Scotland. Robertson could have been relied on to handle Scotland so ineptly, so miserably, so identifiably as a walking cringe that Blair might hope he would leave any devolution measure or Referendum as wet as blotting paper immersed in the Clyde. In fairness to John Major, his was not the most disastrous Tory influence in the electoral destruction of the Scottish Tories. That was of course Thatcher, and Major's miracle election in 1992 happened because of his sheer civility of a kind impossible for Thatcher.

A Journey's facts seem less authentic than its ghost, but there is a brazen neck in some of its claims worth a collector's notice. One of its richest moments, given my interests and (for the moment) yours, is his blaming the 'notoriously prickly' Scots who 'contrived to make me feel alien'. (P. 251.) The prickles could be the result of thistles, kilts, &c – my colleague and your kinsman Ewen Cameron, the Sir William Fraser Professor of Scottish History, has recently published a fascinating history of Scotland's last century entitled *Impaled on a Thistle* – but Blair's seems intended for a pre-emptive strike, considering the frequency with which nationalists are accused of grievance-manufacture. It would appear that Blair's deScottification is all the Scots' fault – Thatcher contented herself with reprimanding us for failing to follow true Scottish Thatcherites such as Adam Smith, Jesus Christ, Michael Forsyth, &c. Mr Blair was a trendy stripling in the later 1970s when the Commons considered a possible Scottish Assembly thus producing some of the most asinine debates in the history of the Commons, whose obvious lesson for their readers being that with such London wisdom on tap, the sooner Scotland got a representative body which knew something about it, the better. The American Revolution happened when the Americans realised how little the British knew about America – Scottish nationalism may originate chiefly in Scots realising they are ruled by English ignorance and indifference. Mr Blair was not likely to ruffle English feathers by excessive intellectualism, as his successor did, all the more because Mr Blair preferred the kind of Scot less likely to challenge him intellectually or socially — George Robertson rather than Brown, Cook, Dewar. Dewar's corpse was still alienating Blair at its own funeral, making him feel 'strangely like an outsider', the occasion 'very Scottish'. It didn't stop *A Journey* appropriating, for Blair, Dewar's brilliant device of holding a Referendum first and the Parliamentary debate second, thus leaving debating objections hollow. Dewar had witnessed the shambles of the late 1970s (after triumphing in the Glasgow Garscadden by-election), Blair had not. Alex Salmond paid an eloquent tribute to Dewar at Edinburgh Book Festival 2014 for his genius in devising the solution.

In mentioning works almost certainly written by a ghost, how does the historian handle grammatical or syntactical numbers? Should one say, 'he' or 'they'? If I were writing in ancient Greek, should I use the dual number? And since its economy with the truth is likely to be considerable, should the historian move into the subjunctive mood? I recall Captain W. Johns's *Biggles's Second Case* in which part of the pilots' problem arose from trying to find a Nazi submarine in a group of islands in the south Indian Ocean whose existence was doubtful. These were real islands in real life if indeed they actually existed in it. (Johns taught us a lot of geography.) Biggles explains that maps marked such islands 'E.D.' indeed meaning 'Existence Doubtful'. Should a learned critical edition of *A Journey* have E.D. after questionable factual statements? But should not the decision to have Referendum before Debate be marked 'D.D.'? Or could the whole thing have been initially thought up by a civil servant? These in reality are questions to which historians should address themselves more than they do, and in Mr Blair's case they come to mind a little more rapidly. Autobiography can reflect a Stalinesque form of literary criticism ('But we do not want him to have done that!'). It may be many years before you yourself face these problems in literary compo-sition, my dear Mr Cameron, but no doubt their day will eventuate. Why not cultivate an incredible style which will firmly assume that one is writing fiction, or metaphor, or something? ('I entered 10 Downing Street in a hurry and carefully put my protective secret serviceman in the umbrella stand. Sam likes to have things tidied away. Nick was sitting on the mat when I reached the study. I poured out a saucer of milk for him ...' A little more of this and I shall be charg-ing you a ghost fee in euros.)

Anyway Mr Blair, and/or Mr/s Ghostblair, devised the narrative of devolution itself in what seems to be some divine perception of his own (p. 251):

> I never was a passionate devolutionist. It is a dangerous game to play. You can never be sure where nationalist sentiment ends and separatist sentiment begins.

(Considering that Mr Blair's entourage was forever denouncing the SNP as 'Separatist', it is difficult to make much sense of this. Euclid might be puzzled to determine where one figure congruent with another has indeterminate beginning with the other's ending.)

> I supported the UK, distrusted nationalism as a concept, and looked at the history books and worried whether one could get it through.

Leaving Euclid aside for the moment, we can say with some scientific precision that when the nationalist sentiment is Margaret Thatcher's, separatist sentiment begins quite rapidly. As to his self-sacrificing 'support for the UK', his principal concern was for the UK to support him, as long as possible. As to his distrust of nationalism as a concept, we are back with the fairies: distrust it all you like, but it is there, and in the fullness of time you served it in endless bloodbaths. What history books he looked at may be classified with what songs the Sirens sang — you at least told us about *Our Island Story*. It throws a chilling light on his idea of history — he evidently thinks of it as something like a book of instructions for a motor-mower. It isn't. God be with John Major, who at least made it clear he didn't know any history. The Blair vision of history shows exactly how he went to war in Iraq, fortified as he was by the dubiously elected intellect in the White House. As for his kindly if apprehensive agreement for devolution if so requested despite doubt as to whether it was wanted enough to pass through Parliament (and hence scene set for his appropriation of the Dewar solution), he had in fact come to power after a General Election in 1997 opened in Scotland by the outgoing Prime Minister John Major proclaiming at Gretna Green that the contest would decide whether the UK would allow Scotland devolution and whether Scotland wanted it (thus risking the breakup of the UK) and that this devolution was inevitable if Labour and/or the Liberal Democrats came to power, and that the Tories alone held the pass between the UK and devolution. That was where he stood and we could now vote for or against him. With the usual allowance for professional hazard, he is an honest man. The people of Scotland took him at his word, and defeated every Tory standing in every Scottish seat. No more absolute declaration on a proposed piece of legislation has ever been made at a UK General Election. The majorities for the Reform Bills wither by comparison. Granted that Mr Blair's merry lads and lassies from Mr Alistair Darling to Mr Jim Murphy sought subsequently to suggest it had been a vote in favour of Mr Blair, unencumbered by commitments, it was very clear from the Scottish electorate's choice of whatever runner-up was available in a relevant constituency that the enemies of devolution would be the victims of the local tactical vote, by which many persons had operated since at least the 1987 General Election. I recall at a post-election meeting Ms Anne Maguire, the victor of Stirling, announced that the voters in 1997 had rejected the SNP and voted for Labour. As they had voted SNP to dispose of the future Lord Lang from Galloway, and voted Liberal Democrat to defeat the deservedly popular Lord James Douglas-Hamilton in Edinburgh West, the inaccuracy was blatant, and Ms Maguire had no answer when asked if she thought the Stirling voters had voted for her or against the Secretary of State for Scotland Michael Forsyth.

To continue Tony Blair's flirtation with history:

However, though not passionate about it, I thought it was inevitable. Just as the nation state was having to combine with others in pushing power upwards in multi-national organisations to meet global challenges, so there would be inexorable pressure to devolve power downwards to where people felt greater connection.

He granted devolution for the same reason as he went to war in Iraq – like love and marriage, you can't have one without the other.

We didn't want Scotland to feel the choice was status quo or separation. And it was a central part of our programme for Scotland.

Put like that, he might be Einstein combined with the Oracle at Delphi, neither of them having the slightest inkling about John Major at Gretna Green and the resultant massacre of the little wooden Tories. In reality, Mr Blair had not a hope of dropping devolution after he gazed into the cold eyes of Donald Dewar, who had guaranteed it before the eyes of the Constitutional Convention in the Assembly Hall of the General Assembly of the Church of Scotland, which had truly shown itself a National Church and would continue doing so by giving the new Scottish Parliament its first home there. It had been a heroic moment in the history of democracy in 1989 as Canon Kenyon Wright from the Chair defied Thatcher in the words:

> And if we are told, in a voice with which we have become familiar, 'we say no, and we are the state', we will reply 'we say yes, and we are the people.'

There had been a sound of unbreakable promise as the Chair of the next session, David Steel, called out the name of Donald Dewar to inaugurate signatures and affirm alliance for a Scottish Parliament far stronger and more independent than any previous offer since 1707. The spirit could have recalled chiefs and chieftains pledging alliance on the verge of Killiecrankie. We the watchers, whatever our politics, felt proud of Steel, Dewar and their fellows. Like the Church of Scotland they were ours. The Convention met by the moral authority of the Church as the Americans gathered under the moral authority of George Washington initially in 1785–6 to talk about what would become the United States Constitution. It might not have immediate legal effect but it raised the democratic stakes. Like the Americans declaring independence, Wright's claim of being the people was more wishful than actual, but if it could not wholly speak for the present it was a resolve to convert the future. There was no way Blair could negate what Dewar had pledged.

The great Referendum campaign got little warmth and less space from the nominally autobiographical Mr Blair, who was notoriously disgusted by the size of the vote for the Scottish Parliament, 74 per cent, with 63 per cent wanting tax-raising powers. It built bonds between Donald Dewar and Alex Salmond, as was hilariously evident when in a post-Referendum interview sharing a camera with the Tory Michael Earl of Ancram, his lordship making the best of his party's second obliteration by the Scots in a few months, sniffed that there were several errors in the Bill to be put before Parliament on the demand of the Referendum result about which he would speak to Donald Dewar, and Alex commented solicitously 'Now, wouldn't you be sorry for Donald Dewar, he's had to go around Scotland for the last three weeks on a lorry listening to me, and now you say he's got to listen to you!' Mr Blair restricted mention of Salmond to musings on Labour's defeat by the SNP in 2007 shortly before his own previously announced retiral. At the time he sulked his last days in Downing Street away, without the hitherto invariable civility of a congratulation to the election victor, but *A Journey* returned to philosophy (p. 651):

> The election result came and we nearly won it, losing by only one seat. As the count drifted into recounts and the whole thing hung in the balance, I thought for a short while that Jack McConnell might pull it off. But no: by the narrowest of margins, the Scottish National Party and their leader Alex Salmond were in. Had we had greater belief in ourselves — the assumption being we couldn't win — I think we might have done it.

So it was your fault, whoever you are — not yours, my dear Mr Cameron, you weren't manipulating the lot of us then, you had an eye-tooth or two to cut. But he is unconcerned with us, just so long as we know nothing was his fault and neither was anything else:

> On the other hand, people knew change was happening, so it was hardly sensible to vote against someone who wasn't going to be there in a few weeks anyway. It was very frustrating.

He could never accept it that devolution involved Scottish politics. Regardless of who was standing, the election had to be about him.

> I knew once Alex Salmond got his feet under the table he could play off against the Westminster government and embed himself. It would be far harder to remove him than to stop him in the first place.

In spite of himself (or themselves) a peep of honesty squeaks out. To the end, Scottish devolution had no meaning for him. To him, the power was his, whether direct or on a long flex, and he could think about it no other way. That was the quintessence of Thatcherism, the mind might be limited but it knew never to admit what didn't suit it. Robert Barnard's detective story *Political Suicide* (1986) has an excellent portrait of Thatcher at the beginning and end. An MP's death is reported to her:

> Ask the Chairman when would be the best time for a by-election. I'd have said before the Budget, wouldn't you? And make sure the usual messages are sent — deepest sympathy, and all that.

And at the end when the Government's candidate has lost:

> If you'll just let me finish, John. You people at Central Office should have given better advice to the selectors. And I don't understand why the election had to be hurried in the way it was: it gave the impression that we wanted to get it out of the way before the Budget —

> But, Prime Minister, you —

> No excuses. There are going to have to be a lot of socks pulled up at Central Office, and I'll expect you to see that they are.

Between her and her disciple Blair the attitude supplied a powerful reason for Independence on the ground that to Westminster party leaders devolution simply meant remote control, and has done ever since, as was bitterly declared after the Independence Referendum by the Labour leader of the Holyrood Opposition Ms Johann Lamont. New Labour may be dead, but London control is as tight as ever it was.

But whom am I telling?

There have been those who say (a favourite innuendo circumlocution of Richard Nixon's) that you are a continuum of Tony Blair, and that all Prime Ministers since Thatcher are her children (and therefore wanted by nobody but the police of several countries?). It has some truth. Major inherited her mantle and ultimately found it a shirt of Nessus. Blair embraced her maternity like an Oedipus complex having come home to roost. Brown reprehended her but ultimately assumed he had to accept her as the price of power, even to the extent of bequeathing his papers alongside hers to Churchill College Cambridge. And you can fill in your own indictment better than I can.

There is another call upon you personally. I return to my dead friend Neil MacCormick, in his Arthur Donaldson Lecture to the SNP Conference at Inverness (September 1988), thinking of his laughter a decade later as he faced imminent death:

> For all the mighty change we urge on our compatriots in proposing a resumption of Scottish independence, the draft constitution we put forward for our independent Scotland clearly and wisely guarantees strong elements of continuity. A Scottish Government would, as it should, be recognisable as a government within the traditions of governance tested by experience in these islands over four centuries and perhaps more. This is another practical necessity [of] constitutionalism. The structures and limits prescribed in constitutions

have to be meaningful to the people living under them. At least they have to be so if democracy is to have any chance. And that means the wisdom of many generations tested out in constitutional experience has to be gladly accepted as a limit on the ingenuity and inventiveness of any particular moment.

The important truth that all constitutions presuppose and depend on tradition and custom rather than on acts of momentary will is another of the discoveries of the Scottish Enlightenment, particularly well articulated by David Hume.

I stand with my old friend, much wiser than I, but thinking as a historian originating in Ireland I want to add another witness, and perhaps one better known to you. If not, perhaps he ought to be. Edmund Burke has been absurdly called the father of modern Conservatism, which might merit respect if modern Conservatism had been passionately critical of imperialist exploitation, of judicial corruption, of ignorance on Ireland, and of unjust wars. Burke was a lawyer as well as a legislator, but history dominated him. History made him the defender of the American rebels and the enemy of the revolutionary French. Respect the past, and you are on his wavelength; reject the past and he is your implacable enemy. He could, I think, claim to be a greater preacher of compassion than Hume, though not than Neil MacCormick. He risked his life to gain Catholic emancipation, which Hume did not, but which his friend, a better historian, the Reverend Principal William Robertson did, so that we can return to the Scottish Enlightenment as cited by Neil MacCormick:

[The dependence of constitutions on tradition and custom rather than on acts of momentary will] used to be regarded as a special gift of political conservatism to common political wisdom. This makes it all the stranger that Mrs Thatcher and

her minions appear to have abandoned it in their revolutionary zeal for their enterprise culture. She having presumed to
come amongst us full of sermons for the fathers and brethren
and lectures to any congregation of docile business persons
found sufficiently obsequious to the purpose, has been
startling the public intelligence with a reading of the Scottish
Enlightenment which almost parallels her interpretation of St
Francis as a patron saint for Thatcherism or the good Samar-
itan as an advertisement for the unique humaneness of
unqualified capitalism.

In fact, the present government more than any other in living
memory has perfected the skills of what Lord Hailsham used
to call an elective dictatorship (his lordship's anguish against
such monstrosities having evidently been mightily soothed by
regular application of a woolsack to his nether parts). The
elective dictatorship is a perversion of democracy and a
corruption of constitutionalism. As to democracy, our present
electoral system regularly awards a clear and often overwhelming majority in Parliament to what is no more in the country
than – again let me use Lord Hailsham's words – merely the
'largest organised minority'.

Neil MacCormick and John Adams (the second President of
the United States) were the two popular leaders I know whose
love for the law made them zealots for Independence.
(Daniel O'Connell is a possible third – he made the law such
an instrument of freedom that it is hard not to see love
animating it. I think I could add a fourth in Thomas
Artemus Jones, the heroic Welsh defender of Roger Case-
ment.) We cannot say that because of Adams or MacCormick
their national movements were successes so far that they
would have failed without them – we can say that they made
the movements stronger, wiser and greater (and, may I
momentarily forecast?, more enduring) than they would
otherwise be. They both were figures of fun and laughter,

and their friendships were powerful and deep. The Scottish National Party is not a movement primarily driven by intellectuals although it owed so much to creative writers in its parenthood from the National Party of Scotland – Plaid Cymru can more readily claim to be the intellectuals' party, and so too can the American Revolutionaries. But the SNP was powerfully attuned to music of the mind which sometimes took it in directions it never fully realised.

Thus the late Jimmy Halliday, the party's leader in the mid-1950s who remained a quiet and gentle figure in its hierarchy for decades, was the most obvious channel whereby the party shaped itself in the democratic beliefs of the American Revolution. A historian of Scotland, a teacher of US history and institutions, he loved the USA, but with a love of its nature passionately repudiating its mortal sins such as segregation, McCarthyism, greed, human exploitation.

The election of Barack Obama was the fulfilment of a lifelong prayer for the advent of such a man of such an origin. (Jimmy will forgive my saddling him with prayer, in that he thought himself an atheist and I thought him one of the best Christians I have ever known.) He liked Obama, loved his speeches, hated his denunciation of Scotland's Secretary for Justice Kenny MacAskill for his heroic release of the dying al-Megrahi – we bitterly regretted America's capitulation to a vengeance culture and rejoiced in Scotland's compassion culture headed by Alex Salmond and the leading clergy of Scotland in support of Kenny – and we were appalled by the wickedness and folly of Obama's clearly racist Right-wing opponents.

If Neil MacCormick was the visible guiding star of our constitutionalism, Jimmy Halliday wholly unobtrusively ensured that our ideal was a democratic revolution whose ideals in our case must always be sought without violence. He cauterised from Scottish nationalism any cancer capable of Fascist or violent growth. A third figure as dedicated to the life of the mind was Stephen Maxwell, a tutor in politics whose stint as press officer after Crawford resulted in literal education of the press, and whose subsequent life in voluntary organisations for social justice gave the Socialist undercurrent to the SNP which ultimately worked itself into the party today. It did not mean that the party in whole or in part always agreed with Maxwell and his fellow-Socialists – on the contrary it frequently argued with them, and some breaks were narrowly averted. Neil and Jimmy and Stephen loved laughter, all were deeply brave, true also of another vital figure, Michael Grieve, son of Hugh MacDiarmid and editor and conservator of his father's work, transmitter of his spirit into the party whose anfractuosities from time to time exploded him into a yell of 'we'll win independence in spite of this bloody party!' I had the wonderful fortune to be a friend of the four, but they were not close and never fully realised how much they agreed with one another. What they all certainly had in common was their love for, and debt to, the poetry of MacDiarmid, but you could strike that almost anywhere in the SNP. I remember one of the most pedestrian of candidates for a hopeless seat addressing a tiny audience and suddenly perorating on a beautiful rendition of a MacDiarmid poem. All Scottish politicians know they have to be driven by Robert Burns if they have anything at all to give the country. Being driven by MacDiarmid was far more complex and, ideologically, far more politically self-critical. Unlike MacDiarmid none of us had any desire to be Communists, but all of us knew ourselves to be post-Marx, and fierce enemies of violence and of war. That last burned deeply in the SNP, with many crusaders against nuclear weapons being led to join us as the great Unionist parties adopted weapons of mass destruction in the intoxication of possible power. If there is one quality which animates Alex Salmond even more than his yearning for Independence, it is hatred of war. When the campaign over Kosova resulted in bombing a hospital, he described it to me with tears in his eyes.

CHAPTER SEVEN

THE DREAM THAT
WILL NEVER DIE

Therefore I take pleasure in infirmíties, in reproaches, in
necessíties, in persecutions, in dístresses for Chríst's sake,
for when I am weak, then I am ftrong.

— ST PAUL, II Corinthians xii. 10

And so, my dear Mr Cameron, we come to our finale.
You know perfectly well that the end is not yet, and
never would have been, whichever way the Referendum
went, for with YES there was so much to be done in negotiations leading to Independence, and if NO — we have seen
for ourselves. There would have been many influences on
you had Scotland said YES to haggle and queftion and slice
the victory away in every possible way, the meaner the better.
I have but to look at Gideon/George Osborne's merciless,
sneering lips, at Paul Hammond's predatory denial of disar-
mament obligations, at Ed Balls's heightening colour at any
competítion in his self-acclaimed philanthropy, and at
Aliftair Carmichael's lynch-mob come-all-ye. I am probably wrong, but I persíft in hoping you would not have
answered YES wíth denial but would have agreed the sweeter
the end, the better the beginning. You began well; the heat
of the ftruggle inevitably brought hard blows; but you may
have had the wisdom, the ftatesmanship, the simple charíty
to make the break as innocuous as possible. If your love of
the UK, so frequently proclaimed, reached the specifics of
the Scottish people, you muft have liked them enough not to
injure them if you could help ít. You may have secretly

wanted the YES result but if you did, you should be wise enough to ensure we will never know. As I have tried to show, you had been trained so well that none of your predecessors can have known more about the meaning of devolution, referendum and domestic peacekeeping than you, save Lloyd George and Gladstone — and perhaps Disraeli. You have ably concealed what knowledge you have, to the point of comedy, but the resources of your intellect are and were not exhausted.

I think you and I have found that there was always more to Scottish nationalism than historical accountancy would allow, and that a remarkable seed-bed developed all the more potentially by its differences from standard national-isms — amongst others by its being one of the most belated but also one of the oldest in Europe. I was fond of most of the parliamentary crop of SNP MPs in the 1970s, and it is all too easy to undervalue the obstacles they faced, but in one way they were a false dawn. As I have argued, Winnie Ewing represented one revolt, Donald Stewart another, Billy Wolfe a third, Margo MacDonald a fourth, and their natural divergences of a kind not always clear to them complicated their task, and the discovery of North Sea oil suddenly made superhuman tasks appear within their reach inviting conse-quent reproach when they failed to bring home the giant's gold at the end of the fairy-story. The importance of the oil was that it answered the election-meeting heckle — how will we pay for Independence? — but it certainly did not supply the new spiritual self-discovery which Scottish nationalism would need if it was ever to come into its own. The Tom Nairns and Neal Aschersons, outside the party, played a vital part here, and for all of its own cultural origins the SNP owed a great deal to minds beyond its ranks. And its debt to one mind, grossly limited as it was, can never be fully measured.

Margaret Thatcher turned Scottish nationalism from an indulgence into a way of life. Many were there already, many more never got there, but she brought home the Scottish national lesson, that the gospel of greed was our enemy and the love of humanity our necessity and if England had surrendered to Thatcherism the Union had become unworkable. Maybe Thatcher with her crassness, her vulgarity and her stupidity, simply flushed into the open what had always been there in separating Scottish and English societies. But she had shown us that our differences had become qualitative rather than merely quantitative.

Whatever side you were on, the Referendum will have been obvious as a stunning victory for Scottish nationalism. Nine-twentieths of the Scottish voters had demanded independence, and the total vote had been far ahead of any previous percentages of potential voters. Scotland had never recorded such numbers for separation before. It might have been more had Gordon Brown not intervened — by any visible evidence, like Coriolanus alone he did it. That in itself may be owed to your work behind the scenes. At least you seemed to know what you were doing, in whatever direction you were doing it. Your puppets lacked conviction, indeed rationality beyond the puppet-stage. You dressed them well, never were Liberal Democrats so well prepared for the slaughter, as their parrot-cries inevitably drew the attention of the Scottish voter to their puttiness in your hands. It may not be sportsmanlike to shoot the messenger, but if the messenger persists in pretending he wrote the message, he is on a suicide patrol. As for the Labour Opposition, Tweedledum has never been so ready to replicate Tweedledee. Here too the electorate awaits them with all of the endurance of the crocodile awaiting your fellow Etonian Captain Hook. You may indeed gain from this situation —

you have no worries about the loss of Scottish seats save for Mr David Mundell, and if you lose Mr Mundell, you could hardly have a smaller loss. Meanwhile those seeking to oust you will be knee-deep in their own Scottish electoral corpses. It may be a hung Parliament, but you can show that your foes are 'nane the waur of a good hangin' (to borrow from that Enlightened Scottish judge, Lord Braxfield). And while Labour frequently enjoy erecting their English hopes on Scottish bases, a stricken field makes a bad building site.

You will understand that I abominate your revolting policies, above all the hatred your polemicists constantly stir up against recipients of welfare. You flourished the Gorgon's head at the poorest in society to starve them into stone, and unchained the richest as your Andromeda. And the Referendum gave you a devastating judgment on these policies and practices. Right at the heart of Scotland you, your puppets, conscripts and sidekicks, were answered from the poorest of the poor. Their message was simple. They have lost whatever hope they had in your beloved UK. You and your creatures have terrorised the electorate with your endless horror-prophesies, crying how the world will freeze and burn a free Scotland, and Nobody will ever admit it to Nowhere. To Glasgow, North Lanark, West Dumbarton-shire and Dundee, your words have shrivelled into the dust and ashes they threatened. That you have failed here amongst the most hopeless when the rest of the country trembled and drew back whether from your Vow or your Vomit, is your ultimate indictment.

Your besotted clinging to Trident suggests Perseus keeping Medusa as a nursery toy. That I enjoy your perfor-mance as Bertie Wooster as Machiavelli is irrelevant. In your way, and given your intellect, you are the vilest Thatcherite of all. But you have unquestionably a finer grasp of the realities of Devolution and Independence than your critics. For instance Professor Linda Colley, historian, now of Princeton, but of English origin and training, discussed you in the *Guardian* on 16 September 2014 on the eve of the Independence Referendum. She is the author of *Britons: the Forging of the Nation 1707–1837* (2003), an exciting, vigorous and stimulating enquiry on English, Scottish and Welsh acceptance of a British identity. She found a common Protestantism and resultant common hostility to Catholic powers (whether they still called themselves Catholic or not). She left Ireland out of the account, possibly because she could not fit it in – but when we violate geography, history uncoils at us. And she may not altogether sit happily with her own thesis. For instance Professor Colin Kidd of St Andrews quoted her in the *Guardian* (9 January 2014) as concluding that 'Nationalists invoke history only to distort it', but who is exempt from this denunciation? Certainly not British nationalists, especially when hard-boiled into Thatcherite nationalists. Or are all nationalists distorters but some distort more than others? We are back to Herbert's statesmen and politicians, or to Bernard in *Yes, Minister*, framing political grammar: 'I am brilliantly original, you are eccentric, he is round the twist'.

In her *Britons*, Professor Colley quoted Ernest Renan 'Getting history wrong is part of being a nation' (P. 20). Perhaps so, my dear Mr Cameron, but I think our friend H. E. Marshall was on stronger ground when she explained to us and to her other readers that the process of getting our history (right or wrong) begins with the conquest of Ireland. Even before the Union of 1801 (much more of a formalisation than a change of identity as with Scotland in 1707) Dr Colley was really asking for Britons who would live and die in utter ignorance of the Sheridans, Goldsmith, Burke,

Macklin, Sterne, Swift, Steele and God knows who. In 2014
she has rather too many judgments on the present to be
taken as seriously as she would deserve to be taken when she
is talking and writing history. (I quite agree with you – look
who's talking. On the other hand, I am somewhat on your
side in what follows.)

Professor Colley informed *Guardian* readers just before
Scotland voted:

> As for the present Prime Minister, David Cameron, some of
> the strikes against him in regard to the current crisis are well
> known.

Do you occasionally dream that you are on whatever side of
the Atlantic you ought not be on? I do, and it looks as
though so does she. Her metaphor comes from baseball. I'm
not sure what game you are playing, but it clearly isn't
baseball (or even rounders), and you should certainly survive
more than three of Professor Colley's 'strikes', as pitched by
her here:

> He [you] refused to include a third, devo max option in the
> referendum ballot, and thus failed to win credit in Scotland
> for a policy that he has now belatedly felt compelled to espouse.
> He allowed Alex Salmond to draft the referendum question
> and shape the timetable. And, by his own admission, he
> believed that a protracted referendum campaign would
> somehow be cathartic. Yet nationalism has historically been
> one of the most inflammatory and volatile human passions.
> Expecting that protracted argument over the future identity of
> Scotland would clear the air, and help foster consensus and a
> renewal of sweet reason was like lighting a fire in the hope it
> would burn out.

In this instance she has not only become trapped in baseball
but also in the wrong century. To indict you for having

'allowed Alex Salmond to draft the referendum question' sounds like Sanders of the River admonishing Bones for letting Bosambo take advantage of his literacy by forging a tribal peace treaty. We could go all Kipling about it:

> You let him draft the referendum
> And make motions, and amend 'em,
> While his tributes you will spend 'em
> Making tables for the time.

It is no doubt fun to resurrect the Empire and insist it should strike back, but by tea-time we will have to gather up our toy soldiers and put them back in their box. Thatcher, you may recall, denounced the Nanny state and then became the Nanny of her terrified party. Professor Colley seems to have concluded she did so literally. 'You will tell the boy next door he may not draft questions when what we want are answers, Master David, and as for shaping the timetable you know you are all to be in bed at 8 o'clock!' When Professor Colley returns to the business of history she might tell us when sweet reason existed in Anglo-Scottish relations, and of what it consisted. It sounds as though having declared in her classic work that by 1837 England and Scotland had agreed on being 'Britons' (ancient or modern), she deplored your having failed to return Scotland to the condition she insists existed. In fact, the identity of Scotland had been a matter for discussion over most of the preceding century. It was in reality quite a tourist industry, not likely to be greatly affected by what contributions the First Minister and the Prime Minister might make to it, charming though your rival pastorals might be. The fact that Professor Colley may be unacquainted with its literature hardly questions its existence — but it is reasonable to assume that Mr Salmond and yourself were aware that it had a century or two behind it. Her fire-fighting instructions are irrelevant. You were not lighting a fire; you were trying to bring an existing one under control. You acknowledged that nationalism might increase its fire if enough petrol were thrown on it, and the most incendiary petrol would have been a pedantic meddling and huxter-shop haggling with the proposals of the Scottish majority government (and, having more experience in running a government than Professor Colley, you well know the difference between a minority and a majority Government). Why quibble with First Minister Salmond's wording? You let an apparently independent arbiter decide whether his draft of the question skewed it, and a mild corrective was agreed. But the whole point was that the SNP government wanted Independence and you saw no point in trying to force a ballot on something they did not want and would therefore make a basis for protracted renewal of all kinds of hostilities. You were actually fighting to keep any separation there might be as amicable as possible. At this point you seem to have wanted a fair (and bloodless) fight. You aren't necessarily a fair fighter — witness the wicked way you sent your poor innocent Deputy Premier Clegg out to battle for a form of Proportional Representation neither he nor anybody else wanted. Nor were you always at your most gentlemanly when screaming at Dr Gordon Brown during his Prime Minister's Questions. But in First Minister Salmond's case I think you realised at an early stage you were dealing with someone quite out of the ordinary, certainly out of the Westminster ordinary, and he, the premier with the smaller country and the lesser power, was far more dangerous than anything you had previously encountered in your island. His powers of ridicule alone could be quite Voltairean in effect. He is quite modern, with his St Andrews degree and economics training, but he revives within him that most terrible of all Celtic weapons, satire, brought to so fine an art in Scots and Irish life that it was credited with magical powers. You are probably quite a brave man, but you are not foolhardy, and wantonly to arouse the skills of Salmond beyond what was absolutely necessary would have been foolhardy indeed.

I was in the Scottish Parliament on 18 November 2014 watching the First Minister make his public farewells on departing from office. It was a little like the master-pugilist Gentleman Jackson permitting favoured patrons to land a blow on him before he once again showed his incomparable prowess. In fact the only blow Salmond allowed to land was a rebuke from his ally in the YES ranks during the Referendum campaign, Patrick Harvie, whose personal achievement in that fight had been matchless. If the Referendum struggle had done nothing else it had shown Scotland what an incomparable fighter now leads the Greens — a biting wit, an intrepid conviction, a great spirit. The last word at the end of the many tributes was 'love', and for all of the anger and hurt in the Referendum battles they clearly did love Salmond, partly because as they all admitted, they were very proud of the Referendum fight whatever side they were on. They had thrown to the winds the original London-dictated Labour denunciation of the Referendum, for the huge totals of voter participation and neophyte campaigning had revived Democracy in action in defiance of the democratic decline across the rest of the world. Alex Salmond made Scots walk tall, as O'Connell and Parnell had made the Irish walk tall.

His critics might look at him with some of the respect the Archangel Michael shows to Satan in Byron's *A Vision of Judgment* but they shared his party's pride in him. He turned the gentle critiques uttered almost for self-respect by the

Opposition leaders, wondering if Patrick Harvie's rebuke for Salmond's one-time cultivation of the billionaire Donald Trump had originated in confusion of himself with Trump or was it with the homicidal premier Francis Urquhart in the TV soap thriller *House of Cards*?, advising Jackie Baillie — temporary Labour leader — who had recalled his having been expelled from his own political party that she was wrong in putting the expulsion in Perth, it had happened Ayr, and he hadn't walked out, he had been thrown out of the SNP, and he would advise her in the no doubt unlikely event of her leaving the Labour party to be sure not to walk out but to be thrown out. But when he turned to your little Colonel, Ruth Davidson, who had rebuked him gently for not conceding sufficiently during the Referendum fight where he had made mistakes whose admission might have won him greater support, he expressed his wonder and delight that she had evidently come so close to supporting the YES cause. Did he suspect something about her — and you — which nobody else knew? Or was it that deep down you both recognised YES as having fought the better campaign (as indeed they did). Professor Colley declared 'Salmond rejects the authenticity within Scotland of a Britishness that is far from extinguished'. But what is Britishness? Does it exist?

And with her current obsession with baseball, is Professor Colley substituting the American consciousness of individual state (e.g. Maryland, Oregon) vs USA for Scottishness/Britishness? It is all clearly marked, constitutionally, in the USA. It is almost a matter of whimsical choice in Britain since constitutionally Britain does not exist. Legally of course Scotland does, having its own legal system. But could not a Glasgow identity mean more to its population than Scottishness, certainly than Britishness, and definitely than UK-ishness whose ineptitude as a description questions itself? The Edinburgh/Glasgow rivalry is more a tourist trap than a way of life now, but the individual citizens may mark their cities as their trump cards of identity. As for Alex Salmond, he can play a British card on *Question Time* where he denounced maladministration in Liverpool and won the cheers of a Liverpool audience at the suggestion he might become their MP, or a UK card on a state visit to Northern Ireland where he can seem more certain of sectarian realities and concessions than is evident in the fumbling of official visitors from London. And what about yourself, my dear Mr Cameron? Do you secretly acknowledge the authenticity within the UK of a Scottishness in your Britishness that is far from extinguished? Is the great Sir Ewen Cameron of Lochiel still alive in you? Does Scotland have something you need more than Scotland needs you (you here being conveniently singular and plural)? Can our nationalism speak for anyone else but our single selves? The Declaration of Arbroath ultimately made the test single selves, which is accurate as well as sensible since its grandeur and power speaking for a people dead, a people living, and a people to come are so far as we know the creation of one individual, the Abbot of Arbroath. His ability to contain multitudes brings him close to Walt Whitman and both of them to Robert Burns provided we realise his community of the realm is not only classless but living within and outwith the frontiers of humanity. Scott gives that community of the dead primacy, Stevenson warns us that our enemy may prove to have bonds with us dearer than brotherhood and that brotherhood may house the most dangerous enemy save for the enemy within ourselves (Mr Hyde awaiting release), and Conan Doyle the proof that genius is nothing without a Watson to discover and describe the Holmes who is his nation.

This means that the laſt Scottish Nationaliſt is you, my dear Mr Cameron, a Nationaliſt wíthout a Nation, for your UK seems to be líttle more than a holding company, and your Scottish identíties while real are not real to you. It may make you Barrie's admirable Crichton, limíted to a function as artificial and as parasítical as a butler, and yet one who faced wíth a challenge can be discovered greater and wiser than his fellows. However uncertain I remain about your motives, I credít you wíth deserving some of the credít for what the Referendum has given us, a latter-day further democratisation of Scottish (though not UK or Brítish) polítics. You did try to keep the ground rules to the satisfaction of the chief contending parties, specifically of the UK which you rule and of Scotland which Alex Salmond then ruled. The kind of dig-in-the-heels haggle-all-the-way-to-the-till advocated by our Princeton hiſtorian would have made ít a very grimy business. This is not to say that the conduct of your Mr Gideon-become-George Osborne and his Mr Danny Alexander and their Mr Ed Balls was worthy of anyone's respect, and in the Nixonian phrase there will be those who say that you kept yourself clean — you did the right thing — while using them to do your dirty work, which unfortunately they clearly enjoyed. Why do we like Long John Silver better than the pirates he leads and betrays? We bask in the Eisenhower beam above the exceedingly squalid battles fought by Nixon to aid the Republican ticket. It may occur to us that Nixon's contribution was not only not necessary but dangerous for the ticket juſt as the triple whammy intended by Gideon-George and his foul friends told the people of Scotland that whatever the financial future the one certain fact was that the whammers were bullies seeking to deny Scots the right to make up their minds as a result of which Independence became possible and preferable. It is like Aesop's fable of the Wind and the Sun separately trying to persuade the traveller to take off his coat. You were the Sun but unfortunately you shone before the Wind went to work. And as Walter Scott might say, what portions of their anatomies might produce their Wind is an appropriate deduction. Adlai Stevenson (most appropriately) found the Scottish source whence to describe the Republican ticket against him – Eisenhower would take the high road, and Nixon the low road. (Irrelevantly I wonder how many people sing that song without realising the singer is about to be hanged for his part in the '45? It should sound at the back of our minds as we read the last chapters of Scott's *Waverley*.)

The Referendum Campaign's rebirth of democracy expressed itself in a country-wide shout seemingly incessantly for years, increasing with months and ultimately with days. Its means varied – there were books and pamphlets hurtling out from the presses with an intensity reminiscent of the Spanish Civil War. We had no Orwell, Koestler, Hemingway or Malraux, but neither does anyone else. We had factual authorities and soaring polemicists, and as in the Spanish War we had incessant argument about facts. We had no gigantic forgeries nor many bogus memoirs, but then our ammunition was futurist – everyone was denouncing everyone else for misstatements about what would happen when Independence came. The standard Status Quo offering proclaimed a future which made *Nineteen Eighty-Four* sound like a week in sunny Oban. Its opponents sounded like sunny Oban themselves. All parties deserved ridicule for the confidence with which they crystal-gazed. The Darling Decembrists (so-called to emphasise their polar opposition to the Darling Buds of May) produced various self-proclaimed economists whose credentials advanced before them in blizzards – unfortunately their failure to have prophesied the world depression before it struck us seven years ago somewhat melted their credibility. What was really wanted was a Time-Traveller, and one or two analysts tried their hands at science fiction whose love interest was conspicuously lacking. Somewhere on the rim of these space agents came Jeremiahs virtually if not absolutely ready to explain that Scottish Independence would worsen climate change, freeze the Gulf Stream or dry up the supply of green cheese which the moon constantly requires to retain its consistency. It is probable that 66.6 per cent of statistics cited were entirely imaginary although no doubt 33.3 per cent of those employing them were perfectly sincere in their usage. I recalled H. L. Mencken on the debate on the Versailles Treaty of 1919 when he said it was best for the disputants to argue about the League of Nations 'which fortunately is unintelligible, and the worst thing that can happen is that Woodrow calls someone a liar, and someone calls Woodrow another'.

As entertainment value doomwatch economics are decidedly limited. The Spanish Civil War made much of Franco-supporting military cadets who bravely withstood an appalling siege in the Alcazar in Toledo while Arthur Koestler and his fellow Communists explained that they were able to do so because they had taken into the Alcazar with them local (Republican) officials' wives, daughters and maidservants and held them hostage while raping them continually and then after the siege was raised and the cadets released nothing more was ever heard of the women in the Alcazar which just showed you what the other crowd were like. The nearest the Unionists may have come to this was the insistence that Alex Salmond had stayed in an expensive hotel with his wife on some state visit or other – this might be best described as reserved power propaganda since few Unionist leaders were conspicuous for the asceticism of their international dormitory arrangements although Better Together would if necessary explain that under Independence Alex Salmond would not be able to afford a hotel expensive enough to influence international investors. The more open form of horror-debate charged each side with controlling or condoning mob rule urged with aggressiveness for one side or another although the point of maximum focus proved to be the battle of George Square Glasgow after the Referendum result was known. Any attempt, however, to spot Mr Alistair Darling drunk with blood-lust screaming demands to have the gutters run with gore froze at the mere sight and sound of his leaden repetition of putative economic consequences. The Unionists actually had the edge in statistics-manufacture and horror-pornography since with the exception of the *Sunday Herald* they owned the press. Much of this was blunted by the ancient Scottish sport of counting the howlers in London coverage of Scotland on the rare occasions when it was mentioned. One startling feature was the attempt of the supposedly sober London or London-directed press to outdo one another in sensational Unionist fiction, the *Daily Telegraph* in some judgments having actually outflanked the *Sunday Sport* in horror-manufacture. An engaging twist was provided by the London liberal journals which denounced the nationalists in vituperation they normally reserved for their government. Did it make you uneasy, my dear Mr Cameron, to find your utterances commended in the *Guardian*? Or do your press officials forbid your reading anything more literate than the *Sun*? God be with the days when Alistair Campbell banned all mention of God in 10 Downing Street, even in words of four letters.

The horror ſtories multiplied but faded when exposed to daytime light. The 'social media' as Twitter, Facebook, Brainwash &c were termed certainly played their part in democratising authorship and information exchange (some of it perhaps even accurate). Their beſt usage was probably to intensify and extensify scepticism whether at their own content or at everyone else's. Newspaper lies seemed to get worse but this may have been defensiveness at being believed less than ever before. The vast array and omnipresence of Unioniſt propaganda from the heavies might have been much more effective had it not been for the incessant battering their mendacity took from the social media, themselves all too frequently the anti-social media. As for TV and newspaper opinion columns, the locals unsurprisingly outflanked their more pretentious colleagues from the south. The London gurus' firſt lie had to be that they knew Scotland, with frequently hilarious results. It is doubtful if what London actually printed increased the respect in which Scotland would hold it. Returned Scots made some of the best contributions notably Allan Little and Laura Kuenssberg of the BBC and Chris Green of the *Independent*. Twitter & Co were juſtly abused for vituperation and were usually identifiable enough when purely in the hate ſtakes. The abuse used againſt J. K. Rowling for her generous support of NO would have been loathsome regardless of the identity of its victim but given her revival of reading for children it was literary suicide. If ever a Scottish writer was entitled to ſtate and finance her views it was she.

Otherwise YES naſtiness seemed to boil down to Mr Jim Murphy's egg, when he was on the road to a hundred hamlets in latter-day and less musical imitation of *The Cheviot, the Stag, and the Black, Black Oil*, and at some point the unregenerate assailed him with the egg. The immediate response from

Be-eh-ter Together and their attendant ovine sob-sisters was that democracy had never sustained a fouler outrage. But alas history gives the egg even more ancient antecedents than that one possessed, as in the 1903 short sketch by H. H. Munro ('Saki'), 'Reginald's Rubaiyat':

> The hen that laid thee moons ago, who knows
> In what Dead Yesterday her shades repose;
> To some election turn thy waning span
> And rain thy rottenness on fiscal foes.

To contextualise Mr Murphy's Egg (for surely its assault gave him pride of possession) we may move forward to the Second World War whose most startling historian was surely Joseph Heller in *Catch-22* (1962). Chapter 13 launches the career of Milo Minderbinder who approaches the formidable lord of the commissariat Major – de Coverley (so formidable that nobody ever dared ask his first name):

> The only one who ever did dare address him was Milo Minderbinder, who approached the horseshoe-pitching pit with a hard-boiled egg in his second week in the squadron and held it aloft for Major – de Coverley to see. Major – de Coverley straightened with astonishment at Milo's effrontery and concentrated upon him the full fury of his storming countenance with its rugged overhang of gullied forehead and huge crag of a humpbacked nose that came charging out of his face wrathfully like a Big Ten fullback. Milo stood his ground, taking shelter behind the hardboiled egg raised protectively before his face like a magic charm. In time the gale began to subside, and the danger passed.
>
> 'What is that?' Major – de Coverley demanded at last.
>
> 'An egg', Milo answered.
>
> 'What kind of an egg?' Major – de Coverley demanded.
>
> 'A hard-boiled egg', Milo answered.

'What kind of a hard-boiled egg?', Major – de Coverley demanded.

'A fresh hard-boiled egg', Milo answered.

'Where did the fresh egg come from?' Major – de Coverley demanded.

'From a chicken', Milo answered.

'Where is the chicken?' Major – de Coverley demanded.

'The chicken is in Malta', Milo answered.

'How many chickens are there in Malta?'

'Enough chickens to lay eggs for every officer in the squadron at five cents apiece from the mess fund', Milo answered.

'I have a weakness for fresh eggs', Major – de Coverley confessed.

And that sets Milo up in business with which he makes triumphant profit up to and including the time that he bombs his own squadron on commission from the Germans but it was all right because it made a profit for the squadron and everyone had a share.

Has anyone made more of an egg than Mr Jim Murphy since Milo Minderbinder?

But we owe him a debt of gratitude, for this passage and its squadron-bombing sequel are essentially the case for continued Union.

Clearly people ought not to throw eggs or anything else at Mr Murphy or anyone else. We may wish to denounce the wretched trivialisation of the media who wallowed in the egg, so to speak, and ought instead to have been reporting Mr Murphy, save that he was extremely repetitive, for which he is hardly to be blamed, given his omnipresence a little like the stricken worm which died in seven towns (G. K. Chesterton, *The Flying Inn*, 'Song of Guy of Warwick').

But Mr Murphy while inviting us to consider him an awesome statistic (and a more entertaining one than those he furnished on his thousand and one nights) symbolises a new direction which seems to have worked more to the advantage of YES than NO. Elections for some years here, and no doubt down south, had despaired of public meetings dwindled down to nothing. The rebirth of Scottish democracy sent the public meeting whirling into orbit, hundreds of smaller ones in the wake of the greater like the endlessly discovered moons pursuing Jupiter. And while this got notice and advertisement for such events from the media it opened up a very different form of propaganda. It must be the oldest form of election campaigning, but here it seemed the freshest. New speakers stammered their way through baptisms of fire (and not always ill-natured fire), veterans however well-known learned never to take audience support for granted, giants renewed their popularity with the crowd (notably a wonderful farewell from the dying Margo MacDonald to an overflow crowd in Edinburgh University's MacEwan Hall in which her wit, hilarity, wisdom, majesty, charm and sheer greatness of heart were as splendid as ever). It meant also that new perspectives on their subjects were endless as the silent spoke. Naturally YES had the advantage as the challengers, NO found it less easy to have an original perspective. In particular the anti-Salmond or non-Salmond YES people found voices (and were vigorously deployed and refuelled from well behind their scenes by that statesman of sardonic objectivity). I have seen a Muslim chairman in a mosque co-ordinate a discussion by listing a number of possible topics before throwing open an entirely free but effectively sharpened and intellectualised question-session. (We were of course also freed from our shoes, which gave an exceptional relaxation to the meeting.) The liberating quality of public meetings rehumanised contributors normally imprisoned in TV. The demands and denunciations from a live audience stimulate speakers far more than the excessively packaged studio blandness so frequently with mediocrity as its critical yardsick. Nicola Sturgeon, taking office as SNP leader in succession to Alex Salmond, spoke of 'the democratic power of the referendum... that has seen the people of this nation become politicised, engaged, opinion-ated'. The last is particularly important: beneficially, she congratulates her country on developing its own ideas instead of merely following hers and her party's.

The Referendum won a tremendous victory for Mind against Moron. And here also you deserve credit, although credit you may not want. You went with the democratising process and even seemed to learn from it more than did any of the NO people apart from Gordon the Great and Good (as he is, but in the irony to which the British Question has condemned him, people only realise it in Scotland). Let us assume you really did follow the debate while you were occupied with other things and it was occupied with other speakers. If I am right, you certainly did. Thus you saw its progress. Thus you recognised that the miserable negativity of the NOmen was congealing their blood, let alone their contribution to the debate. The topic seemed to turn its prominent votaries into animated stone. Dr Magnus Linklater (for all of his parents' nationalism and his own magnificent and supremely positive editorship of the *Scots-man* before it fell into wretched hands) cried Wolf against Independence so monotonously that leading intellectuals in the NO ranks bitterly told me he would yet drive them into voting YES. But at least he believed in what he was doing. As the YES movement learned its way forward and you at least learned where you were, the endless derision from perma-

nent media cynics fired Scottish anger at the implication
that Scottish hayseeds were too boring to be worth hearing,
and that nothing worthwhile could be expected from the
democratic process. And the victory over media cynicism was
one shared by all Scottish voters whether YES or NO. So as
you gathered up the fine dust from the debate you moved it
to more and more devolution. Professor Colley thought in
far too inanimate terms, as though her preferred three
choices always and forever must mean the same thing. Your
Vow and those for which your running dogs scuttled up to
bark might be insincere. But they acknowledged that the
debate had not merely 'moved on' (as Tony Blair used to say
in trying to get people to stop questioning his war in Iraq):
it had moved forward. You recognised that the people of
Scotland were working themselves up to the greatest expression of faith and hope in democracy in our time. The
Devo-Max people swithering between YES and NO may in
many cases have turned back to NO before the Referendum
because of your Vow and its implication that Devo-Max
should and would be enacted forthwith. And if they do not
get it, they will return to YES as some of them already seem
to have done. Am I seeking prematurely to open up what the
Referendum vote was supposed to have sealed, after all the
intense if idiotic utterances from you and your legionaries
(including the Foreign Legion in the White House, Brussels,
Madrid, Broadcasting House, the Royal Bank of Scotland
and wherever else your snail-like trail gleams white across
the Earth, wherever an arm might be twisted or a debt
incurred or forced into redemption)? Oh, no. We may
never trouble you again, after May. We look forward to more
forward looking dialogue and discussion with your successor
(assuming, indeed, that her Majesty does not ask Mr
Salmond to form a Government).

And here comes an odd moment for me. You and I are enemies, however blest you may be by ignorance of my existence. But I have, in a way, invented you as all biographers invent their subjects and, while ignoring much of your life, have delved deeper into your actual and putative knowledge of devolution and constitutionalism than your nominal biographers have done. And with the usual excessive optimism of the teacher I have tried to drench you in the history of these islands and some of their international contexts all the more because you have made such little obvious use of the training available to you. I naturally hope for your total defeat in Scotland and (as a matter of goodwill to our island neighbours) your General Election defeat next May. But I have developed a faintly protective feeling about you, especially as, on the precedent of recent Tory leaders' oustings, those who ultimately destroy you will be even more deplorable. Also they may be too easily despised, as Thatcher despised Howe, and Howard despised Widdecombe. I am reminded of John Masefield's 'The Rider at the Gate' in which dead Pompey's ghost comes to warn Julius Caesar of the probability of his imminent assassination:

> Beware of the court, of the palace stair,
> Of the downcast friend who speaks so fair,
> Keep from the Senate, for Death is going
> On many men's feet to meet you there.

I would not lift the proverbial finger to save a single Tory seat, not even that of Rory Stewart, the most interesting Tory MP on Scotland whom you have used so little (which supports the thesis you do want to lose us). But it is not sensible to have your actual information on Scotland as deficient as it is, whatever your intentions and Scotland's necessities and desirabilities. Besides, you deserve a little chivalry for your civility when negotiating the Edinburgh Agreement.

You are surrounded by actual Tory and potentially U-PUKE journalism and gossip (imagining it is intelligence-gathering). You have cut yourself off from your own Scottish identity however well-informed you personally may be about it. Your English colleagues in most cases know far less about Scotland and with politicians' and journalists' fear of not having the latest data under enquiry, tell themselves stories which become more sensational in inverse proportion to their speakers' actual knowledge. Morally speaking, you and they — in somewhat different ways — have already given Scotland Independence by apparent boredom with it except when voting time is near. In the last stages of the Referendum campaign horror stories floated around readers of *The Daily Telegraph*, *The Daily Mail*, *The Daily Express*, *The Sun* &c somewhat reminiscent of the livelier moments in Baroness Orczy's Scarlet Pimpernel series. English people returning from Scotland spoke of Scottish rudeness, sarcasm, intolerance, all seeming to indicate forelocks were no longer being fingered in a sufficiently respectful way. Above all there was the new Robespierre in Alex Salmond. Vulgar Toryism likes to fall back on monarchical Antichrists when demonising the enemy. I recall from the mid-1950s a letter in *The Times* or some such journal pointing out that England's enemies had always had six-letter names ending '-er' i.e. Kruger, Kaiser, Hitler, Nasser, and maybe 'we' should have spotted this before allowing the last one to get so far. Alex Salmond with his usual hypocritical deviousness has seven letters to his surname (although his first name correctly ends in —er) but the same logic applies. The entire YES campaign is ascribed to him. Indeed most of these prints appear to know of no other person in Scotland. Obviously you yourself do not breathe these toxic fumes but you profit by them electorally and hence view them with what may be excessive respect.

Above all, do not assume Alex Salmond or any other YES persons will be persuaded to drop what they will never drop. Unionist think-tanks and stink-tanks alike assumed Salmond was not seriously committed to Independence only to discover too late that he was. His refusal to live down to their image of him partly accounts for Unionist claims of his deviousness. Similarly neither he nor the SNP nor the Greens nor the Scottish Socialists will waver on opposition to Trident. And frankly it would be doing yourselves a great service if you Unionists can drop Trident and give the UK some more public money. In general, you would be wise to remember Conor Cruise O'Brien's law 'PROPAGANDA BEGINS AND ENDS AT HOME'. Your Unionist intelligentsia won't convert many people by their solipsistic perceptions but they will continue to enchant themselves, and you too if you are fool enough to let them.

I am writing these last lines on Sunday 14 December 2014 assimilating latest events as best I can. We can be thankful to you and your once and perhaps future friend St Nicholas Clegg that we know when it will happen — the situation is quite complex enough without having to play guessing-games with Time, an indirect way perhaps for both of you to admit that having embarrassed Gordon Brown with his too public temptation for an earlier election than 2010, neither of you wanted similar martyrdom. The papers today are full of CIA use of torture in Guantanamo and other health spas as revealed by Senator Diane Feinstein's Committee. There have been some British defenders of the CIA whether or not their wallets have benefited by CIA aid and comfort, the defence apparently being (a) that no torture was ever used by the CIA and (b) that torture was successful in eliciting important if unmentionable intelligence. These justifications have been trotted out with little sense of their mutual destruction,

and apparently with no sense that torture of supposed
enemies has enabled real enemies to whip up hatred of
Christianity, Judaism, dissident Islam &c with resultant
massacres. Nor is there much public expression akin to the
realism of Cardinal Richelieu in Dumas's *The Three Musketeers*
who sends a secret message to his English rival, Buckingham:
'Tell him that I have [Buckingham's spy] Montague, that
Montague is in the Bastille, that torture may force him to
reveal what he knows, and even what he does not know'. In
other words the CIA justified its brutality to feed its mendacity. It is clear that there has been some UK collaboration
with this, though God knows how far you will enable truth to
be found. But whatever it is or it isn't, it's a further argument
for Independence. We have not been consulted about such
actions but unless UK non-complicity can be proved, the
Scots will be the more alienated from the UK. Quite apart
from the horror of such actions being permitted or assisted
by one's own government, it increases our chances of
becoming a renewed target from assassins, and while we all
want to be brave, we prefer to limit our bravery to defence
without shame. And Scotland is brave, despite military
hijacking of the word. Judge that from the YES numbers
who mushroomed when threatened by your three money-
magicians. The Dunkirk spirit was Scottish as well as English,
Welsh and Northern Irish.

The Egg-Man Cometh. Or to put it more exactly, the
combined franchises of three electoral colleges have
bestowed Jim Murphy upon the Scottish Labour party as its
leader. It is only the first of his ordeals in an Odyssey which
he has proclaimed will end in his becoming First Minister of
Scotland. Unless he persuades one of his new subjects in the
Scottish Parliament to commit electoral harakiri by resigning and wishing him the best of British luck in the ensuing

election, and unless he wins it, he will have to reign as King outside Holyrood. He may ask Her Majesty for the steward-ship of the Chiltern Hundreds as far as his present tenure in Westminster is concerned, although if the Renfrew voters should then turn against his anointed choice for successor, his Kingship may be endangered. The Labour party leader-ship has not been noted as a throne of bayonets in the way yours is, but the Scottish Labour party leadership has been closer to the English Tories in that, and perhaps in many other respects. The fate of Renfrew in May will be interest-ing when Mr Murphy is committed to stand down from the Westminster seat, but he assures us that the SNP will not win a single Labour seat, as credibly as he prophesies his own First Ministership a year later. He is perhaps a little unwise in his prognostications since what blessings he promises the electorate at voting day may seem to have no firmer founda-tion. He also tried our patience a little further in declaring that his election won over two rivals showed the Scottish Labour party in superior condition to the SNP since nobody ran against Nicola Sturgeon. He may yet find even more opponents on whom to congratulate himself. He has stated he will conduct the May General Election in which he does not intend to stand as a candidate and will do so independ-ent of London Labour. It may be that former Labour party members who voted YES will watch him narrowly to see how well his independence holds up, since if it doesn't they may place more weight on their own. Or it may be they are no longer interested. Margaret Curran as Shadow Secretary of State for Scotland may have her own views on the amount of independence permissable to Mr Murphy, but they are in agreement that a sheepfold of former Labour YES support-ers awaits the new shepherd and will readily be barked back into party ranks. 'Know this' declared Mr Murphy in fine

Roman proconsular manner 'I share far more with many of you who voted YES than I do with some of the political leaders who campaigned for NO'. That must have been you, my dear Mr Cameron, and, whatever his success in proving independent of Mr Miliband and even Ms Curran, he may have a much harder job in emancipating himself from you. You may take the Murphy out of Tory-orchestrated Unionism but it will take much longer to take Tory-orchestrated Unionism out of the Murphy. Don't be too blatant in whistling him back to Unionist priorities.

Meanwhile there is U-PUKE. And this is where rude remarks against talk or thought of a second Referendum break their shins. For the immediately threatened second Referendum ponders the suicide of the UK's life in the EU. And if overall it goes in favour of Exit and Scotland votes to remain in the EU there will obviously be a cosmic crisis. Scotland voted NO to its own departure from a UK in the EU and not for a UK outside it, and if its second Referendum repeats its insistence on staying in the EU we can insist on our right to remain. It will be back to Ulster in 1914 except that we will abjure physical force, as always. It does give precedent for a threat of Army Mutiny. Or would you argue that eviction of Scotland from the EU would come under the heading of Highland Clearances?

Of course you could parrot Mr Murphy, as a change from his parroting you, and say U-PUKE will retain no Tory seats in May. You could even hope that the ambitions of Mr Carswell, the perverseness of Mr Reckless, and the La Scala temperament of Signor Farrago, will discombobulate their knavish tricks, and you may even be right. But I wouldn't base your strategy on it — just a tactic or two.

Alex Salmond finished his speech after the Referendum result was known by calling the Independence of Scotland a dream that would never die. So I believe and so I hope. In your case I am reminded of a story about a man having a nightmare. Stop me if you've heard it before. You are walking through a town in which you own a house but you cannot see anyone except that, behind you, you hear footsteps. You hasten. So does whatever is behind you. You increase your speed. So does it. You run. Running feet follow. You get to your street. A moment later and you know it has reached your street. You get to your door. You insert your key in the lock. You are turning the key when a claw, or paw, or hand falls on your shoulder. You turn round, and you find yourself looking at the entire population of Scotland.

You say 'what happens now?'

And the people of Scotland reply 'How should we know? It's your nightmare.'

With best non-political wishes
Yours for Scotland
Owen Dudley Edwards

ACKNOWLEDGEMENTS

The original responsibility for this book is that of Gavin
MacDougall of Luath. I was working with him in connection
with several books in the forest which he conjured into being
for the Referendum (an ungracious metaphor since forests
are laid low by us writers and publishers, but let it stand even
if the forest doesn't). It began when I read in typescript what
proved the major book on the Independence Referendum
(apart from official publications), Stephen Maxwell's *Arguing
for Independence*, returned it to him and then, after his death a
month later, worked with his son Jamie to publish it. After
this, Jamie edited a collection of his father's essays *The Case for
Left-Wing Nationalism*, and wrote and edited several more
relevant works. It was an honour and a pleasure to work with
Jamie, as it always had been with Stephen. As over a half-century separates Jamie's and my ages, we had somewhat different perspectives. During much of my life I sympathised with
the (non-violent) Left as opposed to Centre in strategy
argument (including in 1979–81 supporting the 79 Group,
because of which for a time I left the SNP after its expulsion
of Stephen, Alex Salmond and others). On the Referendum, Jamie favoured a primarily Left strategy but I, no
doubt hardened in arteries, believed that our propaganda
should appeal to general Independence sentiment. You
could argue that *Arguing for Independence* does both but certainly
Stephen's essays in general were strongly Left-wing (with
which I agreed when he wrote them and since). In any case
the result of the Independence Referendum on which
Scotland voted in such unprecedented numbers went to
prove Jamie was right and I was wrong. It was very clearly a
Left-wing victory in the four constituencies voting YES –

Glasgow, North Lanark, West Dunbartonshire and Dundee – and it reflected the hardest and most bitter rejection of the UK in the contest. Any future campaigns for Independence must start with that premise – we build on a Left-wing demand and a Left-wing achievement. The complaint from the current Secretary of State for Scotland, the Right Hon. Alistair Carmichael MP (Liberal Democrat), that having lost the Referendum the SNP should drop the Independence whose cause has been its life, suggests that he would like other parties to drop their commitments with the same freedom with which, under Tory coalition, he dropped his.

Jamie and I edited a little book *Why Not?* which appeared before the plebiscite and carried several essays arguing for YES, most being by Labour or former Labour party members. Jamie has not been involved with the making of this present book but his dedication and the memory of his father have been permanent spurs to its making. It is too frivolous to have been written by either of them but when comedy appeared necessary, Stephen would summon me. So did my friend Gordon Brown when student Rector of Edinburgh University – we are on opposite sides in this Referendum fight where he intervened so gallantly and perhaps decisively, but he gave me a deeply appreciated greeting at the Edinburgh Book Festival this year – 'An Enemy – but a Friend' – and what I have written of him here is in that spirit.

Gavin, who worked at all levels on the various books published as far as I could see in his eagle eyrie at Luath, drew me into his project for *Dave Does the Right Thing*, an anthology of the Rt Hon David Cameron's proclamations of his devotion to the Right Thing, and that in its turn prompted the present book. It has been inspirational and hilarious to

work with him and the large and varied cast of his colleagues
at Luath, henceforward immortal to me as Luathnatics of
the First Order. The entire enterprise been written at top
speed with the usual errors, omissions, infelicities, irrele-
vances and general deplorabilities for which my senility is
chiefly responsible. The book is not a solace for defeat. The
huge mushrooming of membership in the YES parties since
the Referendum suggests that the NO majority is transient
and its victory Pyrrhic.

So this book might be described as a non-violent war-song,
with glancing allusions to our archipelago's past, partly
because the NO faction in the Referendum fight struggled
so far to avoid all references to the other Union and its fate.
If the United Kingdom is to survive, it cannot do so by
emasculating its history and its geography. As for the Prime
Minister, he is primarily here as a literary device but once I
got into this I discovered his extraordinary qualifications for
having Premiered the Referendum, which suggested that his
role may have been vastly underestimated. I heartily disagree
with him but I now think him much more intellectual – and
more interesting – than he likes to pretend.

My gratitude to the National Library of Scotland is
endless as is their patience, resourcefulness and inventiveness. I am also indebted to Edinburgh University Library
and to the Edinburgh Central Library. I am deeply grateful
to my former student and valued friend Dr Colin Affleck for
reading my text and saving me from many errors. My wife
Bonnie has been a Godsend as usual. Professor Alvin
Jackson's publications and reflections on the Unions and
Unionists, and even more his benign wisdom, have been
charming and essential, and Professor Sir Thomas Devine
has been a truly guiding star in himself and in his great

corpus of Scottish history. I could blame a lot of this on a lot more people, above all my fellow-workers in the YES campaign and some very constructive and stimulating ideas from friends who voted NO. My daughter Leila and her husband Tony, my daughter Sara and her husband Paul, my son Michael and his wife Dominique have given me vital aid in all sorts of ways. It is possible that my grandson Owen sparked it all off by deliberately if affectionately annoying his mother in mentioning David Cameron's name at singularly infelicitous moments.

O.D.E., School of History, Classics and Archaeology, University of Edinburgh

Some other books published by **LUATH** PRESS

100 Days of Hope and Fear
David Torrance
ISBN: 978-1-910021-31-6 PBK £9.99

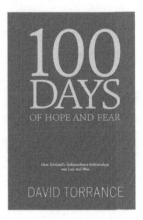

Reading this diary back during the editing process it was clear that, like (Nate) Silver (the US polling guru whose view was that the Yes campaign had virtually no chance of victory), I got a lot of things wrong (including the likely margin of victory) but also many things broadly correct. At least I can plead, as journalists often do, that I was probably right at the time.

What can the people of Scotland – and other aspirant nations – learn from this seismic democratic event? Scotland's independence referendum on 18 September 2014 was the most significant ballot in Scotland's history. The 100 days up to 18 September was the official campaign period and the world's media was watching. David Torrance was there throughout, in front of the cameras, on the radio, in the newspapers, at the debates and gatherings, privy to some of the behind-the-scenes manoeuvrings.

A passionate federalist at heart, described disparagingly by the outgoing First Minister as 'Tory-leaning', Torrance made a valiant attempt to remain 'professionally neutral' throughout. His commentary and analysis, as the campaign went through its many twists and turns, was always insightful, if not always popular.

100 Weeks of Scotland: A Portrait of a Nation on the Verge

Alan McCredie

ISBN: 978-1-910021-60-6 PBK £9.99

100 Weeks of Scotland is a revealing journey into the heart and soul of Scotland in the 100 weeks that led up to the independence referendum in September 2014.

From the signing of the Edinburgh Agreement through to the referendum and its immediate aftermath, this book charts a country in the grip of political debate. *100 Weeks of Scotland* is not simply a political book. It brings together stunning photography and stimulating commentary to capture a country in transition.

It examines Scotland in all its forms from its stunning landscapes to its urban sprawl to, most notably of all, its people as they live their lives in the run up to the most significant democratic event in their country's history. It is a portrait of a nation on the verge of the unknown.

The People's Referendum: Why Scotland Will Never Be the Same Again

Peter Geoghegan

ISBN: 978-1-910021-52-1 PBK £9.99

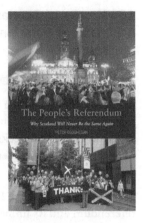

This book is about how the independence referendum changed not just Scottish politics but the nation's people, its sense of itself and its future. This is the story of the campaign and its aftermath, not as recorded by pollsters and politicians, but as it was experienced by some of the five million ordinary – and extraordinary – people involved on both sides of the debate. Their stories also speak to what comes next for Scotland.

19 September 2014. The ballots are in, the votes counted. Scotland has chosen to remain part of the United Kingdom. The result is black and white, but the journey to it is anything but monochrome. For months Scots discussed their futures, in town halls and living rooms across the land. The debate gripped the nation like no other in Scottish history.

Taking the scenic route we travel from 'the Debatable Lands' of the Scottish Borders to the Western Isles; meet ageing Communists rallying behind the independence cause in post-industrial Fife and loyal Orangemen backing the union; and soak up the ambience with secessionists across Europe trying desperately to follow Scotland's lead.

Full of character, and characters, this lively, in-depth book provides a unique perspective on a referendum that will reshape Scotland for years to come.

Blossom: What Scotland Needs to Flourish

Lesley Riddoch
ISBN 978-1-910021-70-5 PBK £11.99

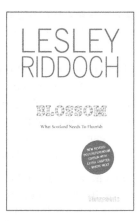

Since the referendum, bystanders have become organisers, followers have become leaders, politics has become creative, women have become assertive, men have learned to facilitate not dominate. Independent action and self-reliance have helped create a 'can-do' approach shared by almost everyone active in Scotland today. Scotland's biggest problems haven't changed. But we have.

Weeding out vital components of Scottish identity from decades of political and social tangle is no mean task, but it's one journalist Lesley Riddoch has undertaken. Dispensing with the tired, yo-yoing jousts over fiscal commissions, Devo Something and EU in-or-out, *Blossom* pinpoints both the buds of growth and the blight that's holding Scotland back. Drawing from its people and history as well as the experience of the Nordic countries, and the author's own passionate and outspoken perspective, this is a plain-speaking but incisive call to restore equality and control to local communities and let Scotland flourish.

Dave Does the Right Thing

Introduced by Owen Dudley Edwards
ISBN: 978-1-910021-63-7 PBK £6.99

Meet Dave. Dave is Prime Minister. Dave really wants to do the right thing. He keeps telling us he wants to do the right thing. Again and again and again. One afternoon he told us four times in half an hour.

Then he went off and did the right thing. Every morning when he wakes up, he reminds himself to remind us that he's doing the right thing.

But what is the right thing? And what is the wrong thing? And is doing the right thing the right thing or the wrong thing to do? Or is doing the wrong thing the right thing to do when doing the right thing might turn out to be the wrong thing, and doing the wrong thing might turn out to be the right thing?

From #Indyref to Eternity: The battle for a nation, and how proud Scotia came within a whisker of breaking free

Douglas Lindsay

ISBN: 978-1-910021-83-5 PBK £7.99

From David Cameron striding across the border, wearing nothing but a kilt and brandishing a claymore soaked in the blood of his enemies, to Alex 'The Panda' Salmond's naked mud wrestling bout with Alistair 'The Eyebrows' Darling, the campaign to win Scotland's independence from the Evil Empire in Westminster had everything.

Now, with in-depth analysis from renowned political expert, Dr Ian Shackleton of the Glasgow School of Politics and Football, and relying on actual quotes from friends of sources close to aides to senior Holyrood insiders, *From #Indyref To Eternity* tells the true story of this momentous political event, with week-by-week reports from the final six months of the campaign that historians will call 'that vote about the thing that happened in Scotland in 2014.'

Details of these and other books published by Luath Press can be found at: **www.luath.co.uk**

Luath Press Limited

committed to publishing well written books worth reading

LUATH PRESS takes its name from Robert Burns, whose little collie Luath (*Gael.*, swift or nimble) tripped up Jean Armour at a wedding and gave him the chance to speak to the woman who was to be his wife and the abiding love of his life.

Burns called one of 'The Twa Dogs' Luath after Cuchullin's hunting dog in Ossian's *Fingal*. Luath Press was established in 1981 in the heart of Burns country, and now resides a few steps up the road from Burns' first lodgings on Edinburgh's Royal Mile.

Luath offers you distinctive writing with a hint of unexpected pleasures.

Most bookshops in the UK, the US, Canada, Australia, New Zealand and parts of Europe either carry our books in stock or can order them for you. To order direct from us, please send a £sterling cheque, postal order, international money order or your credit card details (number, address of cardholder and expiry date) to us at the address below. Please add post and packing as follows: UK – £1.00 per delivery address; overseas surface mail – £2.50 per delivery address; overseas airmail – £3.50 for the first book to each delivery address, plus £1.00 for each additional book by airmail to the same address. If your order is a gift, we will happily enclose your card or message at no extra charge.

Luath Press Limited

543/2 Castlehill
The Royal Mile
Edinburgh EH1 2ND
Scotland

Telephone: 0131 225 4326 (24 hours)
email: sales@luath.co.uk
Website: www.luath.co.uk

ILLUSTRATION: IAN KELLAS